MADHUR JAFFREY'S
FAR EASTERN
COOKERY

Madhur Jaffrey's
Far Eastern
Cookery

BBC BOOKS

To
Sanford
with
all
my
love

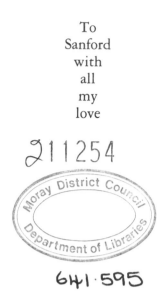

211254

6+1·595

This book accompanies the BBC Television series
Far Eastern Cookery
TV series producer and book editor: Jenny Stevens

Design: Bill Mason
Studio photographs: Martin Brigdale
Food preparation: Berit Vinegrad
Styling: Andrea Lambton
Ingredients photographs: Sue Atkinson, Atkinson Roles Studio
Illustrations: Graham Rosewarne
Map: Tony Garrett
Location photographs:
HONG KONG TOURIST ASSOCIATION page 44; ARNOLD LYE
back cover. The remaining photographs were taken for the
BBC by: JULIAN CHARRINGTON pages 17, 20, 23, 24, 41,
42, 46 and 48; CHONG SEE KWONG page 19; NEIL FARRIN
page 43; JEAN KUGLER page 45; LINDIE LAPIN front cover;
PETER RAMSDEN pages 18 and 47; JENNY STEVENS page 22.

Published by BBC Books,
a division of BBC Enterprises Limited
Woodlands, 80 Wood Lane, London W12 0TT
First published 1989
© Madhur Jaffrey 1989
ISBN 0 563 21364 7 (paperback)
0 563 21365 5 (hardback)

Typeset by Phoenix Photosetting, Chatham in Garamond No 3
Printed and bound in Great Britain by
Mackays of Chatham PLC, Chatham, Kent
Colour separations by Technik Ltd, Berkhamstead
Cover printed by Fletchers of Norwich

CONTENTS

ACKNOWLEDGEMENTS

There were, literally, hundreds of people who helped me through this enormous project. I would like to express my gratitude to all of them, especially to:

HONG KONG: Willy and Mimi Mark, Grace and Kendall Oei, Mrs Audrey Fung, Priscilla Chen, Margaret Leeming, Hong Kong Tourist Association, Irene Ho

PHILIPPINES: Mila Rodriguez, Sandra Cahill, Reynaldo Alejandro, Sandy Daza, Glenda Barretto, Ruby and Buddy Roa, Doreen and Willy Fernandez, Ruska Gamboa, Ramon Hofilena, Doctora Fe Elseyer, Tina Lapres, Philippines Department of Tourism

VIETNAM: Biche Lombatière, Indrajit Ghosh, Ram and Shangri-La Gopal, Richard G. Tallboys, Thuy Pellissier, Lîu Thanh Nhàn, Mrs Vúóng, Ngùyêñ Văn Y, Ministry of Information

THAILAND: Pieng Chom Darbanand, Chompunute and Akorn Hoontrakul, Duangmarn Mekswat, Chalie Amatyakul, Chai and Daeng Jongmu, Kruamas Woodtikarn, Mrs Ubol, Mrs Boonyoun, Tourism Authority of Thailand

INDONESIA: Sri Owen, Mrs Sanuar, Amri Yahya, Jonqui and Sian Januar, Martini Jufri, Usman and Rosalina Beka, Risnawati Agus, Lastri Krisnarto, Department of Tourism, Cri Murthi Adi, Muriel Peters

MALAYSIA: Zainal Arshad, Puan Rashidah, Lim Suan Har, Hasna Abu Bakar, Ahminahbi, Mrs Zaidah Ahmed, Lim Bian Yam, William Chan and the Nyonya Heritage Museum, Zainal Aziz, Penang Development Corporation, Tourist Development Corporation of Malaysia, Boon Cheong

KOREA: Mrs Han Chung Kyu, Mrs Choi Sang In, Sang Kyung Lee, Dr Park Hun-Seop, Chilwon Village, Korea National Tourist Corporation, Mrs Han Chung Hea

JAPAN: Professor Shizuo Tsuji and the staff of the École Technique Hôtelière Tauji, Keiko Okamoto, Tawaraya Inn, John J. McGovern, Tsuruya Ryotei, Japan National Tourist Organisation, and Professor K. C. Chang at Harvard University, Boston, USA

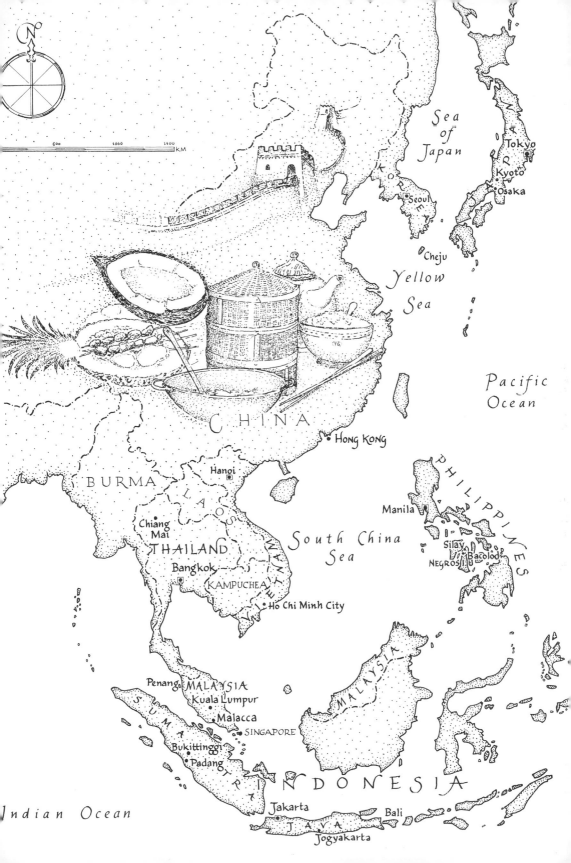

INTRODUCTION

The young women stood poised on the craggy black rocks that edge Korea's southernmost island, Cheju, their trim bodies silhouetted against the blue of the sky and the sea. Then, one by one, they dived off and disappeared into the cold waters. Several minutes later they surfaced with a bounty of abalone, oysters and sea-urchins. These briny creatures were not destined to go far! They were prised open, right there on the rocks, dabbed with a heady sauce made of fermented soya beans, chillies and garlic and sold by the women to waiting customers (including this one) who did not seem to know when to stop eating.

I started travelling to the Far East almost twenty-five years ago, marvelling on each trip at how *well* people ate, at the freshness of their ingredients and at their combinations of cooking techniques and seasonings that produced highly nutritious and delicious foods with such ease. In a market in Indonesia I once bought *gadangan* from a woman with a basket. This was a medley of blanched vegetables tossed lightly with a 'dressing' of grated coconut, red chillies, lime juice, sugar and salt. It was so simple and so utterly glorious. On another occasion I was sitting in a dusty, unpromising office in Vietnam. Some staff members were about to prepare lunch on the premises. Files were cleared off tables and a paraffin cooker lit. Soon an amazing salad emerged. It consisted of plain raw kohlrabi mixed with *very* freshly roasted and lightly crushed peanuts, mint, coriander, vinegar, sugar and chilli powder. It could not have been improved upon. In Japan I have had grilled mushroom caps stuffed with minced chicken and dressed with soy sauce and vinegar; in Thailand I have eaten a superb dish of stir-fried minced chicken blanketed with crisply fried basil leaves; and in the Philippines I have enjoyed an exquisitely delicate first course of mackerel strips 'cooked' in lime juice.

There is so much good food in this region. You might have sampled some Thai, Japanese or Vietnamese dishes in local restaurants and been afraid to try cooking them at home. You should not be put off by the 'foreignness' of some of the ingredients. Just remember that at one time potatoes, tomatoes and corn were 'foreign' (they came from the New World) and so were mangoes, black pepper and cinnamon (they came from Asia). Ingredients, indeed whole dishes, once travelled through the world at the cumbersome pace of the mortals who transported them – on foot, by boat or on horseback. Today a chef can eat a dish in Hong Kong on one day, and recreate it in his kitchen in New York the following week; a recipe for a curry from Malaysia can be 'faxed' to London on the same day and the ingredients for it, what with air transportation and refrigeration, found in many supermarkets.

For this book I have decided to concentrate on eight countries of East Asia – Korea, Japan, Hong Kong, the Philippines, Vietnam, Thailand, Malaysia and Indonesia. The climates of these countries vary from temperate to tropical – Indonesia is actually on the equator – and their cuisines are quite distinct from each other. There are, however, some common elements. What binds all these countries together is their healthy emphasis on grains. Unlike in the West, where the focal point of a meal is meat or eggs, the place of honour in East Asia is given either to wheat, in the form of noodles, pancakes or steamed buns, or it is given to rice.

It is not certain where rice originated, though the latest research seems to point to Thailand. At any rate, rice quickly spread through much of South-East Asia and eventually inched its way north to China and Japan as farming techniques improved. In the entire Far Eastern region, with a few exceptions, rice is synonymous with the meal itself, and an invitation to dine very often translates as 'Come and have rice with me.' In a Chinese dialect, to have a job is to 'have grains to chew', and to have lost it is to 'have broken the rice bowl'. Chinese children are warned that if they leave a single grain of rice in their bowl they will end up with a pockmarked spouse!

While almost all East Asians eat rice, they do not all prefer the same kind. The Chinese generally like a long-grain variety while the Japanese and Koreans frown on anything but their somewhat more glutinous, short-grain varieties. In Bali in Indonesia I have had the fluffiest, lightest rice; in Malaysia I have eaten a pudding made with black rice; in the Philippines, a cake made with purple rice; and in Northern Thailand, following the local custom, I have made small balls out of glutinous rice and eaten them with my pork curry.

The soya bean is another ingredient that gives Far Eastern foods their special character and nutritional value. Pound for pound, it is richer in protein than red meat, richer in digestible calcium than equal amounts of milk, and contains more iron than ox liver. And it has no saturated fat. But it is hard to digest in its normal state and so needs to be processed in some way. This has led to the availability of a host of soya bean products such as bean curd and soy sauce. Made from the beans combined with wheat, barley or rice, briny fermented soy sauce adds protein, flavour and saltiness to thousands of dishes from Korea to Indonesia.

Soy sauce is not the only flavouring-cum-salting sauce in the region. Fish sauce performs a very similar function in Vietnam, Thailand and the

Philippines. Even though this is made from fermented fish, it is neither mal-odorous nor overpowering and it *is* very rich in protein, calcium and phospho-rus! When used properly, as in a Vietnamese dipping sauce that calls for the addition of water, lime juice, sugar and chillies, it is so good as to be almost drinkable.

Then there is that felicitous Chinese creation, the noodle. Originating prob-ably before the start of the Christian era – in fact, as soon as the Chinese were able to grind grains into a fine flour – the noodle quickly made its way into the hearts – and mouths – of the entire Far East. Today there are rice noodles, wheat noodles and buckwheat noodles. These Chinese symbols of longevity may be immersed in soups, stir-fried with meats and put into cold salads. They are as perfect for eating and easy entertaining as Italian pasta.

The one seasoning that is used throughout the Far East is ginger. You prob-ably know it well from Chinese and Indian cookery. Fifth-century Chinese sailors used to carry it on their ships, embedded in earth to make it last. They knew it was rich in vitamin C and prevented scurvy. They also knew that it had 'heating' properties and, to this day, ginger tea is served after a meal of 'cooling' crabs.

The Chinese have, for centuries, felt that the human body functions best when 'cooling' and 'heating' (*yin* and *yang* respectively) forces are properly bal-anced. In 1368 Chia Ming, a medieval foodie, catalogued every edible substance, marking its degree of 'hotness' or 'coolness'. He ate carefully himself and lived to be 106! The Chinese, wherever they are – and as well as populating Hong Kong they have spread widely in the Philippines, Thailand, Malaysia and Indonesia – are very aware of this as they cook and eat. I was offered not only ginger tea after a heady meal of many, many roe-filled crabs but also chry-santhemum tea (it is cooling) after we had gorged ourselves on barbecued beef and chicken (they are heating) at a bayside Hong Kong picnic.

An ancient Chinese poem, attempting to entice the soul back to earth, offers it a meal where dishes of 'all flavours' are present, 'bitter, salt, sour, pungent and sweet'. These are still the five flavours the Chinese try to balance at every meal. The Koreans took cognisance of a flavour the Chinese seemingly missed – the 'nutty' flavour found in sesame seeds. There is, however, a taste that the Chinese and the Koreans were not to know till the sixteenth century – the fire of the red hot chilli.

Chillies came marching into Asia with the Portuguese and conquered the old world forever, transforming the cuisines of Indonesia, Malaysia, Thailand, Vietnam, Korea and some provinces of China such as Sichuan and Hunan. It is hard to say what it is about chillies that causes an addiction. Perhaps it is the exquisite pain they bring that heightens the pleasure of eating, but once you have enjoyed them, there is no turning back: you are hooked forever.

The culinary art of the Far East lies in the magical mingling and balancing of flavours and textures. Western taboos just do not hold: fish and pork strips are thrown together in a fiery stew in Korea; a paste made of minced pork and crab meat is lathered on to triangles of bread before they are fried in Vietnam. The soft, the smooth, the crunchy and the slithery as well as the sweet, salty, hot and sour are all presented in a kaleidoscope of inventive permutations.

The source of meat for much of this region (excepting Japan) has traditionally been the pig. This prolific animal could be raised on scraps while precious grains from the fields could be wisely saved for the growing numbers of humans. Cattle could be saved for ploughing the fields that raised the grains. Changes came to Indonesia, Malaysia and the southern Philippines with the spread of Islam. Pigs, of religious necessity, were out. Goats and, when the people could afford it, cattle were slaughtered instead. As farming methods improved, more and more cows were raised for slaughter. Today Korea has a few cattle farms that rival those in Texas.

What much of this region thrives on, however, is fresh fish. People demand the freshest of fish and get it. The price of fish drops dramatically if it is a day old. Eels, carp, crabs and octopus, all live, wriggle around in tanks and tubs. Even before dawn, hundreds of prawns are lined up on scrubbed counters like repeating commas. By midday the prawns will have been stir-fried with asparagus in Hong Kong, dipped in batter and fried in Tokyo, and stirred into a coconut-enriched sauce in Malaysia.

The demand for freshness extends to vegetables as well. It is said that in China only 60 per cent of the credit for a good meal goes to the person who cooks: 40 per cent goes to the person who shops. Straw mushrooms, it is clear, should be free of spots, and who would buy green beans if they did not snap when they were broken? Vietnam was the poorest country we visited, yet its markets had a fresh herb section that was as verdant as a summer garden.

In Japan the need for freshness is carried a step further. First you buy a very fresh vegetable. Then you make it look even fresher than nature can make it. For example, a cucumber was to be sliced into rounds. It had just been picked; it was perfect. It was, nonetheless, dropped into boiling water for a second and then rinsed in cold water before cutting. The taste remained unchanged but its skin turned a lusher green. Now the cucumber was *more* perfect than perfect!

In spite of their many common ingredients and cooking techniques, the cuisines of each of the eight countries chosen for this book are quite distinctive. Let me tell you a little about each of them.

Malaysia

Malaysian cuisine combines the delicacy of Chinese food with the exuberance of Indian spices and the aromas of South-East Asian herbs. This cuisine has developed interestingly. The original Malay diet consisted mostly of rice and fish. The two could be moistened with coconut and flavoured with a host of local seasonings such as shrimp paste (*blachan*), black pepper, ginger, turmeric, shallots, lemon grass and tamarind. But then things began to change.

A look at a map will reveal that peninsular Malaysia, sticking out like a finger into the sea, seems to be a natural meeting point between East and West Asia. It was actually more than that. From the earliest times favourable northeast and south-west monsoon winds literally blew in the ships of Indian, Arab and Chinese traders. By the early fifteenth century Malacca, a southern port, had become a hotbed of commerce, with trade flourishing in silk, jewels and spices. Each group not only traded but also left behind some of its members who settled and intermarried with local women. Starting with its sultan, a slow conversion to Islam also began. The following century brought the Portuguese, bearing chillies from the West, then the Dutch and English, all of whom stayed on to rule. In the nineteenth century rubber plantations and tin mines needed labour so Hindu and Muslim Tamil Indians and Hokkien-speaking Chinese were imported by the British. The Europeans eventually left but the Asians stayed.

As peoples of all three major races – the Malays, Chinese and Indians – commingled and merged, so did their cuisines. Malaysia is one of the world's few true melting pots. The sharp edges of racialism have been softened by the constant rubbing of multi-coloured shoulders, and the sharp differences in the cuisines have been blurred by the constant exchange of techniques and ingredients. Today one finds that, while some foods have kept their original form, most have been modified subtly or drastically, making it hard to fit many dishes into a clear niche or to pinpoint their exact origin.

I remember once attending a gathering of the Penang Women's Institute, where a dozen women had collected in the home of one of them to prepare a Malay-style meal. Shoes had been left at the front door, as is the custom, and the Muslim Malay ladies, in their long-sleeved, ankle-length dresses and headscarves, were padding around happily, pounding chillies, slicing shallots and squeezing out coconut milk. Hasna Abu Baker was to make a prawn and bottle gourd curry. She boiled the ground spices – ground cumin, coriander, fennel, pepper and chillies – in water, then added the prawns, the gourd and coconut milk. When they were cooked, she heated a little oil, browned shallots, garlic and whole fennel seeds in it, and then threw the oil and seasonings into the curry as a final flavouring. I had never seen this last step done anywhere except in India. The dish was a miraculously good hybrid.

On the other hand, the Indian Muslim community offered me one of their scrumptious marvels, *nasi kandar*, a meal of rice, beef curry, fish curry and hard-boiled eggs, that I had never seen in India. The name of the dish comes from two cultures: *nasi* is the Malay word for cooked rice and *kandar* may come from an Indian word for shoulder. To get this meal you would, some years ago, have to stop a vendor who carried a pole on his shoulder from which were suspended two baskets carrying all the dishes. You would be spooned a little of everything, with the sauce from the meat going over the eggs. Today the itinerant vendors have virtually disappeared, but specialised restaurants and caterers keep up the tradition. In Kuala Lumpur I watched one caterer, Puan Rashidah, prepare the curries. Most of the seasonings were Indian, but not all. For what went into the pots included the very Chinese star anise, the very Malay lemon grass – and soy sauce!

Throughout the nation Muslim Malays, while avoiding pork, have taken to Indian spice mixtures with a passion; Indian Hindus, while continuing to cook their traditional rice and split pea pancakes (*dosas*) and to avoid beef, now routinely add lemon grass and galangal to their coconut-enriched curries; the Chinese, while not giving up their Teo Chew-style duck braised in wine, enjoying eating Hokkien-style noodles with a fiery chutney (*sambal*) made with shrimp paste and red chillies. Today rice noodles can be found floating in a spicy coconut curry sauce (*curry mee*). Western-style cakes and breads are often flavoured with the aromatic pandanus leaves of the region.

The intermarriage between the Malay men and Chinese women in the Straits settlements of Penang and Malacca (as well as Singapore) has led to a new mixed culture – that of the 'Straits Chinese' – and to a style of cooking now gaining much favour in restaurants. Named after the women in the community, this cuisine is known as the food of the Nonyas. The Straits Chinese gave up the use of chopsticks and took to their fingers. They began to perfume and enliven their pork, prawns and chicken with coconut milk, candlenuts and tamarind. They still enjoyed mild gentle dishes such as Chicken with Bamboo Shoots in Black Bean Sauce and their airy stuffed pancakes (*Po piah*) but ate many fiery ones as well. Cooking skills were passed on from mother to daughter, a young girl's eligibility often depending on her ability to chop, cut and pound!

Nowadays the young Straits Chinese spend much less time in the kitchen as the entire nation seems to have become aware of the pleasures of eating out. Malaysia sits just above the equator and the climate is tropical. There are restaurants, of course, to go to, but food can be enjoyed even more as one takes the breeze if bought from obliging hawkers. From breakfast until dinner, hawkers sell an infinite variety of some of the world's most scrumptious snacks. On the way to the office, many workers stop to pick up *nasi lemak*, a banana leaf packet containing, at its simplest, some rice cooked with coconut milk, fried whitebait, a couple of tamarind-flavoured prawns, a few cucumber or pineapple slices and a dollop of fiery chilli sauce made with roasted shrimp paste and pounded red chillies. For lunch you can go to the open-air hawkers' centre on a high-rise rooftop such as the one I visited in Penang. Food here is served on green or orange plates. This is an Islamic nation and green signifies that the food is *halal* – that is, approved for Muslim consumption; orange plates may well have pork on them. This way friends of different faiths can sit together and know instantly what foods they must not touch and which are safe to eat. You might wish to end the day on Penang's seafront, Gurney Drive. Here, calmed by the soft lapping of the waves and the cooling breeze, you can take a last bite from one of those gorgeous sweet pancakes, *ban chan kuay*, spongily light and stuffed with sesame seeds and peanuts.

Recipes from Malaysia in this book include:

Stir-fried Prawns with Tamarind and Chillies *Sambal Udang*
Squid in Chilli and Garlic Sauce *Sotong Dan Chilli Dan Bawang Putih*

Beef Curry with Thick Onion Sauce *Daging Nasi Kandar*

Chicken with Bamboo Shoots and Mushrooms in Black Bean Sauce *Ayam Pongtay*
Hearty Chicken Curry with Potatoes *Lauk Ayam*
Duck Braised in Wine *Teo Chew-style Duck*
Egg Curry *Gulai Telor*

Squid in Black Sauce *Sotong Masak Kicap*
Spicy Prawn and Cucumber Curry *Gulai Labu*

Aubergine in a Thick, Hot, Sweet and Sour Chilli Sauce *Pacheri Terong*
Bean Sprouts with a Spicy Coconut Dressing *Kerabu Tawgeh*
Spicy Yellow Split Peas *Parpu*

Perfumed Rice with Vegetables Nonya-Style *Nasi Ulam*
Tomato Rice *Nasi Tomat*
Rice Noodles in a Coconut Curry Soup *Curry Mee*

Fluffy Pancakes with Sweet Sesame-peanut Filling *Ban Chan Kuay*

THAILAND

Thai food virtually bursts with contrasting hot, sweet, sour and salty flavours. The Thais have taken some of the best ideas from the cooking of the Malays, Chinese and Indians, thrown in their own zesty spirit and their love of the raw, crunchy, aromatic and colourful and have come up with a cuisine that is unmatched in its combination of lightness and seductive earthiness.

Take the Chicken, Prawn and Fruit Salad (*Yam Polamai*, page 52). Who, first of all, would think of putting such disparate ingredients together – shredded chicken, prawns, grapes, oranges, fried garlic, fried shallots and roasted peanuts – and then of dressing them with lime juice, sugar, salt and green chillies? Only the Thais. Yet this salad is so inspired and so good that, when I serve it, my guests cannot stop marvelling – or stop eating. Thailand has such a bountiful repertoire of salads: chicken combined with cucumber and chillies, prawns with oyster mushrooms, minced beef with mint and shallots, each more glorious than the next.

A Thai meal for a fairly well-off family in the Bangkok area is built around rice. Thailand exports its fine rices around the world and yet produces enough to allow each inhabitant to eat about 1 lb (450 g) a day at a very reasonable price. The rice is accompanied by a soup or a soupy stew, a stir-fried dish and a salad-like dish, all served at the same time and eaten either with the fingers or with a fork and a spoon, the fork being used only to shove the food into the latter implement. Many Thai restaurants catering to foreigners serve soups as a first course. All soups, including the stunning Hot and Sour Prawn Soup (*Tom Yam Kung*) with its hot and sour, lemon grass-flavoured broth and its floating prawns and straw mushrooms, are best enjoyed with spoonfuls of plain rice. The neutrality of the soft grain serves to absorb the heat of the soup and accentuate its flavours. Meals here tend to end with fruit: papayas carved like roses, mangoes carved like leaves, pineapples carved like pears and watermelon pieces carved as pineapples. It is quite an art, requiring lethal knives and great patience.

Thai foods can be hot – really hot. Generally hot dishes are balanced with mild ones. There are always side dishes of raw vegetables and fruit to nibble upon – forests of mint, lettuce leaves, long beans and bean sprouts. These often look like garnishes but they are meant to be eaten, offering both a change of texture and taste.

Aromatic herbs grow abundantly in this tropical country and are used generously. They include enormous families of mints and basils, coriander (the leaf and the root), kaffir lime leaves, the highly scented pandanus leaves and lemon grass. 'Indian' spices, such as cumin, coriander, turmeric, cinnamon, cardamom and cloves, *are* used but only for curries and in such small quantities as to leave more of a herby flavour than a spicy one. Gingers are used, particularly galangal, as well as various limes and tamarind for souring. Fish sauce (*nam pla*) and shrimp paste provide saltiness and added flavouring.

Thai curries are exquisite and vary throughout the country. The North, where pork reigns supreme, serves a dark and hearty Indo-Burmese-style curry, filled with large chunks of meat, which is eaten with little balls of hard glutinous rice. The South softens its curries with coconut milk, uses many more fresh herbs and cuts its meats (or prawns or chicken) into small pieces.

Vegetables are often cooked with small amounts of meat, generally pork. In one northern village I was treated to cauliflower stir-fried with minced pork. In Bangkok I often took myself for a cheap meal of green beans, stir-fried with minced pork and chillies, served behind my ritzy hotel; and I remember buying a quite scrumptious dish of *gai lan*, a green leafy vegetable, stir-fried with smoked pork. Pork lubricates the vegetable and gives it an added dimension.

Noodles are eaten in enormous quantities, especially at lunchtime. My favourite was the noodle soup made in two seconds flat by hawkers who sell nothing else. The noodles of your choice are lowered into boiling water and then dropped into your bowl. Green beans, bits of chicken and bean sprouts are lowered into stock until blanched and then draped over your noodles. A ladle of broth goes over everything. You then take this steaming bowl to your streetside table and season it with fish sauce, sugar, crushed chillies and roasted peanuts.

Sometimes a cuisine can best be gauged by its treatment of seafood. Many restaurants in and around Bangkok have large tanks of fresh fish. So first you go and pick it: 'I want *those* prawns, *that* crab, etc.' Then you seat yourself in some airy pavilion and wait. Soon the dishes begin to arrive: small prawns in a delicate broth wherein float little creamy pieces of young coconut; large prawns that have been grilled over wet straw (the smoke penetrates their bodies) and which you eat with fish sauce, vinegar and a chilli dipping sauce; juicy crabs that have been stir-fried with green chillies, mint and lemon grass. There is a phrase in Thailand which says, 'There is rice in the fields and fish in the water.' It means that all is well. Certainly in the culinary sense all seems to be very well in this marvellous country. (Thai recipes are listed on page 25.)

Previous page: Madhur Jaffrey (back to camera)
lunching with the Muslim Sanuar family,
Pandai Sikat, Sumatra, Indonesia

Opposite: Satay-seller, Jogyakarta, Indonesia

Above: Fresh red chillies, Malaysia

Above: Watermelons, Or Tor Kor Market,
Bangkok, Thailand

Opposite: Take-away food stall, Kuala Lumpur,
Malaysia

Opposite: Garlic and fiery red chillies, Chiang
Mai, Thailand

Above: Banana-seller, 1912 Market, Hanoi,
Vietnam

Overleaf: Spring-onion slicing, Chả Cá
Restaurant, Hanoi, Vietnam

Recipes from Thailand in this book include:

Hot and Sour Prawn Soup *Tom Yam Kung*
Chicken, Prawn and Fruit Salad *Yam Polamai*

Thai Pork Curry in the Burmese Style *Kaeng Hunglay*
Spicy Beef Salad *Laab*
Easy Beef Curry *Kaeng Phet Nua*

Red Chicken Curry *Kaeng Pet Kai*
Minced Chicken Stir-fried with Basil *Kai Pad Bai Kaprow*
Chicken with Garlic and Black Pepper *Kai Tod Kratium Priktai*

Squid Salad *Yam Pla Muk*
Fish Poached in Aromatic Tamarind Broth *Kaeng Som*
Fish Steamed with Lemon Grass *Tom Som Pla*

Stir-fried Green Beans with Pork and Chillies *Moo Pad Prik Sai Tua Fak Yao*
Greens with Garlic and Oyster Sauce or 'Flying' Greens *Pak Bung Loy Fa*
Spinach with Garlic and Fish Sauce *Pad Pak Bung*

Coconut Milk Custard *Sankhaya*

$\mathcal{J}$NDONESIA

Mrs Zainar's simple country cottage is built on a high hill overlooking the city.
She waits for us on a bench set under a star fruit tree. We have come to see her
kitchen garden. Unlike gardens in the West, it has no cabbages or cauliflowers.
This is a tropical garden – the equator goes right through the island of Sumatra
– and Mrs Zainar grows turmeric, galangal, ginger, chillies, lemon grass,
tamarind, nutmeg, basils, mints and cloves. She also has coconuts and aubergines. She is pretty self-sufficient – at least, in spices.

It is to Indonesia that traders – Indians, Arabs and eventually the Dutch –
came for spices. They grow easily here and quite abundantly as well. To see
these spices being used in everyday cooking, let us watch a fish curry (*gulai ikan*)
being made farther up the island by Mrs Sanuar. The fish was alive a short while
ago, swimming in the family tank. It has been mercifully dispatched and cut
into steaks. A daughter is grinding the spices on a stone slab set in the counter:

red chillies, shallots, ginger, galangal, fresh turmeric and candlenuts (so called because they can actually be lit). The spice mixture (or *bumbu*) is combined with the fish, coconut milk and herbs such as the leaves of turmeric and mint, and then left to cook. It will be a spectacular curry. I know; I have eaten it before.

The first time I came here was during the Muslim holy days that follow Idul Fitri, when all homes keep glass jars filled with pineapple pastries, little curry puffs and small Dutch-style cakes for visitors who drop by. Mrs Sanuar had treats of her own, including some wonderful peanuts that she had fried with garlic, shallots and Chinese celery. She invited us to stay for lunch. A cloth was spread out on the living room floor (I had seen this Muslim custom in India) and all foods placed, in traditional style, in the middle. Food was to be enjoyed communally. The fish curry was set down. So was some rice (the staple), cabbage greens cooked with a red chilli, shallot and garlic paste, some crisp wafers (*krupuk*) and the most renowed dish of the region, beef *rendang*.

Rendang is cooked for weddings and feasts. It is also called 'traveller's food' because it keeps well. Made with lots of coconut milk and flavoured with lemon grass and chillies, it cooks and cooks until most of the liquid is gone. It is a quite outstanding dish and the best example of West Sumatra's spicy style of food. Strangely enough, Padang, a small town in West Sumatra, has exported its cuisine all over Indonesia through the proliferation of what are now known as Padang restaurants. You can find them in the city. The food is hot, lots of dishes are brought to your table dramatically layered on the arms of the waiters and you pay only for what you eat. It's a good deal!

As it happens, there are more than 13,000 islands in the nation and each has a different culinary slant. Bali, for example, never turned to Islam as the rest of the nation did, so its inhabitants eat pork and turtle with great enthusiasm. The Balinese also specialise in cooking a whole duck or chicken by smothering it with a spice paste of chillies, shallots and turmeric, wrapping up the bird in banana leaves and baking it slowly over charcoal. It is moist, spicy and good. For some reason the Balinese do not like to eat fish; the rest of the islands do, however. From north Sulawesi comes *ikan rica rica* a marvellous fish dish: fish marinated with lime juice and salt is grilled and then smothered with a fried paste of coarsely crushed ginger, shallots and chillies. The Arabs brought skewered kebabs to Java. The East Javanese have now claimed them as their very own, transforming them with their sweet soy sauce (*kecap manis*) into delectable sweet and salty morsels called *satays*. *Satays* are sold nationally with the spicing changing dramatically from region to region.

Among my own favourites in Indonesia are the salads, such as *gado-gado*. Blanched and boiled vegetables – bean sprouts, cabbage, green beans and potatoes – are all arranged on a plate and then doused with a heavenly, hot, sweet, sour and nutty sauce made with peanuts.

Indonesia has no grand cuisine, no special palace dishes. The cuisine is egalitarian: everyone eats the same food. You eat with the right hand and pass food with the left. Food, with the exception of soup, is served at room temperature and is meant to be shared. Sweet teas and ginger coffees are drunk. Muslims generally do not drink alcohol, but the Hindu Balinese have a roaring time with a rice liquor, *brem*. Fruits here are superb and end a meal most satisfactorily. Those with a sweet tooth can take themselves off to the market to buy a sweet *martabak*, a kind of thick light pancake spread with butter and then dusted with sugar, crushed peanuts and tiny chocolate vermicelli. It drips all over the place when eaten but is irresistible.

Recipes from Indonesia in this book include:

Prawn Wafers *Krupuk Udang*
Spicy Chicken Soup with Many Flavours *Soto Ayam*

Beef Chunks Cooked in Coconut Milk *Kaliyo or Rendang Daging*

Stuffed Whole Chicken in a Parcel *Betutu Ayam*
Spicy Chicken Kebabs with a Peanut Sauce *Satay Ayam*

Whole Grilled Fish, Sour and Spicy *Ikan Panggang*
West Sumatran Fish Curry with Coconut Milk *Gulai Ikan*

Salad of Assorted Vegetables with a Delicious Peanut Dressing *Gado-Gado*
Cauliflower and Carrots with a Coconut Dressing *Gudangan*
Spiced Mushrooms in a Packet *Pepes Jamur*
Cabbage Stir-fried with Red Pepper Paste *Sala Lobak*
Green Beans and Carrots with Ginger and Chillies *Tumis Bunchis*

Special Fried Rice with Beef and Prawns *Nasi Goreng Istimewa*

Fluffy Pancakes with Sweet Sesame-peanut Filling *Ban Chan Kuay*
Ginger Coffee *Kopi Jahe*

KOREA

Let me, for a moment, pretend that I am a camera and zoom in – at dinner time, of course – on a middle-class Korean family. All members are seated on the floor around a low rectangular table. Each person has a metal bowl filled with rice. The short-grain rice, of a slightly sticky variety, is being picked up dextrously with strangely thin, knitting needle-like chopsticks. These chopsticks, as well as long-handled metal spoons, now reach out helter-skelter towards the centre of the table where there is a dish of blanched spinach, very lightly seasoned with sprinklings of sesame oil, roasted sesame seeds and soy sauce. In a heavy earthenware casserole can be seen a fiery-looking stew of fish, beef slices and bean curd cubes, still steamy from the retained heat. Near it sits a spicy stir-fried dish of pork and red peppers and, next to that, a bowl of cabbage pickle. Each person has a glass of hot barley tea. The mother of the family, who has cooked dinner, has trendily coiffured hair and pinkish-bronze rouge on her wide cheekbones. She works in a shop that sells jeans and other sportswear. The father's haircut is much more conservative. He works for a company exporting cars to the United States. There are two small children and their grandmother, who cares for them during the day. The flat is modern and small, a ninth-floor refuge in a suburban development, a long bus-ride out of Seoul. Inside the flat it is warm and cosy. Outside it is snowing.

This scene serves to tell much of my story. South Koreans are a rough-tough people of Mongol ancestry who have pushed their country from a developing third world nation into a hive of modern industry. China, which looms further to the north and across the waters to the east, has invaded many times and left a firm imprint. The Japanese were more recent – and much-hated – occupiers. They are rarely mentioned, though their silent mark may occasionally be felt. Today Confucian ideals and modern Mammon are equally revered in a fine balancing act while the Koreans hold on to their unique identity.

As in much of Asia, rice is essential to most meals, having supplanted the millet of ancient times. It is the same sort of rice that is eaten in Japan. Sometimes this rice is cooked together with barley or millet, making it richer nutritionally and nuttier in flavour. Noodles, especially those made of buckwheat and mung beans, are highly popular. On my very first trip to Korea, almost a decade ago, I remember succumbing to the cool flavours of a summer noodle soup, *naeng myon*. Cold buckwheat noodles had been topped with thin slices of cucumber, cold beef and crisp pear-apples. Then the entire lot had been dressed in a cold and utterly delicious meat broth. If this sounds tempting enough, just wait. The soup was meant to be seasoned further at the table with mustard, a sauce of soy and vinegar and some liquid from a pickle. It was heavenly!

At everyday Korean meals, soupy dishes or stews are almost always present. They are served side by side with grilled and stir-fried foods. Some dishes are very hot, others gentle and mild, the latter serving to calm the effects of the former. The seasonings in general use are soy sauce, vinegar, sesame oil, roasted sesame seeds, sugar, ginger, garlic, red chillies and a family of pastes (the *changs*) made of fermented soya beans.

More needs to be said about the last three – and about Korean pickles. First, the garlic.

It is said that the birth of Korea was the direct result of a union between the son of the divine creator, a bear and twenty cloves of garlic. The bear wanted to become human so the god gave it the garlic, suggesting that it retire for 100 days. It emerged as a woman and had a son by the god. This child, Tan'gun, then went on to found Korea. The Koreans may or may not have divinity in their blood. They certainly have a lot of garlic in it. They eat it morning, noon and night, sometimes raw, sometimes grilled, sometimes pickled, and almost always as a seasoning for their marinated and grilled meats and stews. I find it rather amusing that Western nutritionists are now beginning to tell us what Asian folk wisdom has known for centuries – that garlic cleanses the blood and keeps it flowing freely.

I cannot say for sure which country in this world eats the hottest foods, but South Korea must rank easily in the top three. Fiery chilli pods ripen to a rich red colour in the autumn here, at which time they are either cut into hair-thin slices before drying (old women are generally assigned this tedious task) or dried first and then pounded into some of the world's best chilli powder. Its bright carmine colour can be seen smothering squid rings, oysters and all manner of vegetables.

A visit to any Korean home reveals tall ceramic jars standing like silent sentinels on balconies, roofs and yards. These hold the pastes and pickles that give Korean meats their special character. The pastes, such as *toen chang* and *kochu chang*, are made of fermented soya beans and grains. The former, like Japanese *miso*, is mild; the latter, filled with chillies, a virtual firebird. Both may be added to stews to thicken and flavour them, and to boost their nutritional content.

Korean pickles (*kimchee*) are a world in themselves and *no* meal, from breakfast to dinner, is complete without them. There is a *kimchee* museum in Seoul that lists 160 varieties made of vegetables ranging from ordinary pumpkins to the precious ginseng root. The staple, however, remains the *kimchee* made of large Chinese cabbages (rather like Chinese leaves). The vegetables are brined, then stuffed with a mixture containing, among other things, spring onions, ginger, garlic, radishes and red chillies. They are then packed into vats and left to seethe and bubble until they have turned sufficiently sour, by which time they are rich in minerals and vitamin C and are addictively wonderful.

The Korean peninsula is surrounded by the sea on three sides and creatures from these waters are consumed daily, sometimes by themselves, sometimes in the most imaginative combinations with meat. A fish stew may have slices of beef in it and a dozen cockles may be set loose in a sea of pork broth.

Rice, fish and pickles are taken for granted in Korea. It is beef, a relatively new item as far as common consumption goes, that is prized – in particular the marinated and grilled-at-the-table beef strips called *bulgogi*. Tasting of the ginger and garlic, soy sauce, spring onions and sesame seeds that are in their marinade, they hiss and sizzle in front of the diners, teasing them with their heavenly aroma. After a recent poll of children on their likes, the *Korean Times* discovered that mother came first, beef was second and father was third. I feel sorry for father, but here's a hurray for beef – especially *bulgogi*!

Recipes from South Korea in this book include:

Bean Sprout and Radish Soup *Kongnamul Kuk*

Meatball Soup *Wanja Kuk*
Stir-fried Pork with Red Pepper *Twaeji Bokkum*
Marinated and Grilled Beef Strips *Bulgogi*

Chicken Patties with Ginger and Sesame Seeds *Tak Kogi Sopsanjok*
Spicy Chicken Stew with Carrots and Potatoes *Tak Tori Tang*
Savoury Egg Custard with Prawns and Mushrooms *Keran Chim*

Fish, Shellfish and Bean Curd Stew *Saengsun Chigae*

Stir-fired Courgettes with Sesame Seeds *Hobak Namul*
Seasoned Spinach *Sigumchi Namul*

Cellophane Noodles with Beef and Vegetables *Chapchae*
Potato Pancakes *Ganja Buchin*

Hot Fermented Bean Paste *Kochu Chang*
Cabbage Pickle *Kimchee*

Candied Walnut Halves *Hotoo Twikim*

THE PHILIPPINES

It is fiesta time in the small Negros village. Long tables have been set under shady trees and covered over with banana leaves. A whole pig (*lechon*), roasted to a turn on a spit, its skin crackling-crisp, is stretched across the centre like an edible epergne. It has been stuffed in the old traditional manner with sour tamarind leaves. It has been basted, in the new traditional manner, with bottled American-style ginger ale.

On either side of the pig are whole steamed and roasted chickens (*rellenong manok*). They have been boned, marinated overnight in soy sauce and the juice of the small *kalamansi* lime, then stuffed with, among other things, minced meats such as pork, veal, Chinese ham and Spanish sausage, as well as olives, pimentoes, several American-style pickles, sultanas and Parmesan cheese. There are also generous platters of rice *paella*, chock-full of prawns, chicken pieces and sausage.

Ginger ale, Spanish sausage, olives, *paella*?

Like most South-East Asian countries, the Philippines has seen waves of Chinese traders and settlers who brought noodles, bean curd, soy sauce, pancakes and spring rolls in their wake. They intermarried with the local Malays to such an extent that much of the country is of Chinese-Malay extraction. Muslims came too, Arabs and Indians, bearing Islam, cumin and coriander. But the people who had the most influence on the country, its religion, customs – and food – were the ones who followed, the Spaniards and the Americans.

The Spanish came in 1521 and ruled until 1898. At that point the Americans took over, staying through the Second World War until 1946. The Spanish occupation not only gave the Philippines its name (the country is named after Philip II of Spain) and its major religion, Catholicism, but introduced a Mediterranean style of eating. Spanish food was mostly cooked in olive oil, with seasonings limited to garlic, onions, tomatoes, sweet peppers and vinegar. The Filipinos were not about to give up their own Chinese-Malay dishes, but they did begin to add Spanish ingredients to their own recipes and to cook the newcomers' fancy food as well. They thought it rather grand, however, to call most dishes by Spanish names, especially on menus.

With the Americans came a large military presence and vast stocks of exotic goodies such as tinned evaporated and condensed milk, tinned fruit, bottled mayonnaise, hot dogs, sweet bottled pickles and tinned tomato sauce (a kind of thin purée). It was considered a decided improvement to make the Spanish dessert *flan* (caramel custard) with evaporated milk instead of water buffalo milk and quite trendy to eat steaks.

Rice, fish and pork have remained the national staples. Rice is eaten from breakfast to dinner and made into thousands of different cakes, noodles and pancakes. This is a nation of 7,000 islands, and fish – fresh or dried – is eaten daily, especially in the villages. It is also made into fish sauce (*patis*) which is used here almost as much as soy sauce in China. A village meal might well consist of vegetables cooked with cockles, fried dried fish and rice.

Pork is a much-loved meat and is eaten often by those who can afford it. The national dish is probably *adobo*. Even though chicken and squid *adobos* are very popular, pork is the universal favourite. This dish, originally of Spanish extraction, now involves marinating pork pieces in soy sauce and vinegar with garlic, bay leaves and peppercorns, and then cooking them until they brown in their own juices. It is uncommonly good – and lasts well because of the vinegar. (In my house, however, it does not last at all. It gets eaten the minute its made!)

A common breakfast is rice stir-fried with garlic, and cured meat, the two washed down with glasses of ginger tea. Breakfast for the rich, though, could turn into a three-hour meal with thick, frothy chocolate in demi-tasse cups, fluffy, sugared, coiled buns (*ensaimada*), 'sardined' fish cooked with onions and peppers, an array of smoked fish, salted ducks' eggs, fried eggs, Chinese ham, Spanish sausages and glutinous rice lozenges to be eaten with ripe mangoes.

Lunch could bring a stew of mung beans and prawns (*mongo*), often eaten with a few drops of olive oil and lime juice, a goat and potato stew (*caldereta*) and an aubergine salad (*ensaladang balasenas*), all to be eaten with rice.

Filipinos seem to eat all the time and, perhaps finding the gap between lunch and dinner too long, have come up with a whole meal of snacks known as *merienda*. Almost anything can be made to fit here: noodles decked with plump oysters, mango and guapple pies (a guapple being a large, hard, apple-like guava), little ground rice cupcakes (*puto*), stuffed pancakes (*lumpia*) and tiny pastry envelopes filled with mango and banana jam (*panyo-panyo*). To drink there is the refreshing *kalamansi* lime juice and hot chocolate.

The Filipinos are not done. They happily go on to dinner. They might visit a simple *turo-turo* (literally 'point-point') cafeteria to enjoy a hearty pork and chick pea stew (*menudo*), or they might take themselves to a dressier restaurant and start with coconut-enriched seafood soup filled with clams, mussels and prawns and flavoured lightly with ginger, then go on to a deep-fried pork knuckle, beautifully crisp outside and showered with bits of fried garlic and chillies. And for the dessert? Well, how about a large wedge of the American-style lemon meringue pie?

Recipes from the Philippines in this book include:

Mung Bean Soup *Mongo Guisado*
Glorious Seafood Soup *Ama Tito Rey Soup*
Mackerel 'Cooked' in Lime Juice *Kilawing Tanguigue*

Pork Cooked in a Pickling Style *Adobong Baboy*
Lamb or Goat Stew with Potatoes, Peppers and Olives *Caldereta*
Knockout Knuckle *Patang Bawang*
Pork with Calf's Liver and Chick Peas *Menudo*

Piquant Prawns *Gambas Picantes*
Squid with Tomatoes *Adobong Pusit*

Mange-tout Stir-fried with Prawns *Sitsaro Guisado*

Rice with Seafood, Chicken and Sausages *Paella*

Caramel Custard Filipino-style *Leche Flan*
Ginger Tea *Salabat*
Apple (or Guapple) Pie

Vietnam

It was late afternoon in December and uncomfortably chilly. A phalanx of bicycles rushed down a wide Hanoi boulevard. One cyclist, wearing a heavy navy blue jacket, stopped at the entrance to the market and then wheeled his bicycle inside. He bought a huge bunch of swamp cabbage, a green vegetable rich in minerals and vitamins, and strapped it to the back of his bicycle. He intended to cook the vegetables with fish sauce (called *nuoc mam* here) and red chillies, and eat it with fresh noodles. He then walked past the writhing eels and the woman roasting large rice flour wafers encrusted with sesame seeds, stopping once again in front of a woman who squatted before a basket of flowers – pink asters, bright yellow chrysanthemums and an array of the most desirable old-fashioned roses. He put down his money and took the roses. Then, holding them jauntily aloft in one hand and steering with the other, he rejoined the moving river of cyclists and headed home.

Vietnam is indeed a devastated land. Fields are still dotted with bomb craters. But the people have not lost their flair or their style. The country is changing fast. Northern cities, once unable to obtain the more abundant foodstuffs of the south, are doing better as the road system improves. There is much more money in the south, particularly in Hô Chí Minh City, much of it coming in hard currency from relatives abroad. In the warm evenings there, the young zoom round and round the town centre on motor cycles, stopping at one of the many restaurants to listen to Linda Ronstadt or Abba on tape, drink Saigon Beer and eat the world's best spring rolls made with tissue-thin edible rice paper, or spicily cooked chicken pieces flavoured with lemon grass, or whole smoked aubergines smothered with a lime sauce.

The Vietnamese people are of mixed Malay and Chinese stock and have a history of foreign influences. The upper part of the country was either occupied or dominated by China for a thousand years, well into the middle of the tenth century. Indians came – somewhat more peacefully – to the south, where they traded their spices. Western powers, looking first for trade and then colonies, followed, starting around the sixteenth century. France had virtually taken over the country by the late sixteenth century. The Americans came last. Each left their mark.

The Chinese influence is quite pervasive. It can be seen in the use of chopsticks, in the small and delicate spring rolls, in the use of bean curd, fermented soya beans, star anise and Chinese medicinal herbs. It can be seen in the mixture of pork and crab for soups and fillings. It can also be seen in the Vietnamese love of noodles, especially of *phở*. This is a noodle soup, a glorious breakfast soup, though it can be eaten at any time.

The Vietnamese day starts early. Offices open at 7.30 am in summer, 8.00 am in winter. Before that there are exercises to be done and breakfast to be had in one of the many state-run or private restaurants. Most people opt for *phở*^{z}. The stock for this, a meat broth flavoured with roasted ginger and star anise, bubbles in a cauldron. As an order comes in, rice noodles are heated in water and put in a bowl. Cooked beef slices go on top and then slices of raw beef. This is topped with green coriander, mint and spring onions. Boiling stock is ladled over the top. The stock magically releases the fragrances of the herbs and turns the raw beef into rare beef. (In these days of hardship the beef is more often replaced by chicken, which is cheaper.) The soup is seasoned further at the table with a red chilli sauce which adds heat and colour, fish sauce that adds saltiness and rounds off the flavour of the stock, and a generous squeeze of lime. *Phở*^{z} is eaten with chopsticks and a Chinese-style spoon.

The Indian influence can be seen in the use of curry powders in the south, and in the ground rice pancakes. Perhaps the best example of the latter is *banh cuon*, an exquisitely delicate creation. Thin batter is poured on to a piece of muslin to steam briefly. Then the soft pancake is almost scraped off and used to enfold a very Chinese stuffing of minced pork and black fungus. It is served post-haste with crisply fried shallots on the top and a dipping sauce of pork stock seasoned with fish sauce, vinegar, sugar and chillies. If you are lucky, a few drops of jasmine-like essence that comes from a special beetle are put into it as well. It is glorious!

You can tell that the French were here by the dashing berets the men wear. French bread is sold in every city. Quick lunches can be made by splitting a loaf in half, lathering it with butter from the Soviet Union and then stuffing it with slices of pâté or sausage or the Spam-like *chả lụa*. Coffee, once very popular among the Westernised Vietnamese, is hard to find, but tea is drunk all the time. Every office has vacuum flasks of water and a slightly bitter tea is made up quickly in small teapots and served in tiny, Chinese-style, handless cups.

What really distinguishes Vietnam's food from its neighbours' is its use of fresh herbs. Mounds are used for each meal. Every mouthful becomes a little perfumed package. If, say, a piece of fish cooked in coconut milk is to be eaten, a portion is put into a piece of lettuce. This is topped with fresh coriander, mints, basils, spring onions and peanuts. It is wrapped up, dipped in a sauce and *then* eaten. The same happens to a piece of meat that has been marinated with garlic, shallots and lemon grass; and to small, bite-sized spring rolls. Aromatic herbs keep exploding in the mouth, each fresher than the last.

Dill is commonly used, especially in conjunction with fish. One of Hanoi's specialities is *cha² cá*. A restaurant and a street are named after it. Chunks of firm river fish are marinated in a mixture of turmeric, galangal, shrimp paste, lime juice and tamarind, then grilled over charcoal and brought to the table where a frying-pan set over a portable stove awaits. The fish is reheated in lard and fish sauce and then smothered with a blanket of fresh dill and spring onions. As soon as the herbs wilt, the fish can be devoured with the assistance of fresh rice noodles, chopped peanuts and deliciously sour dipping sauces.

It is not just the herbs that give Vietnamese food its special character. It is the mixture of the herbs, the flavours of lemon grass, galangal and fried shallots, the taste of crushed, freshly roasted peanuts, and the use of salty, hot and sour dipping sauces that make Vietnamese food so wonderfully unique.

Recipes from Vietnam in this book include:

Savoury Pork and Crab Toasts *Bánh Mì Chiên*
Pork and Crab Soup *Canh Thịt Nấu Cua*
Small Spring Rolls *Nem Rán*

Aromatic and Spicy Beef Stew *Thịt Bō Kho*
Napoleon Beef on a Skewer *Thịt Bò Lụi*
Easy Beef Kebabs *Bō Nướng Chả*

Spicy Stir-fried Chicken with Lemon Grass *Gà Xào Xẵ Ớt*
Roast Chicken with Five-spice Powder *Gà Xối Mở²*

Steamed Fish with Ginger and Coconut Milk *Cá Lóc Hấp*
Fish Braised in Tea *Cá Kho*
Monkfish with Dill *Chả² Cá*

Kohlrabi or Broccoli Stem Salad *Nộm Su Hào*
Smoky Aubergines in a Lime Sauce *Cà Tím Nướng*
Courgettes with Pork and Prawns *Bâù Xào*

Rice Noodles in Soup with Beef *Phở²*

HONG KONG

The crabs, of leafy green hue, squirm in mild protest. Their fierce claws have been tied to their bodies with matching grass and they have been laid out in baskets with regimental neatness. Each worthy crab is destined for the pot. It is October in Hong Kong and the two-month season for Shanghai's hairy crabs has just started. Trains from the north-east have been rumbling in with their valuable catch. Each small crab is more expensive than a lobster is in the West. Yet three or four per person will be eaten at each meal! The Chinese here know that in October they should eat the females as they just ooze with the much-prized roe; November is the time to tackle the males. They also know that each crab should be steamed alive and that it should be kept tied as it cooks to keep the meat sweet and to prevent the crab from releasing its juices – and its roe – as it struggles. Their cultural traditions have also armed them with the knowledge that crabs are very *yin*, or cooling. So they will eat them with shreds of young ginger, which is *yang*, or heating, and, for good measure, drink ginger tea afterwards.

Hong Kong – big, brash and bustling – is a modern city with an ancient culture. Its 6,500,000 people, who use ferries, buses, underground trains and hydrofoils to zig-zag across its many islands at frenzied speed, know how to make money and how to eat. With the sea on one side and fertile sub-tropical country on the others, they have constant access to a rich supply of the fruits of earth and sea. Spoilt by nature's abundance and fine-tuned by an ancient culinary tradition that is easily one of the world's finest, they demand the best ingredients and are not satisfied unless they get them. They know that a bearded kitchen god watches each hearth, ready to report all errors to his superior above.

Hong Kong, ceded to the British in the nineteenth century, is almost completely encircled by the 3,696,100 square miles that are China. Its cuisine is very much a mirror of the varying cultural traditions of the mother country. Indeed, half of Hong Kong's food and water is brought from there.

Most moderately equipped kitchens here contain certain staples: rice; soy sauces, light and dark; vinegars of varying hues; oil for cooking (peanut) and flavouring (sesame); as well as preserved and pickled foods. The spice rack may hold red chillies, Sichuan peppercorns, star anise, cassia bark and sesame seeds.

Other ingredients must be bought fresh. I have watched prawns being rejected because they were kicking their legs too lazily, lobsters dropped back into tanks because their tails did not curl smartly and crabs failing to find a buyer because their bellies were squishy. Live cockles you buy may be cooked with black bean sauce; prawns may be steamed with garlic oil and spring onions; a whole fish steamed with ginger, pork shreds and sour pickle; and crab may be combined with chicken and winter melon for a soup. Over 30,000 fishermen supply the Hong Kong area with almost 100,000 tons of fish a year.

Daily shoppers are just as choosy about a vast selection of vegetable produce. There are, first of all, herbs and seasonings such as fresh coriander, chives and ginger; bland foods that will serve to absorb flavours and add textures, including bean curd and bamboo shoots; fungi that will add taste as well as protein and vitamin C; gourds to be stir-fried; and cabbages and radishes that can be put into soups and stews.

The day starts early with a choice of breakfasts. Is it to be a bowl of rice porridge (*congee*), a deep-fried Chinese long doughnut (*you tiao*) or a steamed bun (*baozi*)? There would, of course, be tea, the national drink.

For mid-morning tea there is the tea house. Just as there are pubs in England that turn into clubs for the local clientele, so it is with tea houses in Hong Kong. Some are used by wheelers and dealers of the financial world, others by bird fanciers who bring in their pet birds for a bit of appreciation – and perhaps a fight. The business of tea drinking (*yam cha*) is a serious one. First you pick your tea leaves from the many green, half-fermented and fermented teas. Then you go through the motion of 'washing' your cup in a bowl of hot water at the table, then you brew the tea. Regular patrons leave their teas in marked caddies at the tea house. To accompany the tea there is a wide choice of *dim sum*, little snacks whose name means 'order what you fancy': steamed shrimp dumplings with their translucent gossamerlike covering; bits of roast pork baked in savoury pastry; or even a masterfully engineered dumpling filled with soup!

Lunch or dinner could take the form of noodles bought from a neighbourhood stall or it could mean a visit to a restaurant embedded in one of the newer plazas where the meal might be preceded by ice skating, bowling or buying a Gucci handbag! The choice in styles of food available reflects in microcosm what may be found throughout all of China. Lovers of the fiery cuisines of the western regions of Sichuan and Hunan might wish to dine on Cold Chicken with Sesame and Chilli Sauce or the crispy, sweet and hot Fried Shredded Beef with Carrots and Chillies or Pork in Hot and Sour Soup. A Pekinese restaurant might supply the northern delicacies, Lamb with Spring Onions, Spring Onion Bread or Peking Duck. The north eats more wheat than rice, using it to make fried and steamed breads as well as noodles. If you have membership and feel like the mellow, slightly sweet food of the eastern region, you might take yourself to the Shanghai Club and order their Fried Chicken with Spring Onion

Sauce. It is marvellously crisp on the outside and smothered with a sauce of minced fresh herbs.

You could pick Cantonese food, the local cuisine. Mild and gently seasoned, it is designed, as the Cantonese say, 'to let the ingredients shine through'. The freshest of fish fillets are stir-fried with black bean sauce, and young prawns combined with jade-green asparagus.

A few words about etiquette. The Chinese invented chopsticks and use the 'nimble brothers' with masterful ease. Chopsticks should never be left in a crossed position (except after eating *dim sum* to indicate that you have finished). Soup spoons are used not only for soup but also for the liquid in stews. All foods, except the individual bowls of rice, are communal and placed in the centre of the table. Rice bowls should be brought near the mouth when you eat from them, not left on the table. When eating a whole cooked fish, you should never turn it over to get at the flesh on the other side (if you do, a fishing boat will tip over!). And yes, you may slurp your soup!

(The spellings of Chinese words and place names in this book follow the pinyin system of converting Chinese characters to the Roman alphabet.)

Recipes from Hong Kong in this book include:

Summer Soup with Pork and Cucumber *Wei Ling Qinggua Rou Jin Jiang*

Lamb with Spring Onions *Cong Bao Yang Roll*
Glazed Gingery Spareribs *Hong Shao Leigu*
Pork with Long Beans and Chives *Sijidou Chao Zhuliu*
Sichuan-style Fried Shredded Beef with Carrots and Chillies *Gongbao Niuliu*

Cold Chicken with Sesame and Chilli Sauce *Malaji*
Chicken Stir-fried with Celery *Jiancai Jiding*
Fried Chicken with Spring Onion Sauce *Youpi Ziji*

Prawns with Asparagus *Xian Lusun Chad Xiaqiu*
Fish Fillets with Black Bean Sauce *Doushi Yi*

Braised Broad Beans *Shengbian Candou*
Bean Curd with Oyster Sauce *Haoyou Doufu*
Salad of Carrots, Celery, Cucumber and Ham *Liang Ban Yangcai*

Cold Sesame Noodles with Chicken and Vegetables *Bon Bon Jihan Banmian*
Noodles with Pork in Hot and Sour Soup *Suanla Zha Jiangmian*

Sweet Walnut Soup *Waiyou Hetao Tang*

JAPAN

Many years ago my husband and I were taken to one of the better eating establishments on one of the uglier outskirts of Kyoto city. The day was hot and miserable, the city congested and the traffic a nightmare. But the minute we entered the restaurant, our world changed. Our private room was cool and serene. We were seated facing the one large window. All we could see from it was a hill, a stream and an exquisitely proportioned tree. The window frame had been ingeniously placed to crop out all vulgarity and disarray.

Japanese food is meant to serve the same purpose – to create order out of chaos, to bring a sense of simplicity and perfection to a confused and entangled world. The principles belong to Zen Buddhism and apply to most aspects of Japanese culture. Foods are prepared so that their natural flavours remain unmasked and they are served in small, almost austere portions. The arrangement of food on the plate is always three-dimensional – it may be in little hillocks, or one food may lean against another – and, especially in the classy restaurants, it is made to resemble 'nature' as much as possible. Tiny long-stemmed mushrooms float in a soup like fresh-fallen flowers in a stream. Bits of skewered and grilled chicken are set on a plate with leaves and end up by looking like small buds in a tree. It is said that a good Japanese restaurant is rated on three things: a third of the marks go to the cooking, a third to the presentation and the remaining third to the general ambience.

Not everyone can rise to the heights of the great Japanese chefs, but the principles hold true even for everyday meals. A very simple Japanese breakfast might consist of rice, a soup of fermented bean paste (*miso*) with perhaps a few cubes of bean curd floating in it, some pickles and tea. The only eating implement would be chopsticks, the liquid part of the soup being drunk by bringing the soup bowl to the mouth. *Miso* is made of fermented soya beans and grains. There is a world of such pastes in Japan. They range in colour from white to almost black and in texture from smooth to very grainy. With judicious mixing, the flavour of your morning soup can be varied daily.

I find it interesting that many of these breakfast habits are changing. People now walk into coffee shops and order 'morning', which brings them coffee, toast and an egg, if they like! The Japanese have even invented a bread-making machine where all you have to do is put in the right measure of flour and the machine kneads, rests and bakes a loaf!

New-fangled inventions notwithstanding, rice is the staple grain. Japan has very little arable land and rice is made to grow on every available patch, however small it may be. The Japanese pay a lot for their short-grain, somewhat

Previous page: Coconut plantation, Philippines

Opposite: Fish drying, Guinilaharan Village, Negros Island, Philippines

Above: Vegetables, Happy Valley Market, Hong Kong

Overleaf: Dried-food stall, Hong Kong

Previous page: Grilled fish in Nishiki Street,
Kyoto, Japan

Above: Construction workers in Kyoto, Japan,
enjoying a bento box lunch

Opposite: Dried fish stall, East Gate Market,
Seoul, Korea

Overleaf: Fish-seller, Songsan Port, Cheju
Island, Korea

glutinous rice. They could import it; it would be far cheaper that way. But the Japanese are fiercely independent and do not wish to rely on others for a basic foodstuff. Besides, they like the flavour of their own grain.

As in the entire Far East, noodles are very popular. There are restaurants, both humble and expensive, that specialise in them. In the heat of the summer I have sat by a stream and had cold noodles float by me in a moat built into the counter. Once I had fished out the noodles, I had only to dip them in a citron-flavoured dip before devouring them. In the cold autumn I have been served a steaming noodle casserole filled with mushrooms just picked from fallen logs and topped with a poached egg. It is best, my hosts explained, to suck the hot noodles in. The slurping allows an intake of air which cools them off.

The Japanese like to stress the seasons in their meals. In summer a moss-eating fish might be served to you on a bed of cool-looking pebbles; in autumn you might get chrysanthemum petals in your salad; winter might bring steaming savoury custards and bean curd casseroles (bean curd retains its heat for a long time); and spring might produce fiddlehead ferns and young bamboo shoots.

Until the nineteenth century the only flesh consumed by the Japanese came from fish and birds. It then began to be felt that the Japanese race might grow taller and stronger if it ate red meat. So recipes for pork and beef were developed, such as breaded pork cutlets or *tonkatsu*; *sukiyaki*, in which thick slices of beef and vegetables are braised together at the table; and *shabu shabu*, a kind of fondue in which meats and vegetables are dipped at the table into a bowl of simmering kelp stock to cook them and then into a choice of sauces to season them. All these dishes made for delicious meals and tempted many Japanese to eat red meat.

Fish still predominates in the Japanese diet, however. The basic Japanese stock (*dashi*) used in everything from soups to sauces is made from shavings of dried bonito (a large mackerel-like fish) and dried kelp. The nation delights in raw fish, which can come in the form of *sashimi*, thin fish slices eaten with a dip of horseradish-flavoured soy sauce, or in the form of *sushi*, where sliced raw fish of all sorts is put together with small portions of lightly seasoned rice and eaten as *canapés* might be. Fish may be grilled simply with just a sprinkling of salt or basted as it grills with a thicker sauce of soy and sweet rice wine (*mirin*). It may be tossed with rice wine (*sake*), steamed and then served with a sauce of lemon and soy. It may also be dipped in batter and fried, making the glorious *tempura*. There are just as many ways of cooking chicken. Perhaps the most-loved chicken dish, though, is *yakitori*, a kind of chicken kebab dipped into a sweetish soy sauce mixture during the grilling.

It may by now be apparent that Japanese seasonings and sauces are made of careful permutations of the same few ingredients: soy sauce, rice wine (*sake*) sweet rice wine (*mirin*), sugar, fish and kelp stock (*dashi*), the juice of various sour citrus fruits and the occasional use of an aromatic Japanese pepper (*sansho*). The national drink is *sake*; these days, however, whisky or beer may be drunk right through a meal, and French wines, too, are encroaching.

For an informal meal, a family might serve grilled fish, a salad-like dish of spinach or beans dressed with sesame seeds, and perhaps carrots braised in stock. There would also be soup, rice, pickles and tea to round off the meal.

Rice, pickles and tea complete the most formal of dinners as well. I have known Japanese men to eat for three hours at official banquets but refrain from devouring that final triumvirate. 'My wife will be waiting up,' they say. 'I will have my rice with her.' Rice symbolises the meal, and the man who has his rice at home is eating his meal with his wife. Symbols mean a lot in Japan.

Recipes from Japan in this book include:

Stuffed Mushrooms *Shiitake Nikozume*
Fermented Bean Paste Soup with Bean Curd *Miso Shiru*
Cucumber and Prawn Salad *Ebi To Kyuri No Sunomono*

Breaded Pork Cutlets *Tonkatsu*
Breaded Pork Cutlets over Rice *Katsudon*

Chicken Bits on a Skewer *Yakitori*
Chicken with a Sweet Sake Glaze *Toriniku No Teriyaki*

Grilled Mackerel with Sweet Soy Sauce *Sake No Teriyaki*
Prawn and Vegetable Fritters *Tempura*

Green Beans with Sesame Dressing *Sando Mame No Goma Aye*
Mushrooms in a Spring Onion Dressing *Kinoko No Aemono*

Noodles in Broth with Poached Egg and Vegetables *Sansai Udon*
Mixed Rice *Kayaku Gohan*
Ginger Shreds in Sweet Vinegar *Hari Shoga*

Sake

THE
RECIPES

FIRST COURSES

YAM POLAMAI   THAILAND

CHICKEN, PRAWN AND FRUIT SALAD

FROM CHALIE AMATYAKUL AT BANGKOK'S ORIENTAL HOTEL COOKING SCHOOL
There is such exuberance about Thai salads. Not only are meat, fish and fruit
all put together, but they also are seasoned quite brilliantly with hot, sweet,
sour and salty flavours as well as with crisply fried slivers of shallots and
garlic. This salad does have several parts to it but each takes very little time to
prepare. You will, I promise, be more than compensated when your family and
friends cry out with delight at the very first mouthful – this is a superb dish.

In Thailand the fruit in the salad can include such exotic fare as pomelo,
water chestnuts, mangoes, rose apples, mangosteens and litchis, all of which
should be diced. Do use these fruit if you can find them. The amount of sugar,
salt, lime juice and chillies will vary not just according to your taste but also
according to the natural flavours of the fruit. Taste as you mix the salad and make
your own adjustments. If you do not want tiny explosions of 'heat' as you eat, leave
out the green chillies and use chilli powder instead. You may use cooked instead
of uncooked prawns, in which case you will not need to poach them.

All the ingredients and separate parts of the salad may be prepared several
hours ahead of time. The salad should, however, be mixed only at the last
minute so that the texture is crisp.

Salt

1 large, firm, sour dessert
   apple (such as a Granny
   Smith)

5 oz (150 g) medium to large
   red or black grapes,
   preferably seedless

5 oz (150 g) medium to large
   green grapes, preferably
   seedless

1 medium orange

Combine 1 teaspoon salt with 1 pint (600 ml)
water in a small bowl. Peel and core the apple and
cut it into ¼–⅓ inch (0.5–0.75 cm) dice. As you
cut and dice, put the apple pieces into the salted
water. Set aside. Halve the grapes lengthways and
remove the seeds where necessary. Put the grapes
into a bowl. Peel the orange, separate the segments
and skin them as best you can. Cut each segment
crossways at ⅓ inch (0.75 cm) intervals. Lay the
orange pieces over the grapes. Cover and set aside.

5 cloves garlic

3½ oz (90 g) shallots or onions

Oil for deep-frying

4 oz (100 g) chicken breast, boned and skinned

8 medium or 16 small uncooked unpeeled prawns

4 tablespoons Roasted Peanuts (see page 236)

1 teapoon sugar

3 tablespoons fresh lime or lemon juice

2–3 fresh hot green chillies

2 tablespoons fresh coriander leaves

Peel the garlic, cut into thin slices and cut the slices into fine slivers. Peel the shallots, halve them lengthways and thinly slice them.

Pour the oil to a depth of 1 inch (2.5 cm) into a medium-sized frying-pan or wok. Place over a medium-low heat. While you are waiting for the oil to get hot, set a sieve over a bowl and place it on a work-surface near the pan. Spread some kitchen paper over a large plate. When the oil is hot, put in the garlic slivers and stir and fry until they turn golden. Empty the oil and garlic into the sieve; then, when the garlic has drained, spread it out over one half of the kitchen paper.

Put the oil in the bowl back into the frying-pan and set it over a medium heat. Replace the sieve over the bowl. When the oil has reheated, put in the shallots and stir and fry until they are golden-brown and crisp. Empty the contents of the pan into the sieve. When the shallots have drained, spread them out over the remaining kitchen paper. (Save the flavoured oil for cooking other foods.)

Cut the chicken into long thin strips and put these into a clean medium-sized frying-pan. Add water to cover and ¼ teaspoon salt, and bring to a simmer. Simmer gently for about 5 minutes or until the chicken is just done. Remove the chicken from the water and tear it into shreds 1 inch (2.5 cm) long or cut it into ¼–⅓ inch (0.5–0.75 cm) dice. Save the water in which it was cooked.

Peel and de-vein the prawns. Bring the chicken poaching water to a simmer and add the prawns. Turn the heat to medium-low. Stir and poach the prawns for 2–3 minutes or until they are just cooked through. Drain. Cut the prawns into ¼–⅓ inch (0.5–0.75 cm) dice. Combine the chicken and prawns, cover and set aside.

Crush the peanuts lightly – put them into a polythene bag and hit them gently with a hammer. Set them aside. Combine 1 teaspoon salt, the sugar and lime juice in a small bowl and mix. Set aside. Cut the chillies into very fine rounds. Wash and dry the coriander. Cover and set aside.

Immediately before you are ready to serve, drain the apples and and pat them dry. Set aside a little of the fried shallots and coriander for garnishing, then toss all the other ingredients together in a large bowl. Check the seasoning. Bring the salad to the table on individual plates, garnished with the reserved shallots and coriander.

SERVES 6 AS A FIRST COURSE OR 4 AS A MAIN COURSE

SAMBAL UDANG   MALAYSIA

STIR-FRIED PRAWNS WITH TAMARIND AND CHILLIES

Hot, sour and simple to prepare, this is yet another delicious way to cook prawns.

2–10 dried hot red chillies (2 will make a very mild dish, 10 a hot one)

6 candlenuts or 8 cashew nuts

3½ oz (90 g) shallots or onions

1 teaspoon shrimp or anchovy paste

1 lb (450 g) uncooked unpeeled prawns

8 tablespoons vegetable oil

2 tablespoons tamarind paste (see page 272) or 4 teaspoons lime or lemon juice

½ teaspoon salt

2 teaspoons sugar

Crumble the chillies into a cup. Add the nuts and 5 tablespoons water. Set aside for 1 hour. Peel the shallots and chop them coarsely. When the chillies and nuts have finished soaking, put them and their soaking liquid into a blender. Add the chopped shallots and paste. Blend to a smooth paste, adding up to 3 tablespoons water if needed. Peel and de-vein the prawns; wash them and pat dry.

Place the oil in a wok or large frying-pan over a high heat. When it is hot, put in the paste from the blender. Stir-fry for 1 minute. Turn the heat down to medium, and continue to stir-fry for 2–3 minutes. Turn the heat up again and add the prawns. Stir-fry for 1 minute. Lower the heat to medium and add the tamarind (or lime or lemon juice), salt and sugar. Stir-fry for 3–5 minutes or until the prawns are cooked. Check the seasoning.

SERVES 4

BÁNH MÌ CHIÊN   VIETNAM

Savoury Pork and Crab Toasts

FROM THUY PELLISSIER

You may serve these as a savoury at the end of a meal or as a first course. When I invite people over for drinks I find that these toasts are just the perfect nibble to pass around. Rather like the triangles of prawn toast that you might have eaten in Chinese restaurants, they are triangles of minced pork and shredded crab meat. They are simple to prepare. All that they require is that you fry them just before you serve them – usually for less than 2 minutes per batch.

If you are using frozen crab meat make sure that you defrost it completely and squeeze out all the moisture from it beforehand. If you are mincing the pork yourself, put the garlic and shallots into the mincer along with the meat.

2 large cloves garlic

½ oz (15 g) shallot or onion

3 oz (75 g) cooked crab meat, finely shredded

4 oz (100 g) lean pork, very finely minced

1 egg

Freshly ground black pepper

1½ teaspoons sugar

1½ teaspoons fish sauce or salt to taste

About 8 average-sized slices white bread, about ¼–⅓ inch (0.5–0.75 cm) thick

Vegetable oil for frying

Peel the garlic and shallot and mince or chop them finely. Combine the garlic, shallot, crab meat and minced pork in a bowl. Beat the egg in a separate bowl. Add 2 tablespoons of the beaten egg to the pork-crab mixture. (Save the remaining egg for use in another dish.) Add also a generous amount of black pepper, the sugar and the fish sauce. Mix well to form a paste. This mixture may be made ahead of time, covered and stored in the refrigerator.

Stacking a few slices of bread together at a time, cut off the crusts. Now cut the slices in half diagonally, making large triangles, then cut these triangles in half again to make small triangles. Using a knife, spread the prepared paste over one side of each triangle to a thickness of ⅛ inch (0.3 cm).

Pour the oil into a large frying-pan to a depth of just under ½ inch (1 cm) and set it over a medium-low heat. When it is hot (a cube of bread dropped in should begin to sizzle immediately if the temperature is right), put in as many triangles of bread as will fit in a single layer, meat side down, and cook for 1½ minutes or until the meat is golden brown. Turn the bread triangles over and cook on the second side for 30–60 seconds or until golden. Remove them with a slotted spoon and drain on kitchen paper. Fry all the triangles in this way. Serve hot.

MAKES ABOUT 32 TRIANGLES OF TOAST

EBI TO KYURI NO SUNOMONO   JAPAN

CUCUMBER AND PRAWN SALAD

In Japan a *sunomono* is a 'vinegared thing', a salad which is usually served in small portions at the start of a meal. I have used Japanese rice vinegar here; it is milder and slightly sweeter than distilled white vinegar. To make an approximation of it yourself for this recipe, combine 3 teaspoons distilled white vinegar with 1 teaspoon water and a pinch of sugar.

It is best to use small prawns for this dish. You may buy cooked ones, if that is more convenient, or else you could buy raw ones and then drop them into simmering water for a minute or two, after which they will need to be peeled and de-veined. Larger prawns should be cut into ½ inch (1 cm) pieces.

7 oz (200 g) cucumber

Salt

4 teaspoons Japanese rice vinegar

2 teaspoons Japanese soy sauce (shoyu)

½ teaspoon sugar

2 teaspoons Japanese Soup Stock (see page 66) or unsalted chicken stock

½ teaspoon sesame oil

4 oz (100 g) small cooked peeled prawns

Peel the cucumber only if the skin is very thick and cut crossways into very thin rounds. Put the slices in a bowl. Add a very scant ½ teaspoon salt and toss. Set aside for 30–45 minutes. Squeeze as much liquid as possible out of the cucumber slices and pat them dry with kitchen paper.

Mix the vinegar, soy sauce, sugar, Japanese Soup Stock and sesame oil in a small bowl.

Just before serving, drain the cucumber slices again, pat them dry and put them in a bowl. Add the prawns and the vinegar dressing. Toss to mix. Put the salad into the centre of each of four small individual plates or bowls, heaping it up to form little hillocks.

SERVES 4

KILAWING TANGUIGUE   PHILIPPINES

MACKEREL 'COOKED' IN LIME JUICE

WITH HELP FROM RUBY ROA AND SANDY DAZA

In this startlingly good and refreshing first course, particularly suitable for the
summer, the mackerel is actually not cooked at all, making the dish a very easy
one to prepare. The fish does not, however, taste in the slightest bit raw. That
is because it is marinated in lime juice, which firms the flesh and turns it
opaque – in essence doing to the fish what cooking would do to it, only with
less effort on your part. If you have never eaten raw fish, you simply must try
this. It is sour and gingery and best served as a first course over a bed of salad
greens. *Kilawing tanguigue* is not all that different from the Latin American
ceviche and was probably brought to the Philippines by the Spaniards, who
most likely picked it up in Central or Southern America. It is now very popular
in the northern province of Ilocos Norte, where it is sometimes made with a
very special local vinegar.

You may make this mackerel dish a day in advance. Keep it well covered and
refrigerated.

9 oz (250 g) mackerel fillets,
  skinned
4–5 tablespoons lime juice
1 inch (2.5 cm) fresh ginger
1½ oz (40 g) carrot
1 oz (25 g) onion
½ teaspoon salt
Freshly ground black pepper

Mackerel fillets that are supposedly boned inva-
riably have a few bones left in them. Feel for them
with your hands and pull them out either with
your fingers or with a pair of tweezers. Cut the
fillets into ½ inch (1 cm) cubes and put these into a
stainless-steel or non-metallic bowl. Cover with
lime juice. Toss well and set aside for 1 hour.

Meanwhile, peel the ginger and cut it into very
thin slices. Stacking a few slices together at a time,
cut the slices first into very thin strips and then
halve the strips. Peel the carrot and cut first into
thin slices and then into minute dice. Peel the
onion and chop it very finely. Drain the fish
carefully and add to it the ginger, carrot and
onion. Add also the salt and some black pepper.
Toss well. Cover and refrigerate for at least 2
hours. Serve cold.

SERVES 4

SOTONG DAN CHILLI DAN BAWANG PUTIH   MALAYSIA

SQUID IN CHILLI AND GARLIC SAUCE

In Malaysia the sauce for this dish is made with fresh red chillies. Since they are hard to find here, I use a mixture of dried chillies and paprika. The dish still tastes very good.

4–9 dried hot red chillies (4 will make a mild dish, 9 a hot one)

½ teaspoon paprika

½ teaspoon shrimp or anchovy paste

1 lb (450 g) squid, cleaned (see page 291)

3 cloves garlic

4 oz (100 g) onions

5 tablespoons vegetable oil

½ teaspoon salt

½ teaspoon sugar

1 teaspoon lime or lemon juice

Crumble the chillies into a cup. Add 4 tablespoons warm water and set aside for about 30 minutes. Put the chillies and their soaking liquid into an electric blender and blend until smooth. Return the mixture to the cup and add the paprika and shrimp paste. Stir to mix.

Wash the squid and pat it dry. Cut the tubular body of the squid crossways into ¾ inch (2 cm) rings. The tentacles may be left clumped together or separated into 2–3 clumps. Peel the garlic and chop finely. Finely slice the onions.

Place 3 tablespoons of the oil in a frying-pan over a high heat. When it is hot, put in the garlic. Stir and fry for about 30 seconds or until the garlic is golden. Add the squid. Stir and cook for 3–4 minutes or until the squid has turned opaque all the way through. Empty the contents of the frying-pan into a bowl and set aside.

Wipe the frying-pan clean with kitchen paper. Put in the remaining 2 tablespoons oil and set the pan over a medium-high heat. When the oil is hot, put in the onions. Stir and fry for about 3 minutes or until the onions are soft. Add the paste from the cup, the salt, sugar and lime juice. Stir and cook for 1 minute. Add the squid and all the juices in the bowl. Mix, heat thoroughly and serve.

SERVES 4

NEM RÁN   VIETNAM

SMALL SPRING ROLLS

FROM MRS VƯỢNG AT THE THỰC ĐƠN RESTAURANT IN HANOI

Called *nem* in North Vietnam and *chả giò* in South Vietnam, these delicious
bite-sized crab-and-pork-filled spring rolls are usually wrapped in soft lettuce
leaves and dipped into a sauce before being eaten. Fresh herbs such as mint and
basil are put into these lettuce bundles as well.

A word about the Vietnamese spring roll wrappers: unlike the Chinese
spring roll skins, which are made of plain wheat flour, these are made from rice
flour. When bought, they look like round translucent sheets of paper with the
markings of the cross-woven mats on which they dried firmly imprinted on
them. The ideal size is about 4 inches (10 cm) in diameter, but this size is hard
to find in the West. Mrs Vượng, the chef at whose elbow I learned this recipe in
Hanoi, used two very thin wrappers, one placed more or less on top of the
other, to make each spring roll. Since the wrappers were stiff, she softened
them by smearing the outside wrapper with a little caramel-flavoured water. I
find that the wrappers I have managed to obtain at ethnic grocers' in the West
are often much larger and coarser in texture, and need repeated brushings with
caramel water to soften them. They may also need to be halved or quartered.
As they crumble easily, it is best to wet them first, then cut them with a sharp
knife. After they have been stuffed, you will need a little flour paste to stick the
last end of the wrapper down firmly in place.

Vietnamese spring roll wrappers are sold by Chinese and Far Eastern grocers,
where they are usually labelled 'rice paper'. If you cannot get authentic rice
paper wrappers, the best substitute is filo pastry which is sold in many
supermarkets and delicatessens and by Greek grocers. To use the pastry, just
spread one large sheet on a slightly dampened cloth. Brush it with warm
vegetable oil and cover it with another sheet. Brush that with oil as well. Cut
the sheets, in place, into 4 inch (10 cm) squares. As you work with one square,
keep the rest covered with a damp cloth. You will not need the caramel water
or flour paste. Instead of frying the pastry rolls, you can arrange them, one next
to the other, on a baking tray, brush them all with oil and then bake them in
the oven at gas mark 6, 400°F (200°C) for 20–30 minutes, turning them over
half-way through the cooking time.

If you cannot obtain dried black fungus, increase the number of dried
Chinese mushrooms from 8 to 14.

2 tablespoons dried black fungus

8 dried Chinese mushrooms

½ oz (15 g) cellophane noodles

½ spring onion

1½ oz (40 g) onion

4 oz (100 g) lean pork, minced

4 oz (100g) cooked white crab meat, shredded

¼ teaspoon salt

Freshly ground black pepper

1 large egg

1 large head soft lettuce

1 good-sized bunch fresh mint sprigs

4 tablespoons Caramel Water (see page 231)

2 tablespoons plain flour

Vietnamese rice papers

Oil for deep-frying

Fish Sauce Seasoned with Lime Juice (see page 228)

Soak the black fungus in 10 fl oz (300 ml) hot water for 30 minutes. Lift the fungus out of the water and rinse it under cold running water. Feel for the hard 'eyes' and cut them off. Chop the fungus very finely. You should have about 4 tablespoons. Soak the dried mushrooms in a separate 10 fl oz (300 ml) hot water for 30 minutes or until they are soft. Lift them out of the liquid and cut off the hard stems. Chop the caps finely. Soak the cellophane noodles in a large bowl of hot water for 15–30 minutes or until they are soft. Drain and cut them into ½ inch (1 cm) lengths.

Finely chop the spring onion. Peel the onion and chop it finely. In a bowl combine the pork, crab meat (make sure that it has no bits of shell left in it), black fungus, mushrooms, cellophane noodles, spring onion, onion, salt, black pepper and egg. Mix well.

Wash the lettuce, separating all the leaves, and drain it. Wash the mint, break it into very small sprigs, and drain it. Make the Caramel Water (see page 231). Combine the flour with 3–3½ tablespoons water to make a paste.

Add 1 pint (600 ml) hot water to the Caramel Water, which should now be warm. Brush a piece of rice paper on both sides with the diluted Caramel Water. If it turns soft and pliable, proceed with the next step; otherwise brush it again with the Caramel Water. If you have the 4 inch (10 cm) rice papers, leave them as they are. If you have the 9 inch (23 cm) papers, cut them into quarters. Work with one quarter at a time. Put a heaped teaspoon of the pork-crab mixture roughly in the centre, but closer to the edge nearest you (see diagram). Spread the mixture into a sausage shape about 1¾ inches (4.5 cm) long. Fold the side nearest the filling over it. Then fold the two adjacent sides over to the centre. Now roll the parcel away from you and seal the edge with a little flour

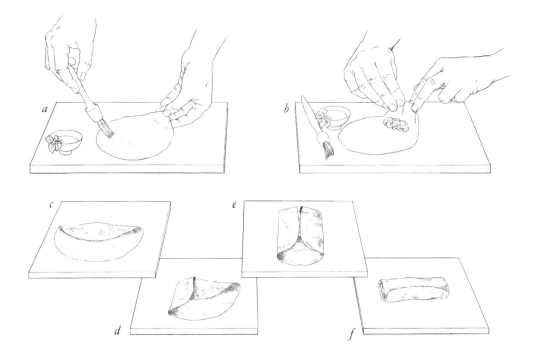

Preparing a spring roll

a) *Brush the piece of rice paper with diluted caramel water on both sides.*

b) *When the rice paper is soft and pliable put a heaped teaspoon of pork-crab mixture near the centre, but closer to one side. The mixture should be in a sausage shape, about 1¾ inches (4.5 cm) long.*

c) *Fold the side nearest the filling right over it.*

d) *Now fold an adjacent side over towards the centre.*

e) *Then fold the opposite side over.*

f) *Finally roll the parcel away from you to use up the remaining rice paper until you are left with a neat parcel.*

paste. Make all the spring rolls in this way and set them aside on a plate. (If you find that the rice paper is too thin and unmanageable, use 2 papers, one on top of the other.)

Heat the oil in a wok or deep-fat fryer over a medium heat. When the oil is hot, put in as many spring rolls as will fit easily in one layer. Fry them until they are golden. Remove them with a slotted spoon and drain them on kitchen paper. Continue until you have fried all the spring rolls in this way.

Arrange the spring rolls on a plate. Arrange the lettuce leaves and mint sprigs on another plate. Put a small bowl of Fish Sauce Seasoned with Lime Juice near each diner, or place a bowl between 2 diners for them to share. To eat, take a lettuce leaf, or part of one, and put a spring roll and a few mint leaves on it; roll it up and dip it into the sauce.

MAKES ABOUT 50 BITE-SIZED ROLLS

STUFFED MUSHROOMS

A *yakitori* bar in Japan produces not just tantalising tit-bits of grilled chicken on skewers (see page 108), but also a whole range of snacks that may be served with drinks or as a first course at a somewhat formal dinner. These mushrooms, for which I must confess a passion, are one such example. They are simple enough to make. Mushroom caps are stuffed with ginger-flavoured minced chicken and then cooked on a hot, lightly oiled surface. What gives them a heady lift is the final dousing they get in a tart sauce of soy and vinegar. A little mustard is served on the side to add further piquancy. A serving in the *yakitori* bars I frequented consisted of three mushrooms – four is considered an unlucky number. You may, of course, serve as many as you please.

1 inch (2.5 cm) cube fresh ginger

1 medium egg

10 oz (275 g) chicken, skinned and minced (use dark or light meat, or a mixture)

Freshly ground black pepper

2–3 blades fresh chives or 1 spring onion (optional)

18 large well-formed mushrooms

1 tablespoon vegetable oil

6 tablespoons Japanese soy sauce (shoyu)

2 tablespoons distilled white vinegar or 3 tablespoons Japanese rice vinegar

English mustard to serve

Peel the ginger and grate it finely. Collect it all on your finger tips. Hold it over a bowl and squeeze as much juice from it as you can. Discard the grated ginger, keeping the juice. Break the egg into the same bowl and beat it lightly. Add the minced chicken and black pepper to taste. Finely chop about 2 teaspoons chives or spring onion and add to the stuffing. Mix gently.

Gently break off the mushroom stems. Wipe the mushroom caps with damp kitchen paper. Stuff each mushroom cavity with a heaped teaspoon of the chicken mixture, flattening off the top.

Put the oil into a large non-stick frying-pan and set it over a medium-high heat. When it is hot, put in the mushroom caps, stuffed side down. Cook for 4–5 minutes or until lightly browned. Turn the caps over, turn the heat down to medium, cover the pan and cook for 3–4 minutes. Meanwhile, mix the soy sauce and vinegar in a bowl.

Put three caps on to each of six individual salad plates, stuffed side up. Spoon an equal amount of sauce over each plate of mushrooms. Serve hot with the mustard handed separately.

SERVES 6

KRUPUK UDANG   INDONESIA

₱RAWN WAFERS

Krupuk are wafers which, rather like the Indian poppadums, add a pleasing crunch to a meal. They may be found sitting neatly at the edge of a plate of *Gado-Gado* (Mixed Vegetable Salad with Peanut Dressing, page 198), their crispness balancing nicely with the blanched vegetables, or on a plate of *Nasi Goreng Istimewa* (Special Fried Rice with Beef and Prawns, page 207). They nearly always appear at festive banquets, are amazingly good with drinks – try them with a dip of *Sambal Terasi* (Red Pepper Sauce with Shrimp Paste, page 233), and may be eaten on their own as a snack. There are many, many varieties of *krupuk*. They may be flavoured with prawns, made of cassava or of nuts. One of my favourites, found only in the hills of Western Sumatra, is made of cassava and comes thinly smeared with a sweet and hot red chilli jam.

Krupuk udang, made of prawns and starch, come in many sizes and colours, some rather startling. I have seen bright blue, pink, green and yellow *krupuk* gracing many a table. *Krupuk* need to be fried quickly – passed through hot oil, you might say – before they are served. To ensure crispness, the wafers must be bone dry before they hit the oil. Indonesian housewives routinely put *krupuk* in the sun for a brief period first. You could place them in a warm oven for 10 minutes. Once they are in the hot oil, they expand quite a bit and assume a lighter, airier texture. Ideally they should be cooked shortly before they are eaten. If you cannot manage that, store them in an air-tight container after they have cooked. Uncooked *krupuk* should also be stored in very tightly lidded jars.

Here is the general method for preparing these wafers. Put enough oil in a wok to have at least 1½ inches (4 cm) in the centre. When it is very hot – about 365°F (185°C) – drop in 2 or 3 small *krupuk* (fewer if they are large). They will sink, rise almost immediately and greatly expand in size. If you are using a wok, spoon oil over them during the few seconds that they take to cook. Do not let them brown. Adjust the heat if necessary. Remove the wafers with a slotted spoon and transfer them to a plate lined with kitchen paper. Cook as many *krupuk* as you need in this way.

CHICKEN STOCK

Good chicken stock is needed for many recipes in this book, so it is useful to keep a supply handy in your refrigerator or freezer. Here are a few tips:

1 Whenever you poach a chicken breast, strain the liquid and save it. Use it when small amounts are called for.
2 Save all chicken bones and carcasses and store in the freezer; they can be added to the pot when making stock.
3 When cooking stock, maintain it at a low simmer or it will turn cloudy. It should bubble only very slightly. Skim the stock frequently as it cooks, especially in the first 30 minutes.
4 Sometimes just a little salt can be added to the stock at the end of the cooking time to bring out its flavour. You should leave the salt out when making stock for use in Japanese cooking.
5 Before freezing stock you can boil it down to half its original quantity so that it occupies less space. It can easily be reconstituted later.
6 Pour cooled, de-greased stock into ice-cube trays and freeze. When frozen, the cubes can be transferred to freezer bags. You will then be able to use small quantities of stock as you need them and will be spared the mess of defrosting large amounts unnecessarily.
7 Frozen stock can be defrosted very quickly in a microwave oven.

3 lb (1.5 kg) chicken necks, wings, backs and bones
2 lb (1 kg) chicken pieces (such as legs)
2 thin slices fresh ginger
2 spring onions
Salt (optional)

Wash the chicken pieces and put them into a large pan. Add 6 pints (3.4 litres) water and bring it to a simmer. Maintain the simmer and do not let the stock boil. Over the next 30 minutes, keep removing the scum that rises to the top. Now put in the ginger slices. Trim the spring onions, discarding the green section, and add the white part to the stock. Cook partially covered, maintaining the heat at a bare simmer for 3–4 hours. Strain into a bowl through a triple layer of dampened muslin, cheesecloth or a large clean handkerchief and add a little salt if required. Stand the bowl in a large basin or sink of cold water to cool it off quickly. Pour the stock into containers, cover and refrigerate. Remove the fat when it has solidified. You can now freeze the stock.

MAKES ABOUT 5 PINTS (2.75 LITRES)

BEEF STOCK

Good beef stock requires both beef bones and meat. While bones provide the body, the depth of flavour can come only from meat. Ideally you should use equal quantities of bones and meat, though you can save a little money by using more bones. I like to save odd bones from roasts, freezing them until I decide to make stock.

If you are starting from scratch, ask the butcher for soup bones (marrow bones are best) and have him saw them into smaller pieces. As far as the meat is concerned, you may use brisket, removing it when it is tender; it takes about 2½ hours to cook. You can also use stewing beef and just leave it to cook for the entire period. Some people like to use shanks, cut up of course, as they provide both meat and bones. You may take the meat off the bone after 2½ hours and let just the bones cook on.

Although it is usually best to salt stock when the cooking is completed, in this recipe I add a small quantity of salt earlier just to give the meat a little flavour. The brisket may be cut into thin slices for use in salads and soups, such as Rice Noodles in Soup with Beef (page 218) and Bean Sprout and Radish Soup (page 68) – but in this case leave out the fish sauce and star anise.

This stock recipe is from Vietnam, but if you make it with salt to taste instead of the fish sauce, it may be used for all recipes in this book that require beef stock.

4 oz (100 g) onions

3 inch (7.5 cm) piece fresh ginger

4 lb (1.75 kg) beef marrow bones, sawed into smaller pieces

3 lb (1.5 kg) beef brisket or stewing beef

2 inch (5 cm) stick cinnamon

2 whole star anise

1 teaspoon salt

2 tablespoons fish sauce or extra salt to taste

Pre-heat the oven to gas mark 8, 450°F (230°C).

Peel the onions. It is not necessary to peel the ginger. Put the onions and ginger in the oven and let them roast for 30 minutes. They should brown a little. Remove them and set aside.

Put the marrow bones and brisket into a very large pan. Add 9 pints (5 litres) water and slowly bring it to a simmer. Over the next 15 minutes, keep removing the scum that rises to the top. Then put in the onion, ginger, cinnamon stick, star anise and salt. Cover partially and cook very gently for about 2½ hours or until the brisket is tender. Remove the brisket and set it aside. Once it has cooled, it can be wrapped and stored in the refrigerator for use in other dishes. Continue to cook the stock gently, with the pan still partially covered, for another 2–2½ hours. Add the fish sauce a little at a time, tasting the stock until it is of the desired saltiness. It should be slightly undersalted.

Strain the stock into a large bowl through a double thickness of dampened muslin, cheesecloth or a large clean handkerchief. Cool it quickly by standing the bowl in a large basin or sink of cold water. Pour the stock into containers, cover and refrigerate. When the stock is cold, remove the fat – if you are in a hurry, you will have to do this with a spoon before the fat has solidified. The stock may now be frozen – see Chicken Stock, points 5–7 (page 64), for instructions.

MAKES ABOUT 4 PINTS (2.25 LITRES)

DASHI   JAPAN

JAPANESE SOUP STOCK

FROM THE ÉCOLE TECHNIQUE HÔTELIÈRE TSUJI IN OSAKA

Unlike much of the world, the Japanese make their basic stock out of fish and sea kelp. The most common fish used for stock is bonito, a member of the mackerel family. It is sold in Japan in a dried, filleted form that looks rather like a piece of smooth, hard, petrified wood, and in fact needs to be shaved with a plane. The delicate, curled shavings are at their best when they are freshly done and when they are a pale pinkish-brown colour. The finest of Japanese food establishments would consider using no other, just as the best French restaurant would always make its stock from scratch. The discriminating Japanese housewife does not shave her own bonito, but she can go into any good market and get it shaved for her on the spot. The average Japanese, on the other hand, either buys packaged bonito shavings, which come in plastic bags or in cornflake-like boxes, or uses instant soup stock (*dashi-no-moto*) which is available in granular form.

The other ingredients used in good *dashi* – and for vegetarians it is often the only ingredient – is *konbu*, a special kelp sold in the form of large, dried leaves. Only sections of it are used at a time. The kelp needs to be of good quality. Its flavour is said to reside on its surface, so it is never washed, just wiped lightly with a damp cloth. This kelp should never be boiled vigorously; it is either soaked overnight or allowed to simmer very gently.

Whether you will be able to get shaved bonito (*hana-katsuo*) and the right kelp (*dashi-konbu*) is another matter. You should make an effort, as their flavours are the purest. If you cannot, use instant *dashi-no-moto*, though it is very often salted. As a last resort, you may use very light, unsalted chicken stock.

The correct way to make authentic *dashi* was demonstrated to me by Mr Saito at the École Technique Hôtelière Tsuji, the largest school training professional chefs in Japan. First, a hunk of wood-like bonito was quickly rinsed and dried. Odd bits of dried skin and dried blood were scraped off. Just before the stock was made, the bonito was shaved with a plane that was affixed to a box. The shavings fell neatly and conveniently into a drawer!

1 oz (25 g) piece kelp (*konbu*)
1 oz (25 g) dried bonito
  shavings (*hana-katsuo*)

Wipe the kelp lightly with a damp cloth and put it into a medium-sized pan. Pour in 1¾ pints (1 litre) water and very slowly bring it to a simmer over a medium-low heat. If you are using the stock to make clear soup, remove the kelp just before the water comes to the boil. If you are using the stock for anything else – such as Fermented Bean Paste Soup with Bean Curd (page 69), noodles, sauces or for cooking vegetables – let the kelp simmer gently for 10 minutes without ever letting the water come to the boil. Remove the kelp and then add the bonito shavings. Immediately take the pan off the heat. Do not stir. Within the next minute or so, the shavings will sink to the bottom. Strain the soup through a piece of dampened cloth.

While stock for clear soups is best when freshly made, all other Japanese Soup Stock may be made ahead of time and refrigerated. It should keep thus for 3 days and may be reheated by being brought to a bare simmer. Japanese Soup Stock is generally seasoned with a little salt and/or soy sauce when it is used for clear soups.

MAKES 1¾ PINTS (1 LITRE)

BEAN SPROUT AND RADISH SOUP

During my very first stay in Korea many years ago I frequently had this soup for breakfast, along with rice, pickles and barley tea. The thin slices of beef in the soup are cut from the brisket used in Beef Stock (page 65). If you are making Beef Stock specially for this soup, leave out the fish sauce and star anise. If you have made a stock using bones but no brisket, you can prepare this soup without including any meat.

Korean white radish is very thick, very long and sweet. The one I used here was 1½ inches (4 cm) in diameter. If the only white radish you can find is very sharp, use the sweeter and more commonly available red radishes instead, cutting them in half lengthways. They will lose a little of their red colour in the soup, but that does not matter. You may also substitute young, sweet turnips.

7 oz (200 g) long white radish (mooli)

1½ oz (40 g) sliced boiled brisket from Beef Stock (see page 65; optional)

2 pints (1.1 litres) Beef Stock (see page 65)

12 oz (350 g) fresh bean sprouts

3 spring onions

Salt

Peel the radish and cut it crossways into 2 inch (5 cm) sections. Cut each section lengthways into ¼ inch (0.5 cm) slabs. If you are using brisket, cut the meat against the grain into very thin slices. Each slice should be about 1½ inches (4 cm) long. Combine the radish, brisket and stock in a pan and bring to the boil. Cover, lower the heat and simmer gently for 15 minutes. The radish should by now be almost translucent.

Meanwhile, wash the bean sprouts and drain them. Pull off their threadlike ends if you feel up to it (see page 260). Cut the spring onions into 2 inch (5 cm) lengths. Cut the white part lengthways into halves or quarters, depending on thickness. When the soup has cooked for 15 minutes, put in the bean sprouts and spring onions. Add salt to taste and simmer for 5 minutes more. Serve hot.

SERVES 4

FERMENTED BEAN PASTE SOUP WITH BEAN CURD

My favourite Japanese breakfast consists of nothing more than a tart preserved plum, so tart that it puckers the mouth and jolts me awake (as well as being full of vitamin C), a hot bowl of this *miso* soup, rice, pickles and tea. Millions of Japanese drink *miso* soup in the morning; those, of course, who have not succumbed to the more modern, fashionable notion of toast and coffee. *Miso* soup may also be served at the beginning or end of a meal.

Miso is a paste made from fermented soya beans, though it can contain mixtures of other fermented grains as well. It is easy to digest, full of protein and, for vegetarians, a major source of nutrients.

There are many different types of *miso* available in Japan. Whole sections of shops contain row upon row of wooden tubs, each heaped with *miso* of a different colour (ranging from white to almost black), a different texture (from coarse grains to a smooth paste) and a different degree of saltiness (from very salty to somewhat sweet – these days there are also low-salt *misos*). Most of these may be used to make soup.

For us in the West, the choice is much more limited. Most of us have access to health food shops which tend to stock three or four varieties. There are nearly always yellowish, brown and reddish-brown *misos*. Start with *aka miso*, the reddish-brown one. You may later even decide to mix several *misos* together, once you get to learn the characteristics of each one.

1 spring onion

4 oz (100 g) bean curd

1¾ pints (1 litre) Japanese Soup Stock (see page 66) or light unsalted chicken stock

4 tablespoons *aka miso* (the reddish-brown one)

Cut the entire spring onion (including the green section) into very thin rounds. Cut the bean curd into ½ inch (1 cm) cubes. Heat the stock in a medium-sized pan until it is hot, but not boiling. Take it off the heat. Lower a small sieve into it so that only its lower half is submerged in the liquid. Put the *miso* into the sieve and push as much of it through as possible. Discard any lumps which may be left in the sieve. Put the soup back on a medium heat and add the bean curd and spring onion. Bring the soup to a simmer. When the first bubbles appear, remove it from the heat and serve.

SERVES 4

AMA TITO REY SOUP   PHILIPPINES

$\mathcal{G}$LORIOUS SEAFOOD SOUP

FROM THE TITO REY RESTAURANT IN MANILA

Seafood is plentiful in the Philippines and at Tito Rey's Restaurant it is cooked to perfection. This soup combines Spanish techniques with Filipino ingredients in the most delectable way. Needless to say, it should be made only if fresh mussels and clams are available. If you can find only one of these molluscs, use it to replace the other. You can improvise freely here and add seafood that you happen to like. I often put in squid, cut into rings, and cubes of filleted white fish, such as sole. When selecting shellfish, avoid mussels or clams which have broken shells.

8 mussels

4 clams

4 oz (100 g) uncooked unpeeled prawns

½ inch (1 cm) cube fresh ginger

1½ oz (40 g) onion

2 pints (1.1 litres) chicken stock

1 teaspoon whole black peppercorns

Salt

1½ oz (40 g) unsalted butter

3 tablespoons plain flour

2 oz (50 g) cooked or uncooked white crab meat

5 tablespoons thick coconut milk (see page 263)

A little fresh parsley

Scrub the mussels and clams well with a stiff brush under cold running water. Pull the 'beards' from the mussels. Peel and de-vein the prawns, wash them and pat them dry. Cut each prawn crossways into 3 segments. Cut the ginger crossways into 4–5 slices. Peel the onion.

Combine the stock, ginger, whole onion and peppercorns in a pan and bring to a simmer. Cover and simmer gently for 15 minutes. Strain the stock and put it back into the pan. Add salt to taste – it should be slightly undersalted as shellfish are briny – and keep it hot.

Melt the butter in a wide heavy pan over a medium-low heat. When it is melted and bubbly, put in the flour and turn the heat to low. Stir and cook for 2 minutes, letting the mixture bubble and froth but not brown. Slowly pour in the hot stock, stirring rapidly with a whisk as you go. Bring the stock to a simmer and then simmer gently for 3–4 minutes. If you see even a few lumps in the soup, strain it at this stage.

Put the mussels and clams into the soup and bring to the boil. Cover, turn the heat to medium and cook for 5 minutes. Remove the lid. The mussels and clams should have opened up. (If some have not, cook for another minute, then discard any that still have not opened.) Put in the prawns, crab meat and coconut milk. Cook for another minute over a low heat.

Meanwhile, finely chop the parsley. Pour the soup into wide soup plates, dividing the shells evenly between them. Garnish with the parsley and serve.

SERVES 4

TOM YAM KUNG   THAILAND

Hot and Sour Prawn Soup

FROM PIENG CHOM DARBANAND AT THE IMPERIAL HOTEL, BANGKOK

I would definitely classify this as one of the world's greatest soups. I have enjoyed it for some twenty years and have never had quite the same version twice. Traditionally the stock is made only with prawns. Whole prawns that still have their flavourful heads attached to their bodies are boiled in water seasoned with aromatic lemon grass and lime leaves. They are then removed, peeled, and their heads and skins thrown back into the stock pot for added flavour. Since most of us cannot find raw prawns with heads, it is best to use a rich chicken stock instead and add the prawn peelings to intensify its taste.

This soup can be made as fiery hot as you can handle. The amount of both the chilli paste and the hot green chillies can easily be increased. My recipe is for a soup of medium heat, though the fresh green chillies, when bitten into, do carry their own explosive power with them. If you cannot find the Thai chilli paste known as *nam prik pow*, use ¼ teaspoon chilli powder combined with ¼ teaspoon sugar and ½ teaspoon vegetable oil.

Although Thai hotels and plush Westernised restaurants tend to serve this soup as a first course. In homes it is usually one of several main dishes served with plain rice.

1 lb (450 g) uncooked
unpeeled prawns

2 sticks fresh or 2 tablespoons
dried sliced lemon grass

4 fresh or dried kaffir lime
leaves or 1 tablespoon finely
grated lemon rind

2½ pints (1.2 litres) chicken
stock

1 tablespoon fish sauce or salt
to taste

3 tablespoons fresh lime juice
or to taste

1 teaspoon chilli paste (*nam
prik pow*; see page 261)

15 oz (425 g) tin straw
mushrooms or 12 medium-
sized fresh mushrooms

3 fresh hot green chillies

3 tablespoons fresh coriander
leaves

Wash the unpeeled prawns well. Peel and de-vein them, saving the peelings. Wash the prawns again, drain and pat them dry. Cover and refrigerate.

If you are using fresh lemon grass, cut each stick into 3 × 2 inch (5 cm) pieces, starting from the rounded bottom end. Discard the strawlike top. Lightly crush the 6 pieces with a heavy pestle, a hammer, or the blade of a knife.

Combine the lemon grass (fresh or dried), the kaffir lime leaves (or lemon rind), the stock and prawn peelings in a pan. Bring to the boil. Lower the heat and simmer very gently for 20 minutes. Strain this stock and to it add the fish sauce, the lime juice and the chilli paste. Mix and taste again, adding more fish sauce or lime juice if you need it. Drain the straw mushrooms and add them to the seasoned stock. (If you are using fresh mushrooms, quarter them and drop them in lightly salted boiling water. Boil for 1 minute. Drain and add to the seasoned stock.)

This much of the soup may be prepared several hours ahead of time and stored in the refrigerator if necessary.

Prepare the garnishes shortly before you are ready to serve the soup. Cut the green chillies into very fine rounds and wash and dry the coriander leaves. Just before serving, heat the stock with the mushrooms in it. When it begins to bubble, drop in the peeled prawns. Cook on a medium heat for about 2 minutes or just until the prawns turn opaque. Put the soup into a large serving bowl or into individual serving bowls. Garnish with the green chillies and whole coriander leaves and serve hot.

SERVES 6 AS A SOUP OR 4 AS A MAIN COURSE

Mung Bean Soup

FROM GLENDA BARRETTO AT THE VIA MARE RESTAURANT

Here is an easy-to-prepare, delicious and very nourishing soup. Generally it is quite thick and is eaten with rice, but many restaurants now serve it in a somewhat simplified version. Fish sauce, olive oil and lime wedges are usually passed around at the table for those who wish to add a little more seasoning. A common garnish for the soup is pork crackling. If you wish to use it, you will need 1 tablespoon crumbled pork crackling per serving.

6½ oz (185 g) mung beans

1½ pints (900 ml) rich chicken, pork or chicken-and-pork stock

3½ oz (90 g) onions

1 large clove garlic

4 oz (100 g) uncooked unpeeled prawns

3 tablespoons olive oil

¾ teaspoon salt

Freshly ground black pepper

Fresh lime or lemon wedges, fish sauce (optional) and extra olive oil (optional) to serve

Pick over the beans and wash them in several changes of water. Drain them and put them into a medium-sized pan. Cover with water by about 2 inches (5 cm) and bring to the boil. Lower the heat and simmer for 2 minutes. Turn off the heat and let the pan and its contents sit for 1 hour. Then drain the beans and put them back into the pan. Add the stock and bring to the boil again. Cover loosely, turn the heat to low and simmer gently for about 1 hour or until the beans are tender. Mash them lightly in the pan.

Peel and thinly slice the onions. Peel the garlic and chop it finely. Peel and de-vein the prawns, wash them and pat them dry. Cut the prawns crossways into ½ inch (1 cm) segments.

Put the olive oil in a medium-sized frying-pan and set it over a medium-high heat. When the oil is hot, put in the onions and garlic. Stir and fry them until they turn golden and are just beginning to brown. Put in the prawn pieces and stir and fry for about a minute or until they turn opaque. Empty the contents of the frying-pan, including the oil, into the pan containing the soup. Add the salt and black pepper. Stir to mix.

Re-heat the soup and serve with lime wedges and, if you like, fish sauce and olive oil.

SERVES 4

CANH THỊT NẤU CUA   VIETNAM

PORK AND CRAB SOUP

FROM MRS VƯỢNG AT THE THỰC ĐƠN RESTAURANT IN HANOI

Here is another pork and crab combination that the Vietnamese do so well. This time it is in a soup which is quite Chinese in its origins. In Vietnam the soup is served with a generous squeeze of fresh lime juice and some Red Pepper Sauce (see page 231) for those who want it.

One of the ingredients this soup calls for is a fungus known variously as wood-ears, cloud-ears, *moer*-mushrooms or just black fungus. Used routinely in Chinese cookery, these 'mushrooms' look like miniature elephant's ears and have a mild earthy taste and a crunchy texture. They are also meant to be very good for the heart! The Vietnamese often use them in their fresh form. In the West, we can obtain them only in their dried form at Chinese grocers'. (Consult page 268 for more details on this interesting ingredient and what variety to look for.) Do try to get it for this soup. If you cannot find it, increase the number of dried Chinese mushrooms to 12, and if you cannot get those either, use 12 good-sized, fresh ordinary mushrooms in the place of both fungi, cutting them into thin slices and putting the slices into the soup at the same time as you would add the dried fungi. The fresh mushrooms will, of course, need no soaking.

8 dried Chinese mushrooms

1 tablespoon small dried black fungus

4–5 oz (100–150 g) lean meat from boneless loin of pork or pork loin chops

2 teaspoons plus 2 tablespoons cornflour

2 teaspoons sesame oil

1 teaspoon fish sauce or ¼ teaspoon salt

1 egg

1 spring onion

2 pints (1.1 litres) chicken stock

Salt

Soak the dried mushrooms in about 8 fl oz (250 ml) hot water for 30 minutes or until they are soft. Soak the black fungus in 8 fl oz (250 ml) hot water for 30 minutes or until it is soft. Cut the pork against the grain into ⅛ inch (0.3 cm) slices. Stacking a few slices at a time together, cut the meat, again against the grain, into long shreds about ⅛ inch (0.3 cm) wide. Put the pork in a bowl. Add the 2 teaspoons cornflour, sesame oil and fish sauce. Mix. Cover and set aside for 20 minutes or longer, refrigerating if necessary.

Lift the mushrooms out of their soaking liquid. Strain the soaking liquid through a cloth and set it aside. Cut off the hard mushroom stems and discard them. Cut the caps into ⅛ inch (0.3 cm) strips. Lift the black fungus out of its soaking

4 oz (100 g) cooked white crab meat, finely shredded

lime wedges and Red Pepper Sauce (see page 231; optional) to serve

liquid and discard the liquid. Feel the fungus for hard 'eyes'. Cut off any you find and discard them. Chop the fungus coarsely.

Put the remaining 2 tablespoons cornflour into a small cup. Add 3 tablespoons of the reserved mushroom-soaking liquid or water. Mix and set aside. Beat the egg lightly and set it aside. Cut the spring onion crossways into very fine rounds.

Put the stock and any remaining mushroom-soaking liquid into a pan. Add the two kinds of mushrooms and bring the stock to a simmer. Cover and simmer on a low heat for 5 minutes. Then put in the pork. Bring to the boil gently and simmer until the pork is just cooked through, stirring and breaking up any meat lumps as you do so. Taste the soup and add salt if it is needed. Put in the crab meat. Give the cornflour mixture a stir and pour that in as well. Stir and cook on a lowish heat until the soup is thick and bubbling.

Take the soup off the heat. Immediately pour in the beaten egg in a slow steady stream using a fork to stir the top of the soup in a figure of eight pattern. This procedure makes perfect 'egg drop' slivers. Put in the spring onion and stir the soup for a few seconds more to allow the onion to wilt. Serve with lime wedges and Red Pepper Sauce.

SERVES 4–5

WEI LING QINGGUA ROU JIN JIANG   HONG KONG

SUMMER SOUP WITH PORK AND CUCUMBER

FROM WILLY MARK

Fresh ingredients and delicate flavours – that is what Cantonese food is all about, and nothing exemplifies it more than this soup. Even though the soup is ideal for summer, you may serve it successfully in winter as well. The cucumber in it, you might be interested to know, does not stay raw. It cooks, however briefly, to turn into a most interesting vegetable. As far as the pork is concerned, you could buy either 8 oz (225 g) of pork tenderloin or 2 pork loin chops weighing in total about 14 oz (400 g) and then just cut the meat off the bone.

You can prepare the stock, marinate and parboil the meat, and slice the cucumbers well ahead of time. The soup should be assembled and heated only at the last minute.

8 oz (225 g) pork tenderloin or 14 oz (400 g) loin chops, boned

½ teaspoon cornflour

2 teaspoons sesame oil

⅔ egg white

Salt

1 inch (2.5 cm) cube fresh ginger

1 oz (25 g) fresh coriander (with stems and roots if possible)

2¼ pints (1.25 litres) chicken stock

6½ oz (185 g) cucumber

Remove any fat from the pork and then cut the lean into thin slices about 1½ × 1 × ¹⁄₁₆ inches (4 × 1 × 0.15 cm). Put the meat in a bowl. Add the cornflour, sesame oil, egg white and ¼ teaspoon salt. Mix well and set aside for 30 minutes or more, refrigerating if necessary.

Peel the ginger and cut it into thin slices. Wash the coriander well and pat it dry. Remove the leaves (reserving the stems and roots), cover them with cling-film and set them aside. Combine the chicken stock, ginger slices and coriander stems and roots in a pan. Bring to the boil, turn the heat to low and simmer for 20 minutes. Strain and add salt to taste.

Pour about ¾ inch (2 cm) water into a medium-sized frying-pan and bring it to the boil. Put in the pork and then turn the heat to low. Stir the pork about until it turns white all the way through. (It is not necessary for the water to come to the boil again.) Remove the pork with a slotted spoon and set it aside. Peel the cucumber and cut it into very thin rounds.

Just before eating, heat the seasoned stock until it is bubbling. Put in the pork and cucumber and let them just heat through. This should take 30–40 seconds. Remove the pan from the heat and put in the coriander leaves. Serve immediately.

SERVES 4–5

SOTO AYAM   INDONESIA

SPICY CHICKEN SOUP WITH MANY FLAVOURS

There are probably as many recipes for *soto ayam* as there are families in Indonesia. This soup can be a light and delicate teaser or it can, with the addition of fried potato balls, noodles and hard-boiled eggs, transform itself into a whole meal. I have decided to place my *soto ayam* smack in the middle of its range of possibilities. It is light enough to qualify as a first course and yet it has enough of the titillating additions – bean sprouts, bits of chicken, crisply fried shallot flakes, spring onions and red chilli sauce – to give it its complex Indonesian flavour.

When this soup is made in Indonesia, a whole chicken is first boiled with a few spices. The liquid becomes the stock and the chicken meat is then pulled off the bone, shredded and put back into the stock. I do not do this for two reasons. I like to cook my stock long and slowly, using necks, backs, wings and odd bones and carcasses I have lying in wait in the freezer. Also, for my taste, good quality chicken meat either gets too tough over such a long cooking period or it is overcooked. I prefer to make my stock separately and then, since we can buy chicken pieces so easily in the West, lightly poach skinned and boned chicken breast to provide the meat content of the soup.

Making the liquid part of the soup, poaching the chicken meat and preparing the bean sprouts, the red pepper sauce, shallots, potatoes and green seasonings can all be done ahead of time. Just before serving, the sprouts can be thrown into boiling water to heat them and the stock can be brought to a simmer.

FOR THE GARNISHES, FLAVOURINGS AND SAUCE:

2 oz (50 g) shallots or onions

3 oz (75 g) potatoes

Vegetable oil for shallow-frying

Salt

1 spring onion

1 handful tender celery leaves or stalks

½ lime or lemon

2 oz (50 g) red pepper, de-seeded

1 tablespoon distilled white vinegar

¼ teaspoon sugar

½ teaspoon chilli powder

FOR THE FLAVOURED STOCK:

3 oz (75g) shallots or onions

3 cloves garlic

½ oz (15 g) candlenuts or cashew nuts

2½ pints (1.5 litres) chicken stock

Salt

YOU ALSO NEED:

4 oz (100 g) chicken breast, boned and skinned

Salt

12 oz (350 g) fresh bean sprouts

First prepare the garnishes, flavourings and sauce. Peel the 2 oz (50 g) shallots and cut them lengthways into fine slivers. Peel the potatoes and cut them first into ⅛ inch (0.3 cm) thick slices and then into ⅛ inch (0.3 cm) wide julienne strips.

Place a bowl on the work-surface near your cooker and balance a sieve over it. Put about ¼ inch (0.5 cm) oil in a frying-pan and set it on a medium heat. When the oil is hot, put in the shallots. Stir and fry until golden-brown and crisp. Empty the contents of the pan into the sieve. Drain the shallots well and then spread them out on a plate lined with kitchen paper. Put the oil back into the frying-pan and heat it again over a medium heat. When it is hot, put in the potato sticks. Stir and fry until they are golden and crisp. Empty the contents of the frying-pan again into the sieve set over the bowl. Drain the potatoes well and spread them out on another plate lined with kitchen paper. Sprinkle the potatoes very lightly with salt. When the shallots and potatoes have cooled, they can be put into small airtight jars until needed. (Save the oil for the flavoured stock.)

Cut the spring onion crossways into very, very fine rounds along its entire length, including the green section. Soak the rounds in cold water (this makes them milder). Coarsely chop the celery leaves. Cover them with cling-film and set them aside. Cut the lime (or lemon) into 4 wedges. Cover and set aside.

Combine the red pepper, vinegar, ½ teaspoon salt, sugar and chilli powder in an electric blender. Blend until smooth. Empty into a small attractive serving bowl. Cover and set aside.

Now make the flavoured stock. Peel the 3 oz (75 g) shallots and chop them coarsely. Peel the garlic and chop it coarsely. Coarsely chop the nuts. Combine the shallots, garlic, nuts and 4 tablespoons water in a blender and blend until smooth.

Put 4 tablespoons of the reserved oil in a medium-sized pan (preferably non-stick) and set it on a medium-high heat. When the oil is hot, add the paste from the blender. Stir and fry for 4–5 minutes or until the paste is lightly browned. Add the stock and bring it to the boil. Turn the heat to low and simmer gently for 15 minutes. Add salt to taste, stir in well, then set aside.

Cut the chicken lengthways into ¾ inch (2 cm) wide strips. Put these into a pan and cover with about ½ inch (1 cm) water. Add ¼ teaspoon salt and bring slowly to a simmer. Simmer gently for 2–3 minutes or until the chicken turns white all the way through. Lift the chicken out of the liquid and let it cool slightly. Using both hands, pull the meat into long – not too thin – shreds. Cover with cling-film. (The poaching liquid can be strained and reserved for use in another dish.)

Trim away the long threadlike ends of the bean sprouts if you feel up to it and drop them into a pan of boiling water for 30 seconds. Drain and immediately rinse under cold water. Drain well, cover and set aside.

All the elements of the soup are now assembled. To serve, uncover the sauce and put it on the table. Drain the spring onion and pat dry. Arrange the fried shallots, fried potatoes, spring onion, celery leaves and lime wedges on a platter. Heat the flavoured stock. Drop the bean sprouts into boiling water for 10 seconds to heat them through. Drain them and divide them between 4 generous soup bowls or plates. Top with the chicken, which should also be divided up equally. Ladle the hot stock over the top and take the soup to the table. Diners should help themselves to some sauce, lime wedges, shallots, potatoes, spring onion and celery, roughly in that order. All are put into the soup.

SERVES 4

MEAT

THỊT BÒ LỤI   VIETNAM

Napoleon beef on a skewer

FROM MRS VƯỢNG AT THE THỰC ĐỒN RESTAURANT IN HANOI

Many Vietnamese in Hanoi refer to this dish either as *boeuf brochette* or *boeuf Napoleon*. (I suppose it is the sort of thing an army on the move might cook!) Thin slices of meat are marinated in a mixture of fried spices, skewered and then grilled over charcoal or wood. The meat is then taken off the skewer and put on to a plate. It is eaten, as many other Vietnames dishes are, in little packages. You take a soft lettuce leaf and put a few pieces of meat on it. On top of the meat you put a few fresh mint leaves, a few small sprigs of fresh coriander, a few fresh bean sprouts, some sliced spring onion, some cucumber slices, some Crisply Fried Shallot Flakes (page 240) and some crushed Roasted Peanuts (page 236). Next you wrap the lettuce leaf round all this to form a bundle, dip the bundle into Fish Sauce Seasoned with Lime Juice (page 228) – and eat it.

If you do not feel like making packages, there is another way of serving the meat, a method that I use quite frequently. I put only ½ teaspoon of salt in the marinade. When the meat is cooked, I take it off the skewers and put it on a plate. I dribble Fish Sauce Seasoned with Lime Juice over it generously, then scatter crushed Roasted Peanuts and some Crisply Fried Shallot Flakes on the top. With this I serve a side salad of lettuce, cucumbers, ripe tomatoes, fresh mint and fresh coriander.

All the cooking in north Vietnam seems to be done in lard. I have used vegetable oil here, but you may use lard if you wish.

1 stick fresh or 2 tablespoons dried sliced lemon grass
3½ oz (90 g) onion
3 oz (75 g) red pepper
1 teaspoon salt
Freshly ground black pepper

If you are using fresh lemon grass, slice it crossways as thinly as possible, starting at the bulbous end and going up about 6 inches (15 cm). Discard the strawlike top. If you are using dried sliced lemon grass, soak it in 4 tablespoons hot water for 1 hour.

¼ teaspoon chilli powder or to taste

4 tablespoons vegetable oil

1 lb (450 g) lean steak, about 1 inch (2.5 cm) thick

Peel the onion and chop it coarsely. Remove the seeds from the red pepper and chop it coarsely. Combine the lemon grass, its soaking liquid (if you are using the dried variety), the onion, red pepper, salt, black pepper and chilli powder in an electric blender. Blend to a smooth paste, adding a few tablespoons of water if necessary.

Put the oil in a medium-sized, preferably non-stick frying-pan and set it over a highish heat. When the oil is hot, add the paste from the blender. Stir and fry for 6–8 minutes or until the paste has darkened in colour. (You may need to turn the heat down towards the end of this cooking time.) Leave the paste to cool.

Assuming that you are right-handed, hold a large knife at a 135° angle to your work-surface (45° for left-handers) and cut the slab of meat against the grain into very thin slices (in other words, you are cutting at a slight diagonal). Cut these slices into 1 inch (2.5 cm) pieces and put the pieces into a bowl. Add the paste and oil from the frying-pan and mix well. Cover and set aside, refrigerating if necessary, for 1–24 hours. (You may put the meat on its skewers before you set it aside, if that is more convenient.)

Pre-heat an indoor grill or an outdoor charcoal grill.

Thread the meat fairly tightly on to 2–4 skewers – the number of skewers required will depend upon their length. Grill the meat about 5 inches (13 cm) from the source of heat for about 5 minutes on one side and for 3–4 minutes on the opposite side. Serve as suggested above.

SERVES 4

BULGOGI   KOREA

MARINATED AND GRILLED BEEF STRIPS

FROM MRS HAN CHUNG KYU

Koreans have a great fondness for beef, especially *bulgogi*. Now, with prosperity high and the price of beef reasonable, many a housewife lovingly cooks it for her husband's dinner. If it is not available at home, there are restaurants a-plenty, scattered across the length and breadth of the land, that specialise in it and, like magnets, draw thousands of eager customers to their smoke-filled rooms.

Bulgogi is a grilled meat. This grilling is done over charcoal or gas and may take place at the table or outdoors. The grill itself is usually portable and varies from a ridged, heavy, metal plate that is raised in the centre to a more conventional cross-hatched surface. Since I do not have a Korean *bulgogi* grill, I use a large, well-heated, cast-iron frying-pan. I happen to have a trusted 14 inch (35 cm) pan that is perfect for the job but a smaller cast-iron frying-pan will do. You could also cook the meat, spread out, under a very hot grill.

In Korea thin slices of meat, marinated in a mixture of soy sauce, sugar, spring onions, ginger and garlic, are flung over the fire. Diners cook the meat themselves, turning it over with their chopsticks until it is cooked as they like it. Other ingredients can be added to the marinade as well, such as roasted sesame seeds and – very uncommon for us in the West – pear. This pear is the hard, round and very crisp 'pear-apple' that is found in Korea and China. It has a mellowing, softening effect on a mixture of somewhat sharper flavours. I use any hard pear that is available and find that it works well as a substitute.

This beef is generally eaten with rice, Cabbage Pickle (page 238) and vegetables such as Seasoned Spinach (page 197) or Stir-Fried Courgettes with Sesame Seeds (page 179). Sometimes leaves of soft lettuce are served on the side for diners to make small packages of the meat, rice and vegetables. A package is usually dipped in soy sauce before it is eaten.

1¼ lb (500 g) lean tender beef steak	Cut the meat against the grain into 3 × 2 inch (7.5 × 5 cm) rectangles that are about ⅛ inch (0.3 cm) thick.
½ medium-sized hard pear	
4–5 cloves garlic	Peel and core the pear half and then chop it
2 inch (5 cm) cube fresh ginger	coarsely. Peel the garlic and ginger and chop them

4 tablespoons Japanese soy sauce (shoyu)

5 medium-sized mushrooms

4½ oz (120 g) onions

3 spring onions

1 medium-sized carrot

2 tablespoons sesame oil

1 tablespoon roasted sesame seeds (see page 270)

2½ tablespoons sugar

coarsely. Put the pear, garlic, ginger and soy sauce into an electric blender and blend until smooth.

Cut the mushrooms into ⅛ inch (0.3 cm) slices. Peel and thickly slice the onions. Cut the spring onions into 2½ inch (6 cm) lengths. Peel the carrot and cut it into 2½ inch (6 cm) chunks. Then cut each chunk lengthways into ⅛ inch (0.3 cm) slices.

Put the meat in a bowl. Add the paste from the blender, the mushrooms, onions, spring onions, carrot, sesame oil, sesame seeds and sugar. Mix well. Cover and marinate for 1–24 hours.

Set a large cast-iron frying-pan on a high heat. Let it get almost white-hot. Put in as many of the meat slices as will fit in one layer. Cook, turning the meat pieces over as soon as they brown a little. You may leave the meat rare if you like. Remove the meat as soon as it is ready. Cook all the meat in this way. Then put in the vegetables and the marinade. Cook on a high heat for a minute or so. Then spoon the mixture over or beside the meat. Serve immediately.

SERVES 4

LAAB   THAILAND

Spicy Beef Salad

As steak tartare, that piquant mixture of raw minced beef and seasonings, is named after the nomadic Asians who thought it up, it should come as no surprise that the Far East has a host of fairly similar dishes. Take *laab*, an exquisite Thai salad. It comes from the north-east part of the country, an area that borders Laos. The minced beef in this case is sometimes left raw or it may be quickly stirred in a very hot wok so that it qualifies as 'rare'. It is then magically seasoned with sliced shallots, lime juice and mint. There is a secret ingredient that binds the salad and gives it a nutty aroma. It is rice – rice which has been roasted and ground!

A plate of *laab* usually has the seasoned meat on one side and a whole forest of fresh herbs and raw vegetables on the other. The two are then eaten together, the spicy meat nicely balanced by the crisp vegetables. Incidentally, you may also make this salad with left-over roast beef. Cut it into very thin slices and then cut the slices into 1 × 2 inch (2.5 × 5 cm) strips. You do not, of course need to cook them.

FOR THE VEGETABLES ON THE SIDE:

About 12 crisp inner leaves of iceberg, cos or other lettuce

4–8 sprigs fresh mint

8 oz (225 g) fresh bean sprouts

12 tender green beans or about 8 long beans

7 fresh hot red chillies or 1 red pepper

FOR THE SPICED BEEF:

3 tablespoons long-grain rice

2½ oz (65 g) shallots or onions (preferably red)

2 cloves garlic

2 tablespoons vegetable oil

1 lb (450 g) tender beef (such as a good-quality steak), minced

4 tablespoons lime or lemon juice

4 tablespoons fish sauce or salt to taste

1 tablespoon sugar

1 oz (25 g) fresh mint leaves

1 fresh hot red or green chilli

¼ teaspoon chilli powder

First prepare the vegetables. Wash the lettuce and pat it dry. Put it in a polythene bag and refrigerate. Remove the large coarse stems from the mint, if any; otherwise leave it in sprigs. Wash these and pat them dry. Put them in a polythene bag and refrigerate. Top and tail the bean sprouts (see page 260) if you are up to it. Wash them and leave them floating in a bowl of cold water. You may refrigerate them. Drain them well before using them. Wash and trim the beans. Long beans should be cut into thirds. Cover and refrigerate. The red chillies may be cut into flowers (see page 262) or into long strips. If you are using a red pepper, de-seed it and cut it into strips. Cover and refrigerate.

Set a small cast-iron frying-pan over a medium-high heat. When it is hot, put in the rice and stir it for 2–3 minutes or until the grains turn golden. Some might even pop. Remove the rice from the pan, cool it slightly and then put it into a clean coffee-grinder or mortar and pulverise it.

Peel the shallots and cut them into very fine, long slivers. (If you are using onions, peel, cut in half lengthways and then crossways into fine half-rings.) Peel the garlic and chop it finely.

Just before eating, put a wok on a high heat. When it is hot, swirl in the oil. Let the oil heat. When it is hot, put in the minced meat and stir-fry for 15–30 seconds. The meat should remain rare. Lift the beef out with a slotted spoon and put it into a bowl. Add the rice, shallots, garlic, lime juice, fish sauce and sugar. Chop the mint leaves coarsely and finely slice the red or green chilli. Add them and the chilli powder to the mixture. Mix well and check the seasoning.

Put the beef on one side of a large serving plate. Arrange the prepared vegetables prettily on the other side of the plate.

SERVES 4

BŌ NƯỚNG CHẢ

EASY BEEF KEBABS

All types of grilled kebabs enjoy great popularity in Vietnam. Here is a very simple version. You could serve this dish with a green salad of lettuce, cucumber, fresh coriander and mint leaves. Fresh rice noodles are generally served on the side in Vietnam. You could serve dried rice noodles or rice itself.

1 lb (450 g) boneless beef steak or beef skirt

4 cloves garlic

2 oz (50 g) onions

2 tablespoons fish sauce or a little salt to taste

1½ teaspoons Chinese light soy sauce

4 tablespoons crushed Roasted Peanuts (see page 236)

Fish Sauce with Vinegar and Lime Juice (see page 228)

Assuming that you are right-handed, hold a large knife at a 135° angle to your work-surface (45° for the left-handers) and cut the slab of meat against the grain into very thin slices (in other words, you are cutting at a slight diagonal). Cut these slices into 1 inch (2.5 cm) long pieces and put them in a bowl. Peel the garlic and onions and chop them very finely. Add these to the meat together with the fish sauce and soy sauce. (If you are substituting salt for the fish sauce, be sure to add only a little as the dish is served with a well-seasoned dipping sauce.) Mix well and set aside for 1–2 hours.

Pre-heat an indoor grill or an outdoor charcoal grill. Thread the meat fairly tightly on to 2–4 skewers depending on their length. Grill about 5 inches (13 cm) from the source of heat for about 5 minutes on one side and 3–4 minutes on the other side.

The meat may be served on or off the skewers, sprinkled with some crushed Roasted Peanuts. Fish Sauce with Vinegar and Lime Juice is poured over the top by each diner.

SERVES 4

Meatball Soup

FROM MRS CHOI SANG IN

A soupy dish in Korea is not always a soup, as we understand it. This meatball soup, for example, is fairly substantial and is usually served as one of the main dishes at a meal that might also include grilled and stir-fried foods. The meatballs here are quite delicate and light. The reason is bean curd – lots of it – which is mashed and combined with minced beef. This results in soft meatballs, the softest you will probably ever encounter.

When I want a light meal, I serve this mild and gentle soup all by itself, with just a green salad on the side for added balance – and crunch.

5–6 oz (150–175 g) bean curd

2 cloves garlic

4 spring onions

8 oz (225 g) minced lean beef

1 tablespoon Japanese soy sauce (shoyu)

2 teaspoons sesame oil

2 teaspoons roasted sesame seeds (see page 270)

2 pints (1.1 litres) chicken, beef or pork stock

½ inch (1 cm) cube fresh ginger

Salt

2½ oz (65 g) plain flour

1 egg

Put the bean curd in the centre of a clean cloth. Gather the ends together and squeeze as much moisture from it as you can. Then mash the bean curd with a fork or push it through a sieve.

Peel the garlic and chop it very finely. Cut 2 of the spring onions crossways into very fine rounds.

In a bowl combine the bean curd, garlic, sliced spring onions, minced beef, soy sauce, sesame oil and sesame seeds. Mix well and then make about 20 meatballs. You might find it helpful to wet your hands as you form the meatballs.

Put the stock in a large pan. Cut the remaining spring onions into 2 inch (5 cm) lengths. Peel the ginger and cut it into thin slices. Put the spring onions and ginger into the stock and bring it to the boil. Lower the heat and simmer gently for 8–10 minutes. Salt the stock to your taste and leave it simmering very gently.

Put the flour on to a plate. Break the egg into a saucer and beat it lightly. Roll each meatball first in the flour and then in the egg, and finally drop it into the simmering soup. After the meatballs are in, continue to simmer for another 5 minutes. You may remove the ginger slices before serving.

SERVES 4–5

GONGBAO NIULIU   HONG KONG

SICHUAN-STYLE FRIED SHREDDED BEEF WITH CARROTS AND CHILLIES

FROM THE AMERICAN RESTAURANT IN WANCHAI

In this spicy, slightly sweet, slightly sour dish, beef and carrot shreds are fried until they turn a bit crisp. They are then stir-fried with hot chillies and spring onions and doused with a light mixture of vinegar, soy sauce and sugar. The result is quite spectacular.

FOR THE BEEF MARINADE:

12 oz (350 g) lean beef steak

2½ teaspoons Chinese light soy sauce

1 small egg white

1 teaspoon cornflour

1½ teaspoons sesame oil

YOU ALSO NEED:

12 oz (350 g) carrots

2 cloves garlic

3–4 fresh hot red or green chillies

4 spring onions

2½ teaspoons Chinese rice wine or dry sherry

1½ teaspoons distilled white vinegar

2½ teaspoons sugar

1 teaspoon Chinese light soy sauce

2 teaspoons Chinese dark soy sauce

Vegetable oil for deep-frying

1 teaspoon cornflour

Cut the beef against the grain into very thin slices about ¹⁄₁₆ inch (0.15 cm) in width. Then stack a few slices at a time together and cut the meat into thin strips about 2½–3 inches (6–7.5 cm) long. Put the meat in a bowl. Add all the other marinade ingredients and mix well, ensuring that you break up the egg white. Cover and refrigerate if necessary.

Peel the carrots and cut them into long thin julienne strips, the same size as the beef. Peel the garlic and chop it finely. Cut the chillies lengthways into fine strips. Cut the spring onions crossways into 3 inch (7.5 cm) lengths and then cut them lengthways with the tip of a sharp knife into long fine strips.

Combine the rice wine, vinegar, sugar, light soy sauce and dark soy sauce in a cup. Mix and set aside.

Put about 1½ inches (4 cm) oil in a wok or large frying-pan and set it over a medium heat, or put the recommended quantity of oil in a deep-fat fryer and heat to 325°F (160°C). When it is hot, put in the carrots. Stir and fry for about 5 minutes or until the carrots are slightly crisp. Remove them with a slotted spoon. Now put all the beef in and turn off the heat. Stir the beef around until all the strands have separated and just turned white. You may have to turn the heat back on low to achieve this. Remove the meat with a slotted spoon and put it into a bowl. Sprinkle the meat with 1 teaspoon cornflour and toss well. Turn the heat under the oil to high. When it is hot, drop the meat in again for 30 seconds and then empty the contents of the wok into a strainer set over a bowl. Drain the meat well.

Put 2 tablespoons of the previously used oil into a clean wok or large frying-pan and set it on a high heat. When it is hot, put in the garlic. Stir and fry for 30 seconds or until it is lightly browned. Put in the chillies. Stir once and then add the spring onions. Stir rapidly once and add the meat and carrots. Stir for 30 seconds and add the rice wine sauce. Stir rapidly for about 30 seconds and serve.

SERVES 3–4

KALIYO OR RENDANG DAGING   INDONESIA

BEEF CHUNKS COOKED IN COCONUT MILK

FROM MARTINI JUFRI AND THE HOUSEHOLD OF RISNAWATI AGUS

Perhaps the most loved dish in Muslim West Sumatra, indeed in all of Indonesia, is beef *rendang*, in which large chunks of beef (sometimes water buffalo) are cooked and cooked in a mixture of coconut milk and spices until all the liquid disappears and the meat takes on a very inviting, dark, dry look. Prepared in this way, the beef lasts for days without refrigeration if kept in air-tight jars, and it is the preferred food taken by Sumatran travellers on long journeys. No wedding or festive occasion is ever without a *rendang*. Indeed, every time I was fêted it appeared on the menu, much to my delight. Once it was even cooked over wood, which gave it a deliciously complex flavour.

Almost a sister to *rendang* is *kaliyo*. It is exactly the same dish, only in a slightly earlier stage of preparation when the meat still has a nicely thickened sauce clinging to it. I love *rendang*, but I have a passion for *kaliyo*. Its sauce goes so well with the accompanying rice. It also takes less time to cook! This recipe is for both *kaliyo* and *rendang*.

3 inch (7.5 cm) cube fresh or 10–12 slices dried galangal

2 sticks fresh or 2 tablespoons dried sliced lemon grass

4–6 dried hot red chillies

2 inch (5 cm) stick cinnamon

12–14 cloves

4 oz (100 g) red pepper

3½ oz (90 g) shallots or onions

1 inch (2.5 cm) cube fresh ginger

7–8 cloves garlic

12 fresh or dried curry leaves or 4 dried bay leaves

8 fresh or dried kaffir lime leaves or 3 × ¼ inch (7.5 × 0.5 cm) strip lemon rind

2¾ pints (1.6 litres) coconut milk (see page 263)

2 lb (1 kg) stewing beef, cut into 1½–2 inch (4–5 cm) cubes

1¼ teaspoons salt

If you are using fresh galangal, peel and coarsely chop it and set it aside. If you are using dried galangal, combine it in a cup with 4 tablespoons water. If you are using fresh lemon grass, cut off the strawlike top, leaving about 6 inches (15 cm) of the bottom. Lightly crush the very bottom with a hammer or other heavy object and set it aside. If you are using dried lemon grass, put it into the water with the galangal.

Crumble or break the dried red chillies and cinnamon into enough water to cover or add them to the dried galangal and dried lemon grass if you are using them. Also put in the cloves. Soak the spices for 30 minutes. Cut the red pepper coarsely into dice, discarding all the seeds. Peel and coarsely chop the shallots, ginger and garlic.

In an electric blender, combine the soaked spices and their liquid, the fresh galangal (if you are using it), the chopped red pepper, shallots, ginger and garlic. Blend until smooth.

Into a wide, preferably non-stick pan put the paste from the blender, the fresh lemon grass (if you are using it), the curry leaves and kaffir lime leaves (or lemon rind). Stir the coconut milk well until smooth and pour that in as well. Bring to the boil, stirring occasionally. Turn the heat to medium and cook the sauce for 15 minutes, stirring now and then to prevent curdling. Put in the meat and salt and bring to the boil again. Reduce the heat to medium. Cook, uncovered, for 1 hour, stirring from time to time. Turn the heat up to medium-high and continue to cook, stirring now and then, for 30 minutes or until the sauce is very thick and brown and the meat tender. (If the sauce begins to splatter too much at any stage, cover the pot very loosely for that period.) This is *kaliyo*. To make *rendang*, continue to stir and cook until all the sauce has disappeared.

SERVES 4

THỊT BŌ KHO   VIETNAM

AROMATIC AND SPICY BEEF STEW

FROM BICHE LOMBATIÈRE

Although the West may not associate hearty stews with East Asia, they are, of course, cooked and eaten there. This stew is, perhaps, Vietnam's *boeuf bourguignon*. Some of the seasonings, such as cinnamon (technically cassia bark, a member of the cinnamon family that is used in China and Vietnam) and black pepper, will be quite familiar. Others, such as lemon grass, star anise and yellow bean sauce, may not be, but it is these which give this stew its Eastern aroma and taste. The yellow bean sauce used here is the one with whole or halved beans in it, usually sold as whole or crushed yellow bean sauce.

In Vietnam, this stew is eaten either with rice or with hunks of crusty French bread that is sold in all markets.

2 medium onions

5 cloves garlic

10–12 medium shallots or pickling onions

1 stick fresh lemon grass or 3 × 1 inch (7.5 × 1 cm) strip lemon rind

7 tablespoons vegetable oil

3 lb (1.5 kg) stewing beef, cut into 1 inch (2.5 cm) cubes

6 tablespoons yellow bean sauce

½–1 teaspoon chilli powder

4 whole star anise

1 inch (2.5 cm) stick cinnamon

½ teaspoon whole peppercorns

2 tablespoons sugar

Peel and finely chop the onions and garlic. Peel the shallots and leave them whole. Cut the lemon grass into 2 inch (5 cm) sections, starting from the bottom and going up about 6 inches (15 cm). Discard the strawlike top. Crush each section lightly with a hammer or other heavy object. (If you are using lemon rind, leave it in one piece.)

Put 3 tablespoons of the oil in a non-stick frying-pan and set it on a medium-high heat. When it is hot, put in the onions, garlic and shallots. Stir and fry for 2 minutes. Add the lemon grass (but not the lemon rind if you are using it as a substitute). Continue to stir and fry until the onions have browned lightly. Turn off the heat. Pick the shallots out of the pan and set them aside.

Put the remaining 4 tablespoons oil in a large, wide, preferably non-stick pan and set it over a high heat. When it is hot, put in as many meat cubes as the pan will hold in a single layer and brown them, turning them over when necessary. Remove the cubes with a slotted spoon. Brown all the meat in this way.

Return all the browned meat to the large pan. Add 1¾ pints (1 litre) water as well as the onion-garlic-lemon grass mixture. Coarsely chop the beans in the yellow bean sauce (if they are not already crushed) and add them as well. Also put in the chilli powder, star anise, cinnamon, peppercorns and sugar. Bring to the boil, then cover, lower the heat and simmer gently for 1¼ hours. Add the reserved shallots (and the lemon rind, if you are using it). Cover again and simmer for another 15 minutes. Remove the lid, raise the heat to medium and cook for a further 15–20 minutes or until sauce has thickened a little and the meat is tender. Spoon the fat off the top before serving.

SERVES 6

DAGING NASI KANDAR   MALAYSIA

BEEF CURRY WITH THICK ONION SAUCE

FROM PUAN RASHIDAH IN KUALA LUMPUR

Daging is beef, *nasi* is rice and as far as *kandar* is concerned – well, herein lies a tale. Early Indian settlers, as many others before them, often turned to hawking as a means of livelihood. The Indians suspended two baskets at each end of a pole and balanced this pole on their shoulders or *kandar*. Among the most popular items sold from these baskets was a particular combination of dishes, a whole meal in fact, that took on the name of *nasi kandar*, or 'rice meal on a shoulder'. There was rice, of course, and a fish curry; hard-boiled eggs, and this beef curry whose thick sauce could also be ladled over the eggs.

Today many hawkers have moved indoors and *nasi kandar* is rarely sold on the move, but there are several restaurants that serve it as their speciality. One, in Penang, is so famous, that government ministers from Kuala Lumpur make a beeline for it when they visit there. Puan Rashidah, who gave me this recipe, makes her own, cooking it when catering for private parties besides selling it at a small stall. This curry, which probably started out being Indian, has by now picked up Malay and Chinese seasonings as well. It is a spectacular dish.

2 lb (1 kg) stewing beef

6–16 dried hot red chillies (6 will make a mild dish, 16 a fairly hot one)

2 sticks fresh lemon grass or 2 3 × ½ inch (7.5 × 1 cm) slices lemon rind

1½ lb (750 g) onions

5 fl oz (150 ml) vegetable oil

5 tablespoons black bean sauce or 3 tablespoons tinned or dried black beans, washed and mashed with 2 tablespoons oyster sauce

2 inch (5 cm) stick cinnamon

20 curry leaves (optional)

3 tablespoons tamarind paste (see page 272) or 2 tablespoons lime or lemon juice

1 tablespoon sugar

1 teaspoon salt

Cut the beef into 1½ inch (4 cm) cubes and set aside. Crumble the chillies into a small bowl. Add 4 tablespoons hot water and set aside for 30 minutes or until the chillies soften. Put the chillies and their soaking liquid into an electric blender and blend until smooth.

Cut the lemon grass sticks into 6 inch (15 cm) lengths, starting from the bottom. Discard the strawlike top. Crush the bulbous bottoms of the lemon grass lightly. (If you are using lemon rind, leave it in one piece.)

Peel and finely slice the onions. Put the oil in a large wide pan over a medium-high heat. When it is hot, put in half the sliced onions. Stir and fry for about 15 minutes or until the onions are reddish brown and crisp. (You will probably need to turn the heat down to medium after about 4–5 minutes.) Remove the onions with a slotted spoon and spread them out on a plate lined with kitchen paper. Put the chilli paste from the blender into the pan. Stir and fry for 30 seconds. Now put in the remaining uncooked sliced onions. Stir and fry for about 5 minutes or until they are soft. Add the black bean sauce and stir for 30 seconds. Next put in the meat, cinnamon stick, curry leaves, tamarind paste (or lime or lemon juice), sugar, whole lemon grass sticks (or lemon rind) and 1½ pints (900 ml) water. Stir and bring to the boil. Cover, lower the heat and simmer gently for 1¼ hours or until the meat is almost done. Remove the lid and taste, adding as much of the salt as you think you need. Stir, turn the heat to high and, over the next 10 minutes or so, reduce the sauce until it is thick. Put in the browned onions and mix. Turn the heat to medium and cook for another 2 minutes.

This dish can be made ahead of time and reheated. Remove the lemon grass (or rind) and cinnamon stick before serving.

SERVES 4

KAENG PHET NUA   THAILAND

EASY BEEF CURRY

I use beef skirt for this curry. It is such a tender cut of meat and requires hardly
any cooking at all. I stand at the cooker for about 12 minutes only, 8 of which
are spent frying the spices, and the other 4 cooking the beef. This is a perfect
dish to serve at a small dinner party. If you cannot get kaffir lime leaves use a
3 × ½ inch (7.5 × 1 cm) strip of lemon rind that is cut into fine julienne strips.
Put it into the curry at the same time as the mint and basil leaves.

1 lb (450 g) beef skirt

4½–5 oz (120–150 g) red
  pepper

4 oz (100 g) onions

4 large cloves garlic

1 teaspoon shrimp or anchovy
  paste

½ teaspoon chilli powder

8 tablespoons vegetable oil

2 tablespoons fish sauce or 1
  tablespoon soy sauce mixed
  with 1 tablespoon water and
  ¼ teaspoon sugar

8 fl oz (250 ml) coconut milk
  (see page 263)

½ teaspoon salt

4 fresh or dried kaffir lime
  leaves or lemon rind (see
  above)

10–15 fresh basil leaves

10–15 fresh mint leaves

Cut the beef against the grain into pieces 2–3
inches (5–7.5 cm) long, 1 inch (2.5 cm) wide and
1/16–1/8 inch (0.15–0.3 cm) thick. If you have
bought the meat in a long, thin, continuous piece,
cut it into 3 inch (7.5 cm) segments first and then
cut each segment against the grain, holding the
knife at a 135° angle to your work-surface. This
will give you the required width.

Core the red pepper, remove the seeds and chop
it coarsely. Peel the onions and garlic and chop
them coarsely. Combine the red pepper, onions,
garlic, shrimp paste and chilli powder in an electric blender. Blend until smooth, adding a tablespoon or so of water only if you need to.

Put the oil in a wide shallow saucepan or frying-
pan and set it over a medium-high heat. When it is
hot, put in the spice paste from the blender. Stir
and fry for 7–8 minutes or until the paste turns
dark and separates from the oil. Add the meat and
the fish sauce (or soy sauce mixed with water and
sugar). Stir and cook for 2 minutes. Stir the
coconut milk and add that, together with the salt
and the dried kaffir lime leaves, if you are using
them. If the kaffir lime leaves are fresh, tear them
in half and remove the centre vein before adding.
Coarsely tear the basil and mint leaves, and add as
well. Stir once, turn off the heat and serve.

SERVES 4

CONG BAO YANG ROLL   HONG KONG

LAMB WITH SPRING ONIONS

FROM THE SPRING DEER RESTAURANT IN HONG KONG

Beijing (Peking) may be best known in the West for its roast duck but Hong Kong's knowledgeable residents often order simpler and equally delicious dishes when they go to northern-style restaurants. Here is a simple dish which is as good to eat as it is easy to make. The only labour required is in slicing the meat and spring onions. The cooking itself takes just a few minutes.

I use leg of lamb for this recipe. I buy a whole leg, asking the butcher to bone it and remove most of the fat. I cut off the amount I need and freeze the rest for future use. In order to make this dish successfully, it is important that you do not overcook the spring onions. They should barely wilt.

FOR THE LAMB MARINADE:

12 oz (350 g) lean tender lamb

2 teaspoons Chinese light soy sauce

2 teaspoons Chinese rice wine or dry sherry

2 teaspoons sesame oil

½ teaspoon roasted and ground Sichuan peppercorns (see page 271) or coarsely ground black peppercorns

FOR THE SAUCE:

1 tablespoon Chinese rice wine or dry sherry

4 teaspoons Chinese dark soy sauce

1 tablespoon sesame oil

1 teaspoon distilled white vinegar

YOU ALSO NEED:

2 cloves garlic

5 oz (150 g) spring onions

2 tablespoons fresh coriander leaves

4 tablespoons vegetable oil

Cut the lamb against the grain into very thin slices. Cut the slices into very thin slivers about 3 inches (7.5 cm) long. Put them into a bowl and add all the other marinade ingredients. Mix well and set aside for 20 minutes.

Combine all the ingredients for the sauce. Mix and set aside.

Peel the garlic and chop it finely. Cut the spring onions, including their green section, crossways into 3 inch (7.5 cm) segments. Then cut each piece lengthways into very fine strips. Wash the coriander and pat it dry.

Put the oil in a wok or a large frying-pan and set it over a high heat. When it is smoking hot, put in the garlic. Stir once or twice and then put in the lamb. Stir-fry for about a minute or until the lamb is no longer pink on the outside. Pour in the sauce and stir briefly. Put in the coriander and spring onion. Stir for 20–30 seconds or until the spring onions just wilt. Serve immediately.

SERVES 4

LAMB OR GOAT STEW WITH POTATOES, PEPPERS AND OLIVES

FROM THE FOOD BASKET RESTAURANT IN SILAY

One version or another of *caldereta* is cooked throughout the Philippines, but here it is prepared in the slightly spicy style well loved in the Western Visayas region. Again, as with many dishes from this former Spanish colony, the Mediterranean influence is very evident in the use of tomato paste, red pepper and olives. Incidentally, bay leaves, cinnamon sticks and peppercorns, fairly common seasonings for stews, are sold here in a combined version and are known collectively as *ricado*.

2 lb (1 kg) boneless lamb or goat meat

3 tablespoons distilled white vinegar

1¼ teaspoons salt

Freshly ground black pepper

5 cloves garlic

4 oz (100 g) onions

4 tablespoons olive oil

3 dried hot red chillies

1 teaspoon whole black peppercorns

2 inch (5 cm) stick cinnamon

2 bay leaves

4 teaspoons tomato paste

12 oz (350 g) potatoes

3 oz (75 g) red pepper

8 whole stuffed green olives or other olives of your choice

Cut the meat into 1½ inch (4 cm) cubes and put it in a bowl. Add the vinegar, salt and ground black pepper. Mix and set aside for 30–40 minutes. Drain the meat (saving the liquid) and pat it dry. Peel the garlic and onions and chop them finely.

Put the oil in a large heavy pan and set it over a medium-high heat. When it is hot, put in the chillies. Stir for a few seconds or until they swell and darken. Remove them with a slotted spoon and set them aside. Put as many cubes of meat into the pan as will fit easily in a single layer. Brown the meat on both sides and then remove it with a slotted spoon. Brown all the meat in this way. Next put the garlic and onion into the oil in which you have cooked the meat. Stir and cook for 2 minutes, scraping up any pan juices as you do so. Put in the black peppercorns, cinnamon and bay leaves. Continue to stir and cook for another minute. Now put in the meat and its accumulated juices, the chillies, the reserved marinade liquid and the tomato paste. Stir and cook for 1 minute. Add 15 fl oz (450 ml) water and bring it to the boil. Cover, turn the heat to low and cook for 15 minutes.

Meanwhile, peel the potatoes and cut them into

1½ inch (4 cm) cubes. When the meat has cooked for 15 minutes, add the potatoes to the pan. Cover again and continue to cook for another 45 minutes—1 hour or until the meat is tender. Deseed the red pepper and cut it into ¼ inch (0.5 cm) wide strips. When the meat is tender, put the pepper strips and olives into the stew. Stir and cook for another 3–5 minutes.

SERVES 4–5

TWAEJI BOKKUM   KOREA

STIR-FRIED PORK WITH RED PEPPER

Easy to prepare and spicily delicious, this dish is best served with plain rice.

12 oz (350 g) boneless loin of pork

1 spring onion

1 large clove garlic

1 X ½ inch (2.5 X 1 cm) piece fresh ginger

2 tablespoons Hot Fermented Bean Paste (see page 230)

3 oz (75 g) red pepper

3 oz (75 g) onions

3 tablespoons vegetable oil

Cut the pork against the grain into slices about 2 X 1 X ⅛ inch (5 X 2.5 X 0.3 cm). Cut the spring onion crossways into very fine rounds. Peel the garlic and ginger and chop them finely. Combine the pork, spring onion, garlic, ginger and Hot Fermented Bean Paste in a bowl. Mix well. Cover and set aside for 30 minutes or longer, refrigerating if necessary.

Cut the pepper into ½ inch (1 cm) squares. Cut the onions into ½ inch (1 cm) cubes and then separate the layers.

Just before serving, put the oil in a large non-stick frying-pan and set it over a high heat. When it is hot, put in the pork together with all its marinade. Stir-fry for 3 minutes or until the pork is white all the way through. Add about 6 tablespoons water and the pepper and onion. Stir and cook for another 2 minutes on a high heat.

SERVES 4

PORK COOKED IN A PICKLING STYLE

FROM SANDY DAZA

One of the most popular pork dishes in the Philippines is *adobo*. It originated well before the age of refrigeration. Meat needed to be preserved and the tastiest way to do it was to cook it with a mixture of vinegar, soy sauce and garlic, thus pickling it into the bargain. Normally belly pork is used, but thin-cut pork loin chops – about ½ inch (1 cm) thick – make a successful substitute. If you wish to use the more authentic belly pork, cut it crossways into 1 inch (2.5 cm) cubes. Pork *adobo* is served with plain rice.

12 large cloves garlic

6 tablespoons Chinese dark soy sauce

6 tablespoons distilled white vinegar

3 bay leaves

1 teaspoon whole black peppercorns

2 lb (1 kg) thin-cut pork loin chops

3 tablespoons vegetable oil

Peel the garlic cloves. Chop 4 of them finely and set them aside for the marinade. Chop the remaining 8 finely and set them aside separately. Combine the 4 chopped garlic cloves, the soy sauce, vinegar, bay leaves and peppercorns in a large bowl and mix well. Add the pork chops and mix again so that they are well coated with the marinade. Set aside for 1 hour, turning the chops over a few times during this period.

Put the oil in a wide saucepan or large frying-pan and set it over a medium-high heat. When the oil is hot, put in the 8 chopped cloves of garlic. Stir and fry until they turn light gold in colour. Add the pork chops, their marinade and 4 fl oz (120 ml) water. Bring to the boil. Cover, turn the heat to low and simmer gently for 30 minutes, turning the chops over a few times during this period. Remove the lid from the pan and turn the heat to medium-high. Cook for another 10–15 minutes or until the sauce is thick and the meat is tender. This dish may be prepared a day ahead of time and refrigerated.

SERVES 4

SIJIDOU CHAO ZHULIU   HONG KONG

PORK WITH LONG BEANS AND CHIVES

FROM WILLY MARK

You could call Willy Mark one of Hong Kong's moving landmarks. He owns restaurants, writes about food and cooks with great knowledge and passion. As it happens, he never seems to cook the same dish twice in exactly the same way. He made this particular Cantonese-style dish for me once with onions and chives, another time with garlic. Each time it was superb and different, which just goes to show that there is great flexibility in Chinese cooking and you should never be afraid to make changes and adjustments.

A note about the ingredients: in Hong Kong, long beans come in two shades of green, light and dark. Willy uses the darker, crisper variety. Use any type of long beans if you can find them. Most Chinese and Indian grocers stock them. If you cannot obtain them, use any tender green beans, cooking them carefully so that they retain their crispness. The chives Willy picked from the market were topped with closed buds. If you grow chives, as I do, and they happen to be budding, do use them, young bud and all. If you do not grow them, use either Chinese chives or ordinary chives.

7 oz (200 g) pork tenderloin, well-trimmed

Salt

4 teaspoons sesame oil

2½ teaspoons cornflour

7 oz (200 g) long or green beans

¾ oz (20 g) fresh chives (Chinese chives, if available)

1 medium onion

¾ inch (2 cm) cube fresh ginger

1 large clove garlic

1 tablespoon oyster sauce

2 teaspoons Chinese light soy sauce

1 tablespoon Chinese rice wine or dry sherry

5 tablespoons vegetable oil

Cut the pork tenderloin into very thin slices about 2 inches (5 cm) long and ½ inch (1 cm) wide. Put them in a small bowl. Add about ⅛ teaspoon salt, 2 teaspoons of the sesame oil, 1 teaspoon of the cornflour and 2 teaspoons water. Mix well. Cover and set aside, refrigerating if necessary.

Trim the beans and cut them into 2 inch (5 cm) pieces. Cut the chives into 2 inch (5 cm) lengths as well. Peel the onion and cut in half crossways, then quarter each half and separate the different layers. Peel the ginger and garlic and chop very finely.

In a small bowl combine the oyster sauce, light soy sauce, the remaining 2 teaspoons sesame oil, the rice wine and 5 tablespoons water. Mix well and set aside.

In a cup, combine the remaining 1½ teaspoons cornflour with 2 tablespoons water and set aside.

Just before eating, put 1 tablespoon oil in a wok or frying-pan and set it over a high heat. When the oil is hot, put in half the finely chopped ginger. Stir once or twice. Then add the onion and stir a few times. Put in the green beans and ¼ teaspoon salt. Stir-fry for a minute. Put in 4 tablespoons water and cover immediately. Lower the heat and cook for 4–6 minutes or until the beans are just tender. Uncover and empty the contents of the wok into a bowl.

Clean and dry the wok. Pour in the remaining 4 tablespoons oil and heat it. When it is very hot, put in the pork. Turn off the heat. Keep moving the pork pieces about until they just turn white. You may need to turn the heat on again to achieve this, but keep it on low. Remove the pork with a slotted spoon and put it into a clean bowl.

Remove all but 1 tablespoon of the oil. Set the wok over a high heat. When the oil is hot, add the remaining ginger and the garlic. Stir for 15–30 seconds. Put in the pork. Stir-fry for 1 minute. Put in the green beans and onion and stir them for 30 seconds. Then add the sauce from the bowl and stir for a minute. Take the wok off the heat. Stir the cornflour mixture in the cup. Make a well in the centre of the wok's contents and pour it in. Put the wok back over a low heat. Stir and cook just until the sauce has thickened.

MENUDO   PHILIPPINES

PORK WITH CALF'S LIVER AND CHICK PEAS

This is an easy stew, hearty and nourishing and comforting all at once. It is, quite clearly, of Mediterranean origin. It may be eaten with a salad and also, if you like, with rice.

Tinned chick peas may be used for this dish: drain them first. If you wish to cook your own from scratch, soak about ½ teacup dried chick peas overnight in cold water. The following day, drain them, put them in a pan, cover with 2 pints (1.1 litres) fresh cold water and bring to the boil. Cover, lower the heat and simmer for 45 minutes. Add ½ teaspoon salt and continue to cook for another 30 minutes–1 hour or until the chick peas are tender. (Older chick peas take longer to cook.) Drain them and weigh them before using them for this recipe. I use the meat from 3–4 thin pork loin chops for this dish.

5 oz (150 g) calf's liver
Salt
Freshly ground black pepper
12 oz (350 g) lean pork meat
8 oz (225 g) potatoes
10 oz (275 g) tinned peeled tomatoes
3 cloves garlic
1 medium onion
4 tablespoons vegetable oil
5 oz (150 g) cooked chick peas
1 teaspoon paprika

Cut the liver into ½–¾ inch (1–2 cm) cubes. Dust it lightly with salt and pepper and toss. Cut the pork into ½–¾ inch (1–2 cm) cubes, discarding most of the fat. Peel the potatoes and cut them into ½–¾ inch (1–2 cm) cubes; place them in a bowl of water and set aside. Crush the tomatoes lightly and leave them in their liquid. Peel the garlic and cut it into fine slivers. Peel the onion and cut it into thin slices.

Put the oil in a large, preferably non-stick frying-pan over a high heat. When the oil is hot, put in the liver. Stir and fry until it has browned on the outside but is still soft and slightly rare inside. Remove the liver with a slotted spoon and set it aside. Put the garlic and onion into the same oil. Stir and fry for 1 minute. Then add the diced pork and stir and fry for 3 minutes. Now put in the tomatoes and their liquid. Keep stirring and cooking on a high heat for 1 minute, then cover, turn the heat to low and simmer for 15 minutes. Drain the potatoes and add them to the pan. Also add the chick peas, 1½ teaspoons salt, some black pepper, the paprika and 5 fl oz (150 ml) water. Stir and bring to a simmer. Cover and cook for 15 25 minutes, or until the potatoes and pork are tender. Put in the liver, plus any juices that may have run out of it, and heat it through. This dish may be made in advance and reheated.

SERVES 4

HONG SHAO LEIGU   HONG KONG

GLAZED GINGERY SPARERIBS

FROM ANDY'S KITCHEN RESTAURANT IN CAUSEWAY BAY

These Shanghai-style pork ribs are braised. There really could not be a simpler way to prepare them. You could also make this dish with thin-cut pork loin chops.

2 lb (1 kg) pork spareribs

6 tablespoons Chinese dark soy sauce

6 tablespoons sugar

2 × 1 inch (2.5 cm) cubes fresh ginger

3 spring onions

3 tablespoons Chinese rice wine or dry sherry

Separate the spareribs individually and then cut them into 3 inch (7.5 cm) lengths. (Persuade your butcher to do this for you if possible.)

Put the spareribs in a wide, preferably non-stick pan. Add the soy sauce and sugar. Peel and lightly crush the ginger cubes and add them to the pan. Add the spring onions also. Pour in the rice wine and 1¾ pints (1 litre) water. Bring to the boil. Cover, turn the heat to medium-low and simmer fairly vigorously for 45 minutes. Turn the meat around every 10 minutes or so to allow even colouring. Remove the lid from the pan and turn the heat to high. Remove and discard the ginger and spring onions. Cook for another 20 minutes or so or until liquid is thick and syrupy. It should coat the ribs with an even, dark glaze. You may need to stir the ribs around a few times during this period.

SERVES 4

KNOCKOUT KNUCKLE

FROM THE ANG HANG RESTAURANT IN MANILA

During my last few trips to the Philippines, I had some of the best food in
Manila at the Ang Hang Restaurant. One of its specialities was this dish. Pork is
a much-loved meat in the Philippines, as it is in many Pacific Islands, and what
often adds to the status of the meat itself is the crispness of the skin on top of it.
In this recipe the meat is juicy and tender and the skin is crackling crisp. This is
achieved by an easily mastered technique of slow braising and double-frying.

It is quite easy to make this dish; it is harder to find the right cut of meat!
What you need is the 3 lb (1.5 kg) front leg of a pig that – in the words of the
chef – 'has not been around'. This, when translated, means a 3–4-month-old
pig. I had great trouble finding the front leg of a pig, let alone that of a pig that
had not been around! You have two choices here: you can either buy what is
sold as a pork half-leg knuckle; or you can do what I did. I went to the butcher
and put in a special order for a front leg. It came, all 5½ lb (2.5 kg) of it. I
wanted only 3 lb (1.5 kg), so I asked the butcher to cut away a portion at the
thicker end. He took an educated guess, hacked down and came in at 3½ lb
(1.65 kg). I took both pieces home, one to cook immediately and the thicker end
to store in the freezer for later use.

My children declared that this was the best pork they had ever tasted.

3½ lb (1.65 kg) pork half-leg
knuckle or portion of front
leg of pork

1 medium onion

2 carrots

2 sticks celery

1 teaspoon whole black
peppercorns

3 bay leaves

1 tablespoon salt

9 cloves garlic

6 fresh hot green chillies

5 fl oz (150 ml) vegetable oil,
plus extra for deep-frying

Put the pork, skin-side up, into a large pan along
with 8 pints (4.5 litres) water. Bring to a simmer.
Maintain a very gentle simmer over the next few
minutes and remove as much scum as you can. Peel
the onion and carrots. Put them, as well as the
celery, peppercorns, bay leaves and salt, into the
pan. Cover partially and simmer gently for about 3
hours or until the meat is tender. Remove the meat
and leave it to drain and cool. (The meat broth may
be strained, cooled, de-greased and saved for use in
other dishes.)

Peel the garlic and cut it lengthways into thin
slices. Cut the green chillies crossways into thin
slices. Put the 5 fl oz (150 ml) oil in a frying-pan
set over a medium-low heat. Put in the garlic. Stir

and fry until it just begins to turn golden. Then add the chillies. Continue to stir and fry until the garlic is golden-brown and the chillies have crisped a little. Remove the garlic and chillies with a slotted spoon and spread them over kitchen paper to drain. Save the garlicky oil.

Heat the oil for deep-frying in a large deep-fat fryer or a large wok to a medium temperature, about 325°F (160°C). When it is hot, put in the pork joint, skin-side down. Cover and cook for 5 minutes. Turn the pork over carefully, cover again and cook the second side for 3 minutes. Transfer the pork to a plate. (This much can be done up to 2 hours ahead of time. Do not refrigerate the meat.)

Just before serving, heat the oil again, this time to a high temperature, around 400°F (200°C). When it is hot, put in the meat, skin-side down. Fry, uncovered, for 2–3 minutes or until the skin is crisp and brown. Now turn the meat and fry the opposite side for 1 minute. Turn the meat again and fry the skin side for another minute. Make sure that the skin on the sides of the meat browns properly too.

Lift the meat out carefully and drain it briefly. Put it on a plate and then cut the meat off the bone lengthways in long strips. Lay the strips back over the bone, forming a kind of tent over it. Pour a little of the reserved garlicky oil over the meat. Scatter the fried garlic and chillies over the top and serve.

SERVES 4

TONKATSU   JAPAN

Breaded Pork Cutlets

WITH HELP FROM THE ÉCOLE TECHNIQUE HÔTELIÈRE TSUJI IN OSAKA

Breaded and deep-fried, these cutlets originally came to Japan from the West but they are now so popular that almost every neighbourhood has a thriving *tonkatsu* restaurant. One reason could well be that fine food in Japan tends to be very expensive. Among the few good, cheaper eating places are *tonkatsu* restaurants, noodle shops and *yakitori* (chicken kebab) bars.

In Japan *tonkatsu* cutlets are diced into bite-sized pieces so that they can be picked up with chopsticks. They are then re-assembled in their cutlet shape and served on a bed of finely shredded lettuce or cabbage. The official dipping sauce, which is available, bottled, all over Japan, seems to be a combination of tomato ketchup, Worcestershire sauce, mustard, soy sauce and *sake*. A soup, a bowl of rice and some pickles are generally served on the side. A Japanese portion would normally consist of one cutlet; I have allowed two per person.

8 boneless pork loin chops or 1¼–1½ lb (500–750 g) pork tenderloin, cut into 8 pieces, each about ½ inch (1 cm) thick

Salt

Freshly ground black pepper

1½–2 tablespoons flour

2 eggs

4–5 oz (100–150 g) fresh breadcrumbs, made from slightly stale bread

4 oz (100 g) cabbage or crisp lettuce (such as iceberg or cos)

Oil for deep-frying

East-West Sauce (see page 226) or tomato ketchup

Lime or lemon wedges

Dust the pork pieces on both sides, first with the salt and pepper and then with the flour. Break the eggs into a shallow bowl and beat them lightly. Empty the breadcrumbs into another shallow bowl. Dip the pork pieces first in the egg and then in the breadcrumbs. Set aside for 30 minutes.

Cut the cabbage or lettuce into fine long shreds and divide between 4 plates.

Heat the oil in a deep frying-pan or deep-fat fryer to a temperature of about 350°F (180°C). When it is hot, put in as many pork pieces as the pan will hold in a single layer and deep-fry for 5–6 minutes or until the meat is brown outside and just cooked through. Drain it on kitchen paper. Cook all the meat in this way. Then cut the cooked meat slices neatly into bite-sized cubes and divide them between 4 plates, reforming them into their original cutlet shape and placing 2 reformed cutlets on each bed of cabbage or lettuce. Serve with East-West Sauce and lime or lemon wedges.

SERVES 4

KATSUDON   JAPAN

BREADED PORK CUTLETS OVER RICE

The Breaded Pork Cutlets (opposite) may be served in another way: over a large individual bowl of hot rice (Japanese rice is best), with a sauce of stock, soy, *sake* and onions poured over the top. This dish is then known as *katsudon* and it is a great favourite of mine.

FOR THE CUTLETS:

8 boneless pork loin chops or 1¼–1½ lb (500–750 g) pork tenderloin, cut into 8 pieces, each about ½ inch (1 cm) thick

Salt

Freshly ground black pepper

1½–2 tablespoons flour

2 eggs

4–5 oz (100–150 g) fresh breadcrumbs, made from slightly stale bread

YOU ALSO NEED:

I medium onion

4 spring onions

1 pint (600 ml) Japanese Soup Stock (see page 66) or light unsalted chicken stock

5–6 tablespoons Japanese soy sauce (shoyu)

8 tablespoons *sake*

2 tablespoons sugar

1 tablespoon vegetable oil

Enough Plain Japanese Rice for 4 people (see page 204)

Make the cutlets in exactly the same way as described in the recipe opposite, keeping them hot.

Peel the onion and cut it in half lengthways. Cut each half crossways into ⅛ inch (0.3 cm) slices. Trim the spring onions and cut them in half lengthways, then cut them crossways into 2 inch (5 cm) lengths. Combine the stock, soy sauce, *sake* and sugar in a bowl.

Put the oil in a medium-sized pan and set it over a medium heat. When the oil is hot, add the onion and sauté it until it is soft but do not let it brown. Add the stock mixture and the spring onions. Bring to a simmer gently and then simmer for 3 minutes.

Assemble the *katsudon* quickly now. Put about 1½ teacups hot Plain Japanese Rice into each of 4 bowls. Lay the pork cutlets over the rice, 2 to a bowl. Then spoon the stock-onion mixture over the top, dividing it evenly among the 4 bowls. The liquid will moisten the rice and add great flavour to it. Serve hot.

SERVES 4

KAENG HUNGLAY   THAILAND

THAI PORK CURRY IN THE BURMESE STYLE

FROM THE HOME OF KRUAMAS WOODTIKARN IN CHIANG MAI

Even before I got to Chiang Mai, I had been told by friends in Bangkok of this northern dish. 'Try and eat it in someone's home,' I had been advised. I need not have worried about how I would manage this: Thais are about the most hospitable people I know. Within a day of arriving in Chiang Mai, I was seated with Kruamas 'Ting' Woodtikarn's family, devouring not just curry but a table-load of northern delicacies, including black button mushrooms and freshly plucked litchis.

Much of north-western Thailand not only borders Burma but has also been ruled by it in previous centuries. The cultural give-and-take can still be seen in the lacquered baskets used for storing cooked glutinous rice (this is the rice eaten for breakfast, lunch and dinner), in the cheroot-smoking women of the villages, and in this curry. Those of you who are familiar with India's hot, sweet and sour *vindaloo* will find that this is almost a sister curry. After all, Burma borders India and the ripple effect of cultural exchanges can be quite far-reaching.

Boneless pork from the loin or shoulder may be used in this recipe. A little fat in the meat will keep it more tender. You could cut the meat off chops, if you like, saving the bones for soup. The curry paste can be made ahead of time and frozen. It will need to be de-frosted and brought to room temperature before it is used.

FOR THE CURRY PASTE:

3–8 dried hot red chillies, depending on hotness required

¾ inch (2 cm) cube fresh or 5 slices dried galangal or ¾ inch (2 cm) cube fresh ginger

2 sticks fresh or 2 tablespoons dried sliced lemon grass

3½ oz (90 g) shallots or onions

10 large cloves garlic

First make the curry paste. Put 8 fl oz (250 ml) water in a small bowl and crumble the dried red chillies into it. If using dried galangal and dried lemon grass, add them to the water as well. Leave the dried ingredients to soak for 30 minutes. If you are using fresh galangal (or ginger), peel and coarsely chop it. If you are using fresh lemon grass, cut it into very fine slices crossways, starting from the bottom and going up the stalk about 6 inches (15 cm); discard the strawlike top. Peel the shallots and garlic and chop them coarsely.

1 teaspoon shrimp or anchovy paste

1 tablespoon ground coriander seeds

2 teaspoons ground cumin seeds

½ teaspoon ground turmeric

YOU ALSO NEED:

1¾ lb (875 g) boneless pork, cut into 1½ inch (4 cm) cubes

1½ tablespoons Japanese soy sauce (shoyu)

3 × 1 inch (2.5 cm) cubes fresh ginger (the younger, the better)

10–12 shallots or small pickling onions

10–15 small cloves garlic

2 or more tablespoons tamarind paste (see page 272) or lemon juice

2 or more tablespoons dark brown sugar

Salt (optional)

When the dry seasonings have finished soaking, put them and their soaking liquid as well as all the other ingredients for the curry paste into an electric blender. If you are using fresh galangal (or fresh ginger) or fresh lemon grass, add them to the blender now. Blend until smooth. This curry paste may be made ahead of time and even frozen.

Next combine the pork, curry paste and soy sauce in a bowl and marinate for 30 minutes.

Meanwhile, peel the ginger and cut it into very thin slices. Stack a few slices at a time together and cut them into matchstick strips. Peel the shallots and the garlic, leaving them whole.

Put the pork and its marinade into a wide, heavy, preferably non-stick pan, set it over a medium-low heat and bring it to a simmer. Simmer gently for 15–20 minutes or until the meat starts to release its fat. Turn the heat to medium-high. Stir and fry for about 10 minutes or until the spice mixture begins to dry out and brown. Now add 15 fl oz (450 ml) water, the ginger strips, the whole shallots and the whole cloves of garlic. Bring the mixture to a simmer. Cover and cook for 45 minutes or until the meat is tender. Add the tamarind paste (or lemon juice) and brown sugar. Mix and taste, adding more of each if you think you need it. Add salt if desired. Cook for another 2–3 minutes to allow the flavours to develop and mingle.

SERVES 4–6

POULTRY AND EGGS

YAKITORI   JAPAN

CHICKEN BITS ON A SKEWER

A *yakitori* bar in Japan, is really a drinking establishment which offers specialised snacks, generally made of chicken and generally cooked on bamboo skewers over charcoal. As offices close in the evenings, men (and nowadays, I noticed, women as well) head towards these bars to drink and have a snack, and even to stay on for a full meal.

Yakitori at its simplest is a chicken shish kebab with a very Japanese flavour. Pieces of dark meat are served either by themselves, neatly speared on to the ends of three small bamboo skewers (three makes a serving), or interspersed with bits of green pepper or spring onion. As the meat is grilled, it is dipped into a sweetened soy-based sauce. The servings are tantalisingly small, but one can have as many as one wants.

Chicken innards seem just as popular as the meat; gizzards, livers and hearts may be ordered. The possibilities grow. There is blanched chicken skin, grilled and served with a sprinkling of salt and pepper; there are chicken meatballs and chicken wings; and, for those who want them, other small birds, such as sparrows. If you are hungry enough for a full meal, you can order any of these served on a bowl of rice (*yakitori donburi*) with tea and pickles on the side.

You may serve the simple *yakitori* described below either with drinks or as a meal. A note about the skewers: most oriental shops sell 6–8 inch (15–20 cm) bamboo skewers. They should be soaked in water for 30 minutes–1 hour before being used. All the meat should be placed at one end and it is that end that should be set directly over or under the heat source. You could use metal skewers instead – the best kind are somewhat flattened, like swords, because the meat does not roll around on them when it is turned. In Japan the small *yakitori* sticks are a little like lollipops. You pull the meat off with your mouth. If longer, metal skewers are used, it would be best to push the meat off on to a plate before serving it.

The chicken can be skewered well ahead of time, covered and refrigerated. You may cook this dish outdoors over charcoal or indoors under your kitchen grill.

4 medium chicken legs (thighs and drumsticks), boned (see page 289)

1 large green pepper

8 tablespoons Japanese soy sauce (shoyu)

4 tablespoons *sake*

3 tablespoons sugar

Cut the boned chicken leg meat into 1 inch (2.5 cm) chunks. If some skin separates from the meat, discard it. Leave any skin that clings naturally. Cut the green pepper in half and discard the seeds. Cut it into 1 inch (2.5 cm) squares.

Thread two pieces of meat on to a skewer followed by a piece of pepper. If you are preparing bamboo skewers, Japanese-style, push the meat to one end and keep alternating two pieces of meat with a piece of pepper until you have loaded about 3 inches (7.5 cm) of each skewer. If you are using long metal skewers, you can thread their whole length, leaving each end empty. Use up all the meat in this way, filling up as many skewers as required. Cover well and refrigerate until needed.

Meanwhile, combine the soy sauce, *sake* and sugar in a small pan and bring to the boil. Lower the heat and cook gently until the sugar has dissolved.

Pre-heat an indoor grill or an outdoor charcoal grill. Rest the skewers 4–5 inches (10–13 cm) from the source of heat and grill for 4–5 minutes on each side or until the meat is three quarters cooked. Brush the sauce over the meat and green peppers and grill briefly on both sides until the meat is almost done. Brush with the sauce a second time and grill for another 30 seconds on each side. Serve hot. If you are serving this *yakitori* with drinks and have cooked the meat on long skewers (and have now removed it), push cocktail sticks into the pieces of meat so that they may be picked up easily.

SERVES 4 AS A MAIN COURSE OR UP TO 8 WITH DRINKS

INDONESIA

Spicy Chicken Kebabs with Peanut Sauce

It is believed that *satays,* or tiny bits of meat threaded on to fine bamboo skewers and grilled, spread throughout much of East Asia from Java. Before they reached Java, their origins can surely be traced to the kebabs of India, and beyond India to the Middle East. *Satays* take different forms in different parts of this vast Indonesian archipelago. In Jogyakarta, for example, they tend to be rather sweet, eaten as they are with ritual dips in a thick, syrupy, sweet soy sauce known as *kecap manis.* Crushed peanuts or sliced shallots and an occasional hot chilli may be added to the *kecap.* As you travel west, the sweetness gives way to greater pungency and nuttiness.

Here follows the recipe for one of my favourite Indonesian *satays.* The peanut sauce is exactly the same as the dressing for the *gado-gado* (Salad of Assorted Vegetables with a Delicious Peanut Dressing, page 198). It needs to be heated, beaten lightly and then poured over the grilled kebabs. You may serve these kebabs as a first course, all by themselves, or as main dish along with rice, a vegetable or salad and perhaps some crisp Prawn Wafers (page 63).

As in the recipe for Chicken Bits on a Skewer (page 108), I prefer to use boned and skinned chicken legs as the meat is more moist. You may, however, use boned and skinned chicken breast. I generally find it easier to use flat metal skewers, but if you wish to use the more traditional bamboo *satay* skewers, soak them in water for 30 minutes–1 hour before threading the meat on to them.

4 medium chicken legs (thighs and drumsticks; see page 289) or 1 lb (450 g) chicken breast, boned and skinned

1 clove garlic

1 inch (2.5 cm) cube fresh ginger

¼ oz (10 g) shallot or onion

4 teaspoons Chinese light soy sauce

1 tablespoon lime or lemon juice

Cut the boned and skinned chicken flesh into 1 inch (2.5 cm) cubes.

Peel the garlic and crush it to a pulp. Peel the ginger and grate it as finely as possible. Peel the shallot and chop it finely. In a medium-sized bowl, combine the garlic, ginger, shallot, soy sauce, lime juice, coriander, sugar and chilli powder and mix well. Put in the chicken and rub the marinade over the meat. Cover and refrigerate for 2–24 hours. (Bring the chicken to room temperature before grilling.) Make the Peanut Dressing as described on pages 199–200.

1 teaspoon ground coriander
  seeds

½ teaspoon sugar

¼ teaspoon chilli powder

Peanut Dressing (see page 199)

Pre-heat an indoor grill or an outdoor charcoal grill. Use bamboo skewers solely for an outdoor grill or for an indoor grill if you can ensure that the heat will hit only the upper 3–4 inches (7.5–10 cm) of the skewer (otherwise the exposed bamboo may burn). If using them, thread about 3 inches (7.5 cm) of chicken pieces on to one end of a skewer. Fill in this way as many skewers as needed. If you are using long metal skewers, use 4 and divide the meat evenly between them.

If you are grilling indoors, balance the skewer ends on the raised edges of a grill rack and place them about 4 inches (10 cm) from the heat source. If grilling over charcoal, balance the skewers about 4 inches (10 cm) from the heat source. Grill for about 5 minutes on each side or until the meat is browned.

Heat the Peanut Dressing and beat it lightly. Place the bamboo skewers (if using) directly on individual plates. Pour a few tablespoons of the dressing over each portion and serve. If you are using metal skewers, remove the meat with the help of a fork and divide it among 4 plates. Spoon a few tablespoons of dressing over each serving.

SERVES 4

GĀ XÀO XẢ ỚT   VIETNAM

SPICY STIR-FRIED CHICKEN WITH LEMON GRASS

FROM THE NHÀ HÀNG NỔI NHÀ BÈ RESTAURANT IN HỒ CHÍ MINH CITY
This was one of the quick, very flavourful, stir-fried dishes served to me in a floating restaurant on Saigon River. Even though the chicken cooks quickly, it is a good idea to let it sit in its marinade for at least an hour. It is important that the chicken (while still on the bone) be cut into fairly small, bite-sized pieces. As chicken bones, especially those in the leg, have a tendency to splinter, it is best to let the butcher cut up the chicken for you.

FOR THE MARINADE:

1 stick fresh or 2 tablespoons dried sliced lemon grass

2 lb (1 kg) chicken pieces, cut into small pieces

1 large clove garlic

½ inch (1 cm) cube fresh ginger

1 tablespoon sugar

1½ teaspoons tomato paste

½ teaspoon salt

¼ teaspoon chilli powder

¼ teaspoon ground turmeric

YOU ALSO NEED:

5–6 cloves garlic

3 tablespoons vegetable oil

1 tablespoon fish sauce or salt to taste

4–8 tablespoons chicken stock

3½ oz (90 g) onions

First prepare the marinade. If you are using fresh lemon grass, cut it crossways into very thin slices, starting at the bulbous bottom end and going up about 6 inches (15 cm). Discard the strawlike top. If you using dried sliced lemon grass, soak it in 4 tablespoons hot water for 1 hour.

Put the chicken pieces in a bowl. Add the fresh lemon grass, if you are using it. If you are using dried lemon grass, remove it from its soaking liquid and add it to the chicken. (Save the soaking liquid.) Peel the large garlic clove and crush it well. Peel the ginger and grate it finely. Add the garlic, ginger, sugar, tomato paste, salt, chilli powder and turmeric to the chicken. Mix thoroughly. Cover and set aside for 1–24 hours, refrigerating if necessary.

Peel and finely chop the remaining 5–6 garlic cloves. Put the oil in a wok or large, lidded frying-pan and set it over a high heat. When it is hot, put in this garlic. Stir and fry for 30 seconds or until the garlic is golden. Add the chicken and all its marinade. Stir and fry for 5–6 minutes or until the chicken browns a little. Then add the fish sauce and either the lemon grass soaking liquid or 4 tablespoons stock. Stir once and cover. Cook on a high heat for 5 minutes. Lift the lid and stir, and then add another 4 tablespoons stock. Cover, turn the heat to low and cook for 5 more minutes.

While the chicken cooks, peel the onions and cut them into ¾ inch (2 cm) dice. Separate the onion layers within the diced pieces. Remove the lid from the wok containing the chicken and turn the heat to high. Put in the onion, and stir and fry for 1 minute. Lift the chicken out of its oil and serve.

SERVES 4

Bottom: *Glorious seafood soup (page 70)*; top: *Small spring rolls (page 59)*; centre left: *Fish sauce seasoned with lime juice (page 228)*

Bottom: *Chicken, prawn and fruit salad (page 52);*
top right: *Stir-fried prawns with tamarind and chillies
(page 54);* top left: *Savoury pork and crab toasts (page 55)*

Napoleon beef on a skewer (page 80)

Bottom: *Stir-fried pork with red pepper (page 96);*
top: *Knockout knuckle (page 102)*

Bottom: *Breaded pork cutlets over rice (page 105)*;
top: *Glazed gingery spareribs (page 101)*

Top: *Stuffed whole chicken in a parcel (page 136)*;
bottom: *Spicy chicken kebabs with a peanut sauce*
(page 110)

Top: *Savoury egg custard with prawns and mushrooms* (page 142); bottom: *Egg curry* (page 144)

Fish, shellfish and bean curd stew (page 161)

KAI PAD BAI KAPROW   THAILAND

Minced Chicken Stir-Fried with Basil

FROM PIENG CHOM DARBANAND AT THE IMPERIAL HOTEL, BANGKOK

Here is an exquisite, quick-cooking dish that is made with fresh holy basil (*bai kaprow*). As I cannot always obtain it, I use ordinary basil and find that it makes a superb substitute. The green herb is used in two ways: it is stir-fried with the chicken and it is also shallow-fried until crisp and used as a generous topping. The result is uncommonly good. (If red chillies are unavailable, increase the number of green chillies accordingly.)

4 oz (100 g) leaves fresh holy basil (*bai kaprow*) or ordinary basil (net weight without stems)

Vegetable oil for shallow-frying

5 cloves garlic

3 oz (75 g) shallots or onions

2 fresh hot green chillies or to taste

2 fresh hot red chillies or to taste

1 inch (2.5 cm) cube fresh ginger

1 lb (450 g) minced chicken (from boned and skinned breast or legs or both)

5 teaspoons fish sauce or salt to taste

1½ teaspoons dark brown sugar

Break off and discard the stems of the basil leaves. Wash the leaves and pat them dry. Divide them into two equal parts. Chop one part very coarsely and then set both parts aside.

Pour the oil to a depth of ½ inch (1 cm) into a medium-sized frying-pan and set it over a medium-high heat. Put a plate lined with kitchen paper near your hob. If you wish, have ready a splatter screen or an upturned sieve to cover the pan as soon as you have put in the leaves; this will prevent your being splashed with hot oil. When the oil is hot, place a smallish handful of whole leaves into the frying-pan. Cover immediately with the screen or sieve. As soon as the intense sizzling has died down (this takes only seconds), remove the cover and stir the leaves once or twice. They will turn crisp very quickly. Remove them with a slotted spoon and spread them out on the kitchen paper to drain. Fry all the whole basil leaves in this way. Replace the kitchen paper under the basil leaves several times to prevent the crisp leaves from becoming soggy.

Peel the garlic cloves and chop them finely. Peel and finely slice the shallots. Cut the green and red chillies into fine rounds. Peel the ginger and grate it finely. Once the oil used for frying the basil leaves has cooled a little, strain it and save it.

Just before serving, put 4 tablespoons of this oil in a large frying-pan or wok and set it over a medium-high heat. When it is hot, put in the garlic and shallots. Stir and fry for about 2 minutes or until the shallots are a medium brown. Add the chillies and ginger and give a few vigorous stirs. Now turn the heat to high and put in the chopped basil. Stir once and add the minced chicken. Stir and fry for about 3 minutes, breaking up the chicken lumps as you do so. The chicken should turn white all the way through. Add the fish sauce and sugar. Mix, then transfer to a serving dish. Top with the crisp basil leaves and serve.

SERVES 4

JIANCAI JIDING   HONG KONG

CHICKEN STIR-FRIED WITH CELERY

FROM THE AMERICAN RESTAURANT IN WANCHAI

Some of the best food that I have eaten in Hong Kong has been at a restaurant that calls itself, strangely enough, the American Restaurant. It specialises in northern food and its offerings, particularly its breads, are quite unbeatable.

Not all the chefs in the kitchen, however, are from the north. After feeding the clients superlative Beijing-style food, the chefs settle down to a meal of their own which is often a mixture of northern and their own Cantonese food. Here is a Cantonese dish that I caught the staff eating one day.

10 oz (275 g) chicken breast, boned and skinned

1 egg white

3 teaspoons cornflour

¼ teaspoon salt

6 tablespoons chicken stock

½ dried hot red chilli

1 tablespoon Chinese light soy sauce

Spread the chicken breast out and hit it with a mallet in order to flatten it. It should end up being about ¼ inch (0.5 cm) thick. Cut it into 1 inch (2.5 cm) squares. Combine the egg white, 2 teaspoons of the cornflour and the salt in a small bowl. Beat lightly to mix. Toss the chicken in the egg mixture until it is well coated. Cover and set aside for 2 hours or longer.

2 teaspoons Chinese rice wine
or dry sherry

2 teaspoons lemon juice

1 clove garlic

5 oz (150 g) sticks celery (about
4 – preferably from the
middle of the bunch)

2 tablespoons vegetable oil

Now prepare the sauce. Put the remaining teaspoon of cornflour in a cup. Slowly add 5 tablespoons of the chicken stock, mixing well between each addition. Crumble in the red chilli. Add the light soy sauce, rice wine and lemon juice. Mix and set aside.

Peel and finely chop the garlic. Cut the celery sticks crossways into 1 inch (2.5 cm) pieces.

When the chicken has marinated for 2 hours, bring about 1½ inches (4 cm) water to the boil in a medium-sized frying-pan or a wide shallow saucepan over a high heat. As soon as it starts bubbling, put in all the chicken, separating the pieces with a spoon. Let the pan sit over the heat for about 30 seconds. The chicken should turn white. (If the water returns to the boil before that, turn the heat to low.) Drain the chicken and set it aside – do not refrigerate.

Just before you are ready to serve, set a wok over a high heat. When it is hot, put in 1 tablespoon of the oil. When the oil has heated, put in half the chopped garlic. Stir once or twice and add the chicken. Stir and cook for about 1 minute. Remove the chicken and set it aside in a bowl.

Wash out the wok and dry it. Heat it again over a high heat. When it is hot, put in the remaining tablespoon of oil. When the oil has heated, put in the remaining chopped garlic. Stir once or twice and add the chopped celery. Stir it around for 30–40 seconds. Put in the remaining tablespoon of chicken stock and cover immediately. Turn the heat to low and cook for about 3 minutes or until the celery is just tender. Take the wok off the heat. Stir the sauce and put it into the wok. Put the wok over a low heat. Add the chicken. Stir and cook until the sauce has thickened. Serve immediately.

SERVES 2–4

TAK KOGI SOPSANJOK   KOREA

CHICKEN PATTIES WITH GINGER AND SESAME SEEDS

These delightfully seasoned chicken hamburgers are easy to prepare for light informal meals and picnics. While they may be grilled indoors under the kitchen grill or outdoors over charcoal, here I have cooked them in a frying-pan.

Boned and skinned minced chicken is required for this dish. I get my butcher to mince a half-and-half combination of light and dark meat for me as that gives the best texture. These patties are normally served with Korean Dipping Sauce and rice. You could, if you like, spoon a generous amount of the sauce over them and then slap them inside a hamburger bun.

1 spring onion

1 large clove garlic

1 inch (2.5 cm) cube fresh ginger

1 lb (450 g) minced chicken

1 tablespoon roasted sesame seeds (see page 270)

1 tablespoon sesame oil

1 tablespoon soy sauce (preferably Japanese – shoyu)

Freshly ground black pepper

¼–½ teaspoon chilli powder

Korean Dipping Sauce (see page 229)

1–2 tablespoons vegetable oil

Cut the spring onion crossways into very fine rounds along its entire length, including the green section. Peel the garlic and crush it to a pulp. Peel the ginger and grate it very finely. Put the chicken in a bowl. Add the spring onion, garlic, ginger, roasted sesame seeds, sesame oil, soy sauce, black pepper and chilli powder. Mix thoroughly and make 5 patties that are about 3½ inches (9 cm) in diameter. Put them in a single layer on a plate and cover with cling-film. Set the patties aside until you are ready to eat. Prepare the Korean Dipping Sauce.

Just before eating, grease the bottom of a large non-stick frying-pan very lightly with about 1 tablespoon of the vegetable oil and set it over a medium-high heat. When it is hot, put in the patties in a single layer. Cook for 1–1½ minutes or until they are medium-brown on one side. Turn the patties over and cook the second side the same way. Turn the heat to medium and cook both sides of the patties again for about 1 minute or a little more on each side so that they are nicely browned and cooked through. Pierce the centre of one patty with the point of a sharp knife to check it. If it is no longer pink inside, it is ready. Serve hot.

MAKES 5 PATTIES

KAI TOD KRATIUM PRIKTAI   THAILAND

CHICKEN WITH GARLIC AND BLACK PEPPER

At simple family meals this quick-cooking chicken is usually accompanied by plain rice and a soupy dish or a curry. I find that a green salad, with lots of fresh basil, mint and green coriander thrown in, also goes very well with it. The chicken takes about 9 minutes to cook and is best made just before eating. The dipping sauce that accompanies it can be made several hours in advance.

4 chicken thighs, weighing about 1 lb (450 g), boned (see page 289)

1½–2 teaspoons coarsely ground black pepper

4 large cloves garlic

About ½ packed teacup fresh coriander leaves

1½ tablespoons fish sauce or 1 tablespoon soy sauce mixed with 1 tablespoon water and ¼ teaspoon sugar

1 teaspoon sugar

¼ teaspoon chilli powder (optional)

2 tablespoons vegetable oil

Sprigs of fresh herbs, such as mint, coriander and basil, to garnish (optional)

Fish Sauce Seasoned with Lime Juice and Chilli (see page 227)

Make sure that you do not pierce the skin when boning the chicken thighs. Rub the chicken on both sides with the black pepper and set it aside.

Peel the garlic and crush it to a pulp. Finely chop the coriander leaves. Combine the garlic, coriander leaves, fish sauce (or soy sauce mixed with water and sugar), sugar and chilli powder and mix well. Rub this mixture over the chicken and let it marinate for 1 hour.

Put the oil in a non-stick frying-pan and set it over a medium-high heat. When it is hot, put in the chicken pieces, skin-side down. Cook for about 5 minutes, or until the skin is brown and crisp. Turn the chicken over and reduce the heat to medium-low. Cook the second side for 3½–4 minutes, or until the chicken is just cooked through. Remove the pieces with a slotted spoon and place them on a chopping board, skin-side up. Cut each thigh with a sharp knife into 3 strips, re-form it into the original shape and arrange on a serving plate. Garnish with fresh herbs, if desired, and serve with Fish Sauce Seasoned with Lime Juice and Chilli.

SERVES 2–4

CHICKEN WITH A SWEET SAKE GLAZE

ADAPTED FROM A RECIPE OF THE ÉCOLE TECHNIQUE HÔTELIÈRE TSUJI IN OSAKA
Under the guidance of Mr Saito, I learned much at Professor Tsuji's cookery school in Osaka. To turn out simple dishes – like this *teriyaki* – trusted techniques are used with precision, and simple logical steps are followed methodically. For example, only chicken thighs are used in this recipe. Thigh meat is juicy and moist, much more so than breast meat. The thigh is boned, which allows the meat to be cooked evenly and quickly. It also allows the meat to be sliced after it is cooked so that it can be picked up easily with chopsticks. The chicken is marinated for an hour so that the flavours of the sauce can penetrate the meat. Even though chicken *teriyaki* is generally cooked on a grill, Mr Saito favours another method. He browns the chicken first in a frying-pan and then lets it cook very briefly in a moderately hot oven. The chicken is marvellous; it is moist, slightly sweet, slightly salty, crisp on the outside and meltingly tender inside. Once you have learned this method of preparing it, I am sure you will want to use this technique to cook chicken thighs with other seasonings of your choice.

The Japanese tend to eat small portions of meat. One thigh would be just enough for a single serving at a fine restaurant. It would sit alone on a plate in glorious splendour, garnished perhaps with a few young bamboo shoots leaning against it, a few lime wedges and a few boiled pods of freshly plucked green soya beans. (You may substitute green beans – page 243 – or carrots – page 242 – as a garnish.) There should be Plain Japanese Rice (page 204) on the side. Keeping Western appetites in mind, I've allowed two thighs per person. You will need to cook them in a large frying-pan, or in two batches.

Sweet Glazing Sauce (see page 235)

8 chicken thighs, weighing 2 lb (1 kg), boned (see page 289)

About 2 tablespoons vegetable oil

First make the Sweet Glazing Sauce. Put it in a bowl and let it cool.

Make sure that you do not pierce the skin when boning the chicken thighs. Put the boned and unskinned thighs in the bowl with the Sweet Glazing Sauce. Mix and set aside for 1 hour, turning the pieces over now and then so that they absorb the flavours and colour evenly. Set a shelf in the top third of the oven. Pre-heat the oven to gas mark 6, 400°F (200°C).

Fifteen minutes before you wish to eat, put the oil in a very large non-stick frying-pan and set it over a medium-high heat. When it is hot, lift the chicken pieces out of their sauce. Put the sauce aside. Place the chicken pieces, in a single layer and skin-side down, in the frying-pan. Cook for 5–6 minutes or until the skin is browned. Turn the chicken pieces over and cook them for another 30 seconds only. Lift the chicken pieces out with a slotted spoon and put them skin-side up in a single layer on a roasting rack set over a roasting tin. Bake in the oven on the prepared shelf for 8 minutes, basting the skin 3 times during this period with the Sweet Glazing Sauce.

Put the chicken pieces on a chopping board and cut each lengthways into 3 segments. Re-assemble each thigh into its original form and place 2 thighs in the centre of each of 4 plates. Garnish as suggested above.

SERVES 4

MALAJI   HONG KONG

COLD CHICKEN WITH SESAME AND CHILLI SAUCE

FROM MRS FUNG

Known also as Bon Bon Chicken (from the sound of the pounding once required to shred the chicken) and Strange Taste Chicken (it has the highly aromatic Sichuan peppercorns in it), this spicy dish from the Sichuan province of China is just superb. It is generally served as a first course, though you could have it for lunch with a simple salad.

It is the Sichuan peppercorns that give the dish its special flavour. Even though you could, at a pinch, substitute black peppercorns, here is a spice that you should get to know. Pick up some Sichuan peppercorns when you are next in a Chinese grocer's shop or else send for them by mail order. You will find yourself using them in salads, over eggs, over oily fish (such as mackerel) and in hearty meat stews.

In Hong Kong a whole chicken is steamed, plunged into cold water and then shredded. I simply poach boned and skinned chicken breasts in order to make the preparation of this dish *very* easy. The sesame paste is sold by Asian, Chinese and Greek grocers, as well as by health food shops. (It is sometimes labelled as *tahini*.) Please note that the stalks of fresh coriander are used in this recipe as well as its leaves. This dish is usually served at room temperature, not icy cold.

FOR THE SAUCE:

1 inch (2.5 cm) cube fresh ginger

1 clove garlic

2 tablespoons sesame paste

1 tablespoon sesame oil

1 teaspoon sugar

2½ teaspoons Chilli Oil (see page 227)

4 teaspoons Chinese light soy sauce

½ teaspoon roasted and ground Sichuan peppercorns (see page 271) or coarsely ground black peppercorns

YOU ALSO NEED:

14 oz chicken breasts, boned and skinned

Salt

1 spring onion

⅛ inch (0.3 cm) slice fresh ginger

1 stick celery

1½ oz (40 g) fresh coriander (stalks and leaves)

First make the sauce. Peel the cube of ginger and grate it finely. Peel the garlic and crush it to a pulp. Combine the ginger, garlic, sesame paste, sesame oil, sugar, chilli oil, soy sauce and roasted and ground Sichuan (or black) peppercorns. Mix well.

Cut the chicken breasts lengthways into ½ inch (1 cm) wide strips. Put the strips into a medium-sized frying-pan. Pour in just enough water to cover by ¼ inch (0.5 cm). Add a generous pinch of salt and put in the spring onion and the slice of ginger. Bring to the boil, then turn the heat to low immediately and simmer very gently, turning the pieces over, until the meat becomes white all the way through – this happens very quickly, so keep watching it. Remove the chicken with a slotted spoon and rinse it under cold running water. (Save the poaching liquid.) Using both hands, pull the chicken into long shreds; they do not have to be very fine.

Cut the celery into very fine dice. Cut the coriander stalks crossways into very fine pieces. Coarsely chop the coriander leaves, cover with cling-film and set aside. Add 3 tablespoons of the poaching liquid to the sesame sauce. Stir to mix.

To serve, combine the chicken, celery, diced coriander stalks and sesame sauce and mix well. Put the mixture in a serving dish and sprinkle the chopped coriander leaves over the top.

SERVES 4–6

GÀ XỐI MỠ   VIETNAM

ROAST CHICKEN WITH FIVE-SPICE POWDER

This dish, very popular in South Vietnam, is traditionally made by first roasting a whole marinated chicken over charcoal, just to dry it out, and then deep-frying it. Vietnamese with Western kitchens take the easy way out and simply roast the whole bird in the oven. That is what I have chosen to do.

Five-spice powder, a Chinese spice mixture, contains star anise, fennel, cloves, cinnamon and Sichuan peppercorns. It is sold by Chinese grocers in a powdered form. (For instructions on how to make your own, see page 265).

3½ lb (1.65 kg) chicken

2 cloves garlic

1 oz (25 g) onion

2 tablespoons Chinese rice wine or dry sherry

2 tablespoons Chinese light soy sauce

2 tablespoons Chinese dark soy sauce

2 teaspoons sugar

1¼ teaspoons five-spice powder

2 tablespoons sesame oil

Soft lettuce leaves and fresh mint sprigs

Fish Sauce Seasoned with Lime Juice (see page 228)

Wash the chicken and pat it dry. Peel the garlic and onion and chop them finely. Combine the garlic, onion, wine, the two soy sauces, sugar and five-spice powder in a bowl. Stir until the sugar has dissolved. Put the chicken into a bowl and rub the marinade generously both inside and all over the outside of the bird. Pour any remaining marinade over the chicken and set it aside for 2–3 hours. Turn the chicken around every 20 minutes so that it evenly absorbs the flavours and colour of the marinade.

Pre-heat the oven to gas mark 7, 425°F (220°C). Lift the chicken out of its marinade and lay it, breast-side down, on a rack set in a roasting tin. Roast for 10 minutes. Brush the back with the marinade and turn the chicken over so that the breast is now facing upwards. Brush the breast with the marinade and roast it for 15 minutes. Then brush the chicken with the marinade again, turn the heat down to gas mark 4, 350°F (180°C), and continue to cook for 45 minutes, brushing with the marinade every 15 minutes or so. After this period, brush the chicken generously with the sesame oil and cook it for another 2–5 minutes or until the juices run clear when you pierce the flesh with a fork or skewer. Let the chicken rest for 10 minutes before carving.

Serve the roast chicken with lettuce leaves and mint sprigs as well as the Fish Sauce Seasoned with Lime Juice. Pour a little of the sauce over the chicken once it has been put on its serving plate. The leaves can either be nibbled or the lettuce can be used to make mint-and-chicken-filled parcels.

SERVES 4

LAUK AYAM   MALAYSIA

Hearty Chicken Curry with Potatoes

FROM PUAN RASHIDAH IN KUALA LUMPUR

Malaysian curries are among the best in East Asia and Rashidah's, which are extra spicy and rich, are better than most. She prepared this for a casual lunch and served it with a local bread. It could be served with almost any bread, from crusty French or Italian loaves to *pitta* breads, and Indian *chapattis*. It may also be served with rice. This curry seems to get even better with time, so it can easily be made a day in advance and refrigerated. Use less than the recommended quantity of chilli powder if you prefer a mild curry.

6–8 cardamom pods

6 whole cloves

2 whole star anise

2 X 2 inch (5cm) sticks cinnamon

2 tablespoons whole fennel seeds

1½ tablespoons whole cumin seeds

4 tablespoons ground coriander seeds

1½–2 teaspoons chilli power or to taste

Put the cardamom pods, cloves, star anise, cinnamon, fennel and cumin into the container of a clean coffee grinder or spice grinder. Grind as finely as possible. Empty into a bowl. Add the coriander, chilli powder, paprika and 8 tablespoons water. Mix to a thick paste.

Peel the ginger, garlic and 3 of the onions. Chop them coarsely. Peel and finely slice the fourth onion; set this aside. Combine the chopped onions, ginger and garlic in an electric blender together with about 4 tablespoons water. Blend until you have a smooth paste.

1 tablespoon paprika

4 × 1 inch (2.5 cm) cubes fresh
ginger

3 large cloves garlic

4 medium onions

4 lb (1.75 kg) chicken pieces
(preferably legs)

1 lb (450 g) potatoes

6 fl oz (175 ml) vegetable oil

1 tablespoon salt

7 fl oz (200 ml) coconut milk
(see page 263)

Good handful fresh mint
leaves

Skin the chicken and cut it into smallish serving pieces. (A whole leg should be cut into thigh and drumstick; a breast should be cut in half.) Peel the potatoes and cut them into 1 inch (2.5 cm) cubes. Put the cut potatoes into a bowl of water.

Pour the oil in a large wide pan and set it over a medium-high heat. When the oil is hot, add the sliced onion. Stir and fry until the onion is golden-brown. Put in the paste from the blender and the spice paste from the bowl. Stir and fry for 10–12 minutes or until the mixture is well fried and dark in colour. Put in 1¼ pints (750 ml) water, the chicken, the drained potatoes and salt. Stir and bring to a simmer. Cover, lower the heat and simmer gently for 30 minutes or until the chicken is tender. Stir the coconut milk and pour it in. Stir and cook for another minute. Coarsely chop the mint leaves and stir them in. The oil floating on the top of the curry may be removed before serving.

SERVES 6

AYAM PONGTAY   MALAYSIA

CHICKEN WITH BAMBOO SHOOTS AND MUSHROOMS IN BLACK BEAN SAUCE

FROM THE HYATT SAUJANA'S SRI MELAKA RESTAURANT IN KUALA LUMPUR
The food of the Straits Chinese – the Chinese who migrated to the Straits
settlements of Penang, Malacca and Singapore and who married local Malay
women – has become very popular of late in this region of South-East Asia.
Known as the cooking of the Nonyas (the Straits Chinese women), it can now be
found in elegant trendy restaurants such as the Sri Melaka in Kuala Lumpur.

Ayam pongtay is a Nonya classic. Do not be fooled by its simple ingredients.
Subtle, gentle, full of rich flavour and absolutely addictive, it is, to my mind,
one of South-East Asia's finest dishes.

Ingredients are, of course, important. You need chunky tender bamboo
shoots, which are available in tins. Soft, rounded, cone-shaped 'tips', usually
about 1½–2 inches (4–5 cm) long are ideal, if you can find them. The best
mushrooms to use for this recipe are dried Chinese mushrooms. At a pinch you
could use fresh button mushroom caps which do not, of course, need to be
soaked. Sauté them lightly in oil and then put them into the pan 10 minutes
before the end of the cooking time. Instead of using the mushroom-soaking
liquid for the cooking use 1 pint (600 ml) water or light chicken stock. As a
substitute for black bean sauce you can use 2½ tablespoons tinned or dried
fermented black beans, washed and mashed with 1 tablespoon oyster sauce.

10–12 large dried Chinese
   mushrooms (the thicker the
   caps, the better the quality)

4 oz (100 g) shallots or onions

6 cloves garlic

3 tablespoons black bean sauce

2 lb (1 kg) chicken pieces
   (preferably legs)

3 tablespoons vegetable oil

10–12 chunky pieces good-
   quality tinned bamboo
   shoots

1½ teaspoons dark soy sauce

1½ teaspoons molasses

Quickly rinse the dried mushrooms in cold water
and then soak them in 1 pint (600 ml) hot water for
30 minutes or until the caps are soft. Lift the
mushrooms out and save the soaking liquid. Cut
off the hard stems and discard them. Strain the
soaking liquid through a clean cloth.

Peel the shallots and garlic and chop them
coarsely. Put them into an electric blender along
with 3 tablespoons water and the black bean sauce.
Blend thoroughly.

Peel off the chicken skin and separate the whole
legs into 4 pieces: divide them into thighs and
drumsticks and then divide each thigh and drum-

stick in half using a cleaver or heavy knife to cut through the bone. Alternatively, ask your butcher to do this for you. If you are using chicken breasts, cut each in half.

Put the oil in a wide, heavy, lidded frying-pan and set it over a medium-high heat. When the oil is hot, put in the paste from the blender. Stir and fry for 2–3 minutes or until it has reduced a little and has a slightly fried look. Put in the chicken, bamboo shoots, mushrooms caps and strained mushroom-soaking liquid. Stir and bring to the boil. Cover and cook over a medium heat for 15 minutes. Remove the lid, turn the heat to high and cook for another 6 minutes or until the sauce is reduced and thick. Then combine the soy sauce and molasses and add the mixture to the pan. Stir in well and serve.

SERVES 4

FRIED CHICKEN WITH SPRING ONION SAUCE

FROM THE SHANGHAI CLUB

Some of the best Shanghai-style food can be found today at the Shanghai Club in Hong Kong. Here is one of its recipes. A whole chicken is opened up at the breast bone, marinated with (among other things) Sichuan peppercorns, and deep-fried, beak, feet and all. The crisply fried bird is then cut up, re-assembled to look like itself, head chirpily upright, and doused with an unusual sauce, chock-full of fresh herbs and seasonings. The dish is uncommonly good.

I have simplified it somewhat here. I am assuming that you, like me, have difficulty in obtaining a chicken with head and feet and that, if you did, your heart might yearn for the safer look you know and understand! I have used chicken pieces as they are easier to fry in hot oil. If you prefer, you can grill them and then smother them with the sauce.

If you can find Chinese celery at a Chinese grocer's, do buy it. Only the stems are used here. If you cannot obtain it, ordinary celery, especially its upper portion with the generally unused thin stems, makes a good substitute. This recipe requires many stalks and stems of herbs, items that might normally be thrown away.

FOR THE MARINADE:

1 inch (2.5 cm) cube fresh ginger

1 spring onion

3 lb (1.5 kg) chicken pieces (preferably legs – thighs and drumsticks)

2 teaspoons roasted and ground Sichuan peppercorns (see page 271)

2 tablespoons Chinese light soy sauce

½ teaspoon sugar

First prepare the marinade. Peel the ginger and grate it as finely as possible. Cut the spring onion crossways into very fine rounds. Divide the whole chicken legs into thighs and drumsticks. If you are using chicken breasts, cut each breast in half. Put the chicken in a bowl. Prod the areas without skin with the point of a sharp knife. Sprinkle the ground roasted Sichuan peppercorns, ginger, spring onion, soy sauce and sugar over the chicken. Rub this marinade in as well as you can with your hands. Cover and set aside for 2–4 hours, refrigerating if necessary.

Meanwhile, combine the ingredients for the sauce in 2 separate bowls. Peel the garlic and chop

FOR THE SAUCE:

3 cloves garlic

2 spring onions

Few sticks Chinese celery or
part stick ordinary celery

Few stems fresh coriander or
parsley

1 inch (2.5 cm) cube fresh
ginger

2 tablespoons Chinese light soy
sauce

2 teaspoons distilled white
vinegar

4 tablespoons chicken stock

1 tablespoon tomato ketchup

½ teaspoon sugar

2 tablespoons sesame oil

YOU ALSO NEED:

About 3 tablespoons cornflour

Oil for deep-frying

it as finely as possible. Cut the spring onions crossways into the finest possible rounds. If you are using Chinese celery, cut its stems into very fine rounds. If using ordinary celery, cut it into minute dice (you need about 3 tablespoons). Hold several stems of coriander together and cut crossways into minute pieces (you need about 1 tablespoon). Peel the ginger and cut it into paper-thin slices. Stacking a few slices at a time together, cut the slices first into thin slivers and then into minute dice. Combine the garlic, spring onions, celery, coriander and ginger in a small bowl. Cover and set aside.

In another bowl combine the soy sauce, vinegar, stock, ketchup, sugar and sesame oil. Stir well to mix and set aside.

Lay the chicken pieces out in a single layer and dust both sides with the cornflour. Pat the cornflour in and set the chicken aside for 20 minutes.

Put the oil for deep-frying in a large wok over a medium heat or in a deep-fat fryer. When it is hot, put in the chicken pieces and fry them. If you are using a wok, turn them when necessary. Cook for about 15–20 minutes or until the chicken pieces are nicely browned on the outside and cooked all the way through. Drain them on kitchen paper and put them in a serving dish. Mix together the 2 bowls of sauce ingredients and pour over the chicken. Serve at once.

SERVES 4

BETUTU AYAM   INDONESIA

STUFFED WHOLE CHICKEN IN A PARCEL

Many years ago a large banana-leaf package was unwrapped before me on the beach in Bali to reveal a whole cooked chicken, beautifully red and aromatic from all the spices still clinging to it. The chicken was heavenly. I usually cannot obtain fresh banana leaves so I use the more prosaic aluminium cooking foil. The chicken still tastes very good. If you cannot get any lemon grass use 1½ tablespoons grated lemon rind, adding it to the blender when mixing the ingredients.

1 stick fresh or 2 tablespoons dried sliced lemon grass or lemon rind (see above)

4 dried hot red chillies

4½ tablespoons lime or lemon juice

1 tablespooon plus 1 teaspoon dark brown sugar

2 teaspoons salt

½ teaspoon ground turmeric

¼ teaspoon chilli powder

3½ lb (1.65 kg) chicken

8 oz (225 g) red pepper

3 oz (75 g) shallots or onions

1½ inch (4 cm) cube fresh ginger

8 cloves garlic

1 oz (25 g) candlenuts or cashew nuts

1½ teaspoons coarsely ground black pepper

5 tablespoons vegetable oil

If you are using fresh lemon grass, cut it crossways into the thinnest possible slices, starting at the root end and discarding the strawlike top. Crumble the dried red chillies into a small bowl. Add 5 tablespoons water, and set aside for 30 minutes. If you are using dried lemon grass, add it to the water along with the chillies.

Meanwhile, combine 3 tablespoons of the lime juice, 1 tablespoon sugar, 1 teaspoon of the salt, the turmeric and the chilli powder in a small bowl, and mix.

Put the chicken, breast down, in a large bowl or deep dish. Cut 4 deep diagonal slits on the back, 2 on each side. Rub some of the lime juice mixture into the slits and all over the back. Turn the chicken over. Cut 2 diagonal slits on each side of the breast, 2 slits on the wings, 2 slits on each side of both thighs and 2 slits on each side of both drumsticks. Rub the remaining marinade over the rest of the chicken, working it deeply into all the slits. Set aside for 40 minutes–1 hour.

Coarsely chop the red pepper, discarding all the seeds. Peel and coarsely chop the shallots, ginger and garlic. Coarsely chop the nuts. In an electric blender, combine the red pepper, shallots, ginger, garlic, nuts and the remaining 1½ tablespoons lime juice. Blend until smooth. Add the remaining teaspoon of salt, 1 teaspoon sugar and the black pepper as well as the fresh or soaked dried lemon grass and red chillies and their soaking liquid. Blend again.

Put the oil in a medium-sized non-stick frying-pan and set it over a medium-high heat. When the oil is hot, put in the paste from the blender. Stir and fry for about 15 minutes or until the oil separates from the spices and the paste is a dark reddish-brown.

Pre-heat the oven to gas mark 4, 350°F (180°C).

Spread out a large piece of heavy-duty aluminium foil about 30 inches (75 cm) long and put the chicken, breast down, in the centre. Rub about a quarter of the fried spice mixture on to the back of the chicken. Turn the bird over and rub another quarter of the spice mixture over the front. Stuff the remaining spice mixture inside the chicken. Now fold the foil over the bird, crimping the edges together at least 2 inches (5 cm) above the bottom of the parcel to prevent leakage of juices. Put the chicken parcel on a baking tray and bake in the oven for 1¾ hours.

Open the parcel carefully and pour out the collected liquid into a small pan. Spoon off the fat. Take all the stuffing out of the bird and add it to the pan of liquid. Stir to mix, heating it if necessary. Put the whole chicken in a dish, pour the hot sauce over it and serve.

SERVES 4

TAK TORI TANG   KOREA

Spicy chicken stew with carrots and potatoes

FROM SANG KYUNG LEE

This lightly spiced, hearty and warming stew gets its flavours from Hot Fermented Bean Paste (see page 230), an inspired mixture of fermented beans and red chillies, as well as from soy sauce and sesame seeds. It has a thinnish sauce and is best eaten with plain rice. I skin the chicken pieces before I stew them. The Koreans tend to leave the skin on. You may do whichever you prefer.

3½ lb (1.65 kg) chicken pieces (preferably legs – thighs and drumsticks)

4 tablespoons Japanese soy sauce (shoyu)

2 tablespoons sugar

2½ tablespoons Hot Fermented Bean Paste (see page 230) or to taste

1 lb (450 g) potatoes

12 oz (350 g) carrots

4 spring onions

2 oz (50 g) red pepper

2 oz (50 g) green pepper

Salt (optional)

1 tablespoon roasted sesame seeds (see page 270)

Freshly ground black pepper

Combine the chicken, soy sauce and sugar in a large wide pan. Put the Hot Fermented Bean Paste in a bowl and slowly add 15 fl oz (450 ml) water, mixing as you go. Add this combination to the chicken and bring it to the boil. Cover, turn the heat to medium-low and simmer for 10 minutes.

Meanwhile, peel the potatoes and cut them into 1½ inch (4 cm) cubes. Peel the carrots and cut them crossways into 2 inch (5 cm) lengths. Cut the spring onions into 2 inch (5 cm) lengths. Cut the red and green peppers into ½ inch (1 cm) squares.

When the chicken has simmered for 10 minutes, put in the potatoes, carrots and spring onions. Stir gently and bring to the boil. Cover, turn the heat to medium-low and simmer for 15–20 minutes or until the chicken and potatoes are tender, stirring occasionally. Taste and add salt if you think it is needed. Put in the red and green peppers. Stir and cook for 1–2 minutes. Lift out all the solid ingredients with a slotted spoon and put them into a serving bowl. Boil the sauce for a short time in order to reduce it a little and then pour it over the chicken. Top with the roasted sesame seeds and some freshly ground black pepper.

SERVES 4–6

RED CHICKEN CURRY

FROM PIENG CHOM DARBANAND AT THE IMPERIAL HOTEL, BANGKOK

The people of this world can probably be divided into those who like chicken legs and those who like chicken breasts. For curries I prefer dark meat as it remains more moist; that is what I have used in this recipe. The meat needs to be boned and skinned. My butcher very kindly does this for me but you could do it yourself at home. Just follow the simple directions given on page 289. If you wish to use boned and skinned breast meat, buy 1¼ lb (500 g), dice it and poach it in the coconut milk on *low* heat for just 5 minutes. This way it will remain soft and tender.

This dish is absolutely the best of Thai curries. You may use the recipe to cook chunks of fish or prawns as well as chicken – simply adjust the cooking time so that the fish does not fall apart or turn rubbery.

Most Thai curries are made with a basic paste of ground spices. Tinned and bottled Thai curry pastes are sold by many Asian grocers, but their quality varies. If you wish to try them, look for red curry paste, but it is best to make your own (see the recipe on page 232).

14 fl oz (400 ml) coconut milk (see page 263)

4 medium whole chicken legs (thighs and drumsticks), boned (see page 289)

½ teaspoon salt

4 tablespoons vegetable oil

4 tablespoons Red Curry Paste (see page 232)

1–1½ tablespoons fish sauce or salt to taste

1 teaspoon dark brown sugar

4 fresh or dried kaffir lime leaves or 2 teaspoons finely julienned lemon rind

15–20 fresh sweet basil leaves (*bai horapha*) or ordinary basil or mint leaves

If you are using fresh coconut milk, let it stand until the cream rises to the top. Whether using fresh or tinned milk, skim off 4 tablespoons of the thick cream and set it aside. Stir the rest of the milk to mix.

Skin the boned chicken legs and cut the flesh into 1 inch (2.5 cm) cubes.

Put the thin coconut milk (not the cream) into a medium-sized frying-pan. Add the salt and mix. Now put in the chicken pieces and bring the milk to the boil. Stir and cook on a medium-high heat for about 20 minutes or until the chicken is just done. Remove from the heat and set aside.

Put the oil and the reserved coconut cream in a heavy wok or wide heavy pan. Bring it to the boil. Put in the curry paste and stir and fry on a medium-high heat until the oil separates and the paste is lightly browned. Lower the heat and add the fish sauce and sugar. Stir to mix. Now put in the chicken and the coconut milk it was simmered in. Bring to the boil. Simmer on a low heat for a minute. (All this can be done several hours ahead of time.)

To serve, proceed as follows. If you are using fresh kaffir lime leaves, remove the centre vein and cut the leaves crossways into very fine strips. If you are using dried leaves, you will need to soak them in a little water for 30 minutes first. Break the basil (or mint) leaves off their stems and discard the stems. Put the hot curry into a serving dish. Scatter the basil (or mint) leaves over the chicken and then, with the back of the spoon, submerge them slightly in the sauce. Scatter the kaffir lime leaves (or julienned lemon rind) over the top.

SERVES 4

TEO CHEW-STYLE DUCK   MALAYSIA

DUCK BRAISED IN WINE

Duck is good cooked in most ways but I find that braising – a much underused technique for cooking this bird – brings out its flavours best. All of it remains moist; even the bones become eminently suckable. You may make this dish ahead of time and then reheat it. In fact I prefer to do this as it is much easier to de-grease the sauce once it has been chilled. The duck is normally cooked whole in Malaysia. I quarter it only to make it easier to handle; you could ask the butcher to do this for you.

Served with stir-fried greens, such as spinach, and an elegant rice dish, this duck becomes decidedly festive.

4 lb (1.75 kg) duck, quartered

¼ teaspoon five-spice powder (optional)

2 tablespoons vegetable oil

3 cloves garlic

Examine your duck. If parts of it seem like nothing but skin or fat, cut them off. Wash the duck and pat it as dry as you can. Dust the five-spice powder over it on both sides. Put the oil in a large frying-pan and set it over a high heat. When the oil is hot, put in as many duck pieces as it will hold easily,

6 spring onions

2 cups Chinese rice wine or dry sherry

4 tablespoons Chinese dark soy sauce

1 tablespoon Chinese light soy sauce

3½ tablespoons sugar

3 inch (7.5 cm) stick cinnamon

½ teaspoon Sichuan or black peppercorns

3 whole star anise

8–10 slices fresh or dried galangal or fresh ginger

skin-side down. (The aim here is to sear the skin.) Turn the pieces around so all the skin gets browned. Remove the browned pieces of duck with a slotted spoon. Brown all the duck pieces in this way.

Peel the cloves of garlic and mash them lightly.

Lay the spring onions over the bottom of a wide pan large enough to hold the duck easily, preferably in one layer. Now put the duck pieces on top of the onions, skin-side down. Pour the wine and 1 pint (600 ml) water over the duck. Add the garlic and all the remaining ingredients, and bring to a simmer. Cover and simmer gently for 45 minutes. Turn the duck pieces over and simmer, covered, for another 45 minutes. Remove the cover and turn the heat up to medium. Turn the duck pieces over again and continue to cook for 6–7 minutes. Turn the duck pieces over a third time and cook for another 6–7 minutes. Remove the duck pieces carefully and put them on a plate to cool.

Strain the duck broth. (You should have about 1 pint (600 ml).) Remove the grease from the top if you wish to eat immediately. If you plan to eat the duck the next day, cover the duck pieces well after they have cooled and refrigerate them. Cool the broth and put it in a covered container. Refrigerate that as well.

To serve, de-grease the duck broth and put into a large pan. Add the duck pieces, cover the pan and heat through. Lift the duck pieces out and arrange them on a plate. Pour just a little of the broth over the duck. The rest of the broth can be handed round separately in a sauce boat.

SERVES 4

KERAN CHIM KOREA

SAVOURY EGG CUSTARD WITH PRAWNS AND MUSHROOMS

WITH HELP FROM MRS HAN CHUNG KYU

Savoury egg custards, quivering, soft and soothing, are eaten in many areas of China, Japan and Korea. They can be very delicately flavoured or quite robust in their seasonings. In Japan, where they are called *chawanmushi*, they are steamed in individual cups and served almost as a soup course. In Korea, where most dishes at a meal (except rice) tend to be communal, a large bowl is generally put in the centre of the table and then everyone reaches out with soup spoons. You may serve this custard in any way you like; though, with Western table settings, individual servings are much easier to handle. Incidentally, egg coddlers are ideal for cooking single portions.

To steam *keran chim* properly, the dish containing the custard should never be set on the bottom of your steaming pan. It should be placed on a rack or trivet. Water should come three quarters of the way up its sides and should simmer gently in order to prevent bubbles from forming in the custard. Do not overcook it or the custard might separate. The custard should be cooked just before it is eaten. All the ingredients can, however, be prepared ahead of time but *not* mixed. The cooking time is 13–25 minutes, depending on the size of dish you use. The Koreans use fresh oyster mushrooms. About 4–5 would be enough, but as they are hard to come by, I have used ordinary mushrooms.

1 clove garlic

3 spring onions

6–8 medium mushrooms

4 oz (100 g) uncooked unpeeled prawns

5 large eggs

1 pint (600 ml) unsalted chicken stock or water

1 tablespoon sesame oil

¾ teaspoon salt

4 teaspoons Japanese soy sauce (shoyu)

1 tablespoon roasted sesame seeds (see page 270)

Peel the garlic and crush it to a pulp. Cut the spring onions into very fine rounds along their entire length, including the green section. Slice the mushrooms finely. Peel and de-vein the prawns, wash them and pat them dry. Cut the prawns crossways into ½ inch (1 cm) sections. Beat the eggs lightly in a bowl. Add the chicken stock or water, the sesame oil, salt and soy sauce. Mix and then strain to make sure that the egg whites and yolks are thoroughly blended.

Set some water to heat in a wok, large saucepan or steamer wide enough to hold a custard bowl or individual egg coddlers easily. (Remember that the bowl in which you cook will also be your serving bowl). Bring the water to a simmer. Set a rack or trivet on the bottom of your steaming pan.

Stir the egg mixture again and add to it the garlic, spring onions, mushrooms and prawns. Pour the mixture into the custard bowls or spoon evenly into the coddlers. Sprinkle sesame seeds over the top and cover. (You could cover the bowl with a plate or the individual coddlers, if using, with foil.) Stand the bowl or coddlers on the rack. The simmering water should come three quarters of the way up the sides of the bowl or coddlers, so top it up if necessary. Cover the steaming pan and simmer gently for 13–25 minutes. Check whether the custard is set by inserting a knife into it. The knife should come out clean. If it does not, cook for another minute or so. Remove carefully from the water and serve.

SERVES 4–5

GULAI TELOR   MALAYSIA

EGG CURRY

Here is one of my favourite egg curries. It is hot and spicy, and quite typical of Malaysian food. Served with plain rice and a salad, it is perfect for a Sunday lunch. I have even been known to serve it with crusty bread or with thick toast. In Malaysia the spices are pounded very finely on stone. Since I can never quite manage to get the same effect in a blender, I strain the coarse particles out of the curry sauce before putting the eggs into it.

A note about the hotness of this dish: in Malaysia, it is prepared with 20–30 dried red chillies. It *is* hot *and* good. I tone it down by using 10–15 chillies and I would describe my dish as fairly hot. You may use as few as 2 chillies, if you want it very mild. The fresh red and green chillies added at the end are more of a garnish than anything else. They give the dish a Malaysian look. If fresh red chillies are unavailable, simply use twice as many green ones. You may use slivers cut from fresh red and green peppers, if you prefer. If you cannot get lemon grass, use 1 tablespoon of grated lemon rind, adding it to the curry at the same time as the tomato. This curry may be made a day in advance, refrigerated and then reheated.

2–15 dried hot red chillies

½ teaspoon whole black peppercorns

2 tablespoons whole coriander seeds

1 stick fresh or 3 tablespoons dried sliced lemon grass or lemon rind (see above)

1½ inch (4 cm) cube fresh or 8 large slices dried galangal (optional)

1½ inch (4 cm) cube fresh ginger

¾ teaspoon ground turmeric

18 eggs

3½ oz (90 g) shallots or onions

5 cloves garlic

9 tablespoons vegetable oil

1¾ pints (1 litre) coconut milk (see page 263)

Crumble the dried red chillies and put them in a bowl. Add the peppercorns, coriander seeds, dried lemon grass (if you are using it) and dried galangal (if you are using it). Add about 12 fl oz (350 ml) water and leave to soak for at least 1 hour.

If you are using fresh lemon grass, slice it crossways very finely, starting at the root end and going up about 6 inches (15 cm). Discard the strawlike top. If you are using fresh galangal, peel it and chop it coarsely. Peel the ginger and chop it coarsely.

Combine all the soaked seasonings, their soaking liquid, the fresh lemon grass and fresh galangal (if you are using them), the ginger and the turmeric in an electric blender. Blend thoroughly, adding another few tablespoons of water if needed to make a pastelike consistency, and stopping the machine to stir with a spatula if required.

3 tablespoons tamarind paste
  (see page 272) (or 2
  tablespoons lime juice)
2½ teaspoons salt
1 teaspoon sugar
10 oz (275 g) tomatoes
4 fresh hot green chillies
4 fresh hot red chillies
Few sprigs fresh mint

Put all the eggs in a large pan. Cover well with water and bring to the boil. Turn the heat to very low and simmer until the eggs are hard-boiled (about 12 minutes). Shell them under cold running water. Peel the shallots and slice them finely. Peel the garlic and slice it finely.

Put the oil in a large, wide, preferably non-stick pan and set it over a medium-high heat. When the oil is hot, put in the shallots and garlic. Stir and fry until they are golden. Pour in the paste from the blender. Stir and fry for about 10 minutes or until the oil separates from it and the paste turns dark. Stir the coconut milk and pour it in. Add the tamarind paste (or lime juice), salt and sugar. Mix well and taste, adjust the seasoning if necessary. Bring to a simmer, stirring as you go. As soon as the sauce begins to bubble, turn off the heat. Strain it through a sieve, pushing out as much liquid as possible. Put the sauce back in the pan and add the hard-boiled eggs. (This much of the dish can be prepared a day ahead of time and refrigerated.)

If the tomatoes are small, cut them into wedges; if they are large, cut them into 1 inch (2.5 cm) dice. Wash the fresh chillies and mint sprigs. Remove the coarse stems from the mint sprigs. Just before serving, bring the egg curry to a simmer. Put in the tomatoes and stir a few times. Let the sauce come to a simmer again. Empty the curry into a serving bowl. Garnish with the fresh chillies and the mint sprigs.

SERVES 6–8

FISH AND SEAFOOD

IKAN PANGGANG   INDONESIA

WHOLE GRILLED FISH, SOUR AND SPICY

FROM MARTINI JUFRI AND THE HOUSEHOLD OF RISNAWATI AGUS

It was a warm day. A fire of coconut shells had been lit under a spreading star fruit tree to grill the fish. I was in the seafront town of Padang in Western Sumatra but the fish we were to eat was *gurami*, a freshwater creature. It had already been bathed in two marinades – one of lime juice and salt and the other of coconut milk and hot spices. Then it was put between the twin racks of a hinged grilling contraption and cooked slowly about 6 inches (15 cm) above the fire with frequent and lavish bastings of the marinade. The basting brush was unusual: it consisted of a stick of lemon grass whose bulbous end had been lightly mashed, so that it basted the fish and flavoured it at the same time.

This fish may be grilled either outdoors over charcoal or indoors. If you are grilling indoors, it is important to keep the fish far enough from the heat so that it cooks without charring on the outside. Alternatively, you could brown the fish on both sides and then put it into the oven at gas mark 4, 350°F (180°C), for 10–15 minutes or until it has cooked through.

Whether grilling outdoors or indoors, it helps to have a hinged double-racked 'holder' which makes turning the fish much easier. Mine is rectangular and can hold two medium-sized fish. Such gadgets are available from kitchen supply shops, but if you cannot obtain one, just oil your grill rack well and lay the fish directly on it.

The quantities in this recipe may easily be doubled.

1¼ lb (500 g) fish (such as small salmon, trout, salmon trout, bass, sole or turbot), scaled and cleaned

¾ teaspoon salt

3 tablespoons lime or lemon juice

Cut 3 or 4 deep slightly diagonal slits across both sides of the fish. Rub ½ teaspoon of the salt and 1 tablespoon of the lime juice over the entire fish, working the mixture well into the slits and the stomach cavity. Set aside for 20–30 minutes.

Meanwhile, if you are using dried galangal and

½ inch (1 cm) cube fresh or 3 slices dried galangal

1 stick fresh or 1 tablespoon dried sliced lemon grass

2–3 dried hot red chillies

2 oz (50 g) shallots or onions

3½ oz (90 g) red pepper

½ inch (1 cm) cube fresh ginger

3 cloves garlic

¼ teaspoon ground turmeric

7 fl oz (200 ml) coconut milk (see page 263)

About 2 tablespoons vegetable oil

Lime wedges to serve

dried lemon grass, put these into a cup with 4 tablespoons water. Crumble the dried red chillies into the water as well. Set aside for 20–30 minutes. If you are using fresh galangal, peel and coarsely chop it. If you are using fresh lemon grass, cut off about ¼ inch (0.5 cm) of its very bottom tip and then lightly crush about 1 inch (2.5 cm) of the bulbous bottom to open it up like a brush.

Peel the shallots and chop them coarsely. Coarsely dice the red pepper, discarding all the seeds. Peel the ginger and garlic and chop them coarsely.

Put the soaked spices and their soaking liquid, the shallots, red pepper, ginger, garlic, turmeric and the remaining 2 tablespoons lime juice and ¼ teaspoon salt into an electric blender. If you are using fresh galangal add it too. Blend until smooth.

Pre-heat an outdoor charcoal grill or an indoor kitchen grill. Put the spice paste into a wide shallow dish large enough to hold the fish. Stir the coconut milk, add it to the paste and stir to mix. Put the fish into the dish. Spoon some marinade over it, making sure that it penetrates all the slits and cavities. Set aside for 10 minutes, turning the fish over a few times during this period.

Brush the grill rack lightly with oil to help prevent the fish from sticking. Remove the fish from the marinade and place it on the rack about 5–6 inches (13–15 cm) from the heat source. Baste the fish frequently and generously with the marinade using the lemon grass brush, if you have it. Turn the fish every 5 minutes or so if you can. Cook for about 20–30 minutes or until the fish has cooked through. It should be nicely browned on the outside but still soft and tender inside. Do not baste during the last 5 minutes so that the spices can form a nice crust. Serve with lime wedges.

SERVES 2–3

CHẢ CÁ   VIETNAM

MONKFISH WITH DILL

FROM THE CHẢ CÁ RESTAURANT IN HANOI

There is a street in Hanoi, Chả Cá Street, which is named after this famous dish. Here fresh, firm, river rish is marinated with turmeric and tamarind, grilled over charcoal or wood and then brought to the table. The diners take over and cook it briefly again, tossing it with a mound of fresh dill and spring onions.

At the suggestion of Vietnamese living in the West, I have used monkfish as a substitute for the fish used in Vietnam. This dish is traditionally eaten with thin fresh rice noodles, which we in the West can find only at some Chinese and Far Eastern grocers'. (Look for rice vermicelli noodles.) Ground dried galangal is also needed for this recipe. Since I have not suggested that you use this form of galangal for any other dish in this book, I suggest that you take just a little of the dried sliced galangal and whirr it to a powder in a clean coffee grinder. Of course, if you *can* get ground galangal (sometimes called Laos powder), do use it.

The way to eat this is as follows: you prepare one mouthful at a time by first putting a few noodles in your bowl. On top of the noodles goes the dilled fish which you may or may not dip first in the anchovy-lime sauce or the Fish Sauce with Vinegar and Lime Juice. On top of this you put some fresh mint or green coriander, the white part of spring onions and some peanuts. You may spoon some more of any sauce you like on top of all this. You could also squeeze some lime juice over it. You then pick up this combination with chopsticks and eat.

1¼ lb (500 g) monkfish fillet

½ teaspoon ground turmeric

1 teaspoon anchovy paste

3½ tablespoons lime juice

½ teaspoon vinegar

½ teaspoon ground galangal (Laos powder)

1 tablespoon tamarind paste (see page 272) or ½ tablespoon lime juice mixed with ¼ teaspoon sugar

2 oz (50 g) fresh dill

8–10 spring onions

Wash the fish and pat it dry. Cut it into 1 inch (2.5 cm) chunks. In a wide shallow dish mix together the turmeric, anchovy paste, 2 tablespoons of the lime juice, the vinegar, galangal and tamarind paste (or lime juice and sugar). Put in the fish and rub the mixture over it. Cover the dish and refrigerate for 2–3 hours.

Wash the dill and pat it dry. Trim away all the coarse stalks. You should have only very fine sprigs left. Put these on one side of a large plate. Separate the green and white sections of the spring onions. Cut the green sections into 2 inch (5 cm) lengths and put these beside the dill. Cut the white part of

Several sprigs fresh mint

Several sprigs fresh coriander

10–12 tinned anchovy fillets

8 oz (225 g) dried fine rice noodles (rice vermicelli)

1 tablespoon lard

Few tablespoons fish sauce

Fish Sauce with Vinegar and Lime Juice (see page 228)

Roasted Peanuts (see page 236)

Lime wedges

About 2 tablespoons vegetable oil

the spring onions into very fine rings and put these into a small bowl. Wash and pat dry the sprigs of mint and coriander. Put each herb into a separate bowl.

Next make the anchovy-lime sauce. Wipe the oil off the anchovies and put them in a blender along with the remaining 1½ tablespoons lime juice. Blend until smooth, and then put the mixture in a small bowl.

Soak the noodles for 2 hours in cold water. Drain them and then drop them into boiling water for a minute or less, until they are just tender. Rinse under cold running water. Drain them again and put them into a serving bowl.

If you wish to cook at the table, put an electric frying-pan in the centre. Put the lard in a small bowl and place this next to it. Put the fish sauce in another small bowl also next to the frying-pan. Near the lard put the plate of dill and spring onion greens. Arrange the bowls of mint, coriander, spring onion whites and anchovy-lime sauce on the table. Set out the cold noodles, the Fish Sauce with Vinegar and Lime Juice, the Roasted Peanuts and lime wedges as well.

Pre-heat an indoor or an outdoor grill. When it is hot, brush the fish lightly with the vegetable oil and grill it about 5 inches (13 cm) from the heat source for 4–5 minutes on the first side and about 3 minutes on the opposite side. Now bring the fish to the table if you aim to continue the cooking there, or complete the cooking in the kitchen. Heat the lard in the frying-pan. When it is hot, put in the fish. Stir it once and then pile in all the dill and spring onion greens. Moisten with a tablespoon or so of fish sauce and stir. The fish is now ready to be eaten with the various herbs, sauces and seasonings as described above.

SERVES 4

FISH FILLETS WITH BLACK BEAN SAUCE

Here is southern Chinese food in its simplest and most divine form. I love salted black beans whenever they make an appearance, but have always had trouble stir-frying delicate fish fillets as they have such a frightening tendency to crumble. I now have to worry no more: having learnt the tricks from Chinese masters, I realise how easy the technique really is.

When the fish is put in a marinade of egg white and cornflour, there has to be sufficient cornflour to hold the fish together when it is cooked. The fish also has to be allowed to sit in this marinade for at least 2 hours. I frequently leave it to marinate in the morning and cook it in the evening. The fish also needs to be pre-cooked, very briefly, in water. This has to be done tenderly, just before it is put in its sauce. For those who like fish, I cannot recommend a better way to prepare it. It is light, delicate and full of flavour.

FOR THE MARINADE:

14–15 oz (400–425 g) flat white fish fillets (such as flounder or sole)

¼ teaspoon salt

1 tablespoon Chinese rice wine or dry sherry

Freshly ground black pepper

1 egg white

4 teaspoons cornflour

2 teaspoons sesame oil

FOR THE SAUCE:

1 teaspoon cornflour

4 fl oz (120 ml) chicken stock

2 teaspoons Chinese rice wine or dry sherry

¼ teaspoon salt

2 tablespoons sesame oil

Freshly ground black pepper

1 dried hot red chilli

Cut each fish fillet in half lengthways. Then cut it crossways into 2 inch (5 cm) wide strips. Next marinate the fish. Put it in a wide bowl and add the salt, rice wine and black pepper. Stir gently to mix. Beat the egg white lightly (not to a froth) and add that as well as the 4 teaspoons cornflour and 2 teaspoons sesame oil. Mix. Cover with cling-film and refrigerate for 2 hours or longer.

Now make the sauce. Put the 1 teaspoon corn-flour in a cup. Slowly add the stock, mixing as you go. Add the rice wine, salt, sesame oil and black pepper. Crumble in the dried red chilli. Set aside.

Rinse the black beans and chop them coarsely. Peel the garlic and ginger and chop them finely. Cut the spring onions crossways into very fine rounds along their entire length, including the green section.

Just before eating, put about ¾ inch (2 cm) water into a large, preferably non-stick frying-pan and bring it to the boil. Turn the heat down to a bare simmer. Put the fish into the water, separating the pieces very gently and spreading them

YOU ALSO NEED:

1½ tablespoons salted black beans

2 cloves garlic

1 inch (2.5 cm) cube fresh ginger

2 spring onions

3 tablespoons vegetable oil

around in the pan. Even before the water comes to a simmer again, the fish pieces will turn nearly white. Remove them gently with a slotted spoon and put them on a plate.

Discard the water in the frying-pan and wipe the pan dry. Put 2 tablespoons of the oil in the frying-pan and set it over a medium-high heat. When the oil is hot, put in the garlic, ginger and black beans. Stir once or twice or until the garlic turns golden. Take the pan off the heat, stir the sauce and pour it in. Put the pan back on a medium-low heat and stir gently until the sauce thickens. Put the fish gently back in and spread it out in the pan. Spoon the sauce over the fish, turning over the pieces carefully just once. Slide the contents of the pan on to a warm serving plate. Scatter the spring onions over the top. Quickly put the remaining tablespoon of oil into a small pan and heat it. Pour the hot oil over the onions to wilt them slightly and to make the fish glisten. Serve immediately.

SERVES 3–4

TOM SOM PLA   THAILAND

ISH STEAMED WITH LEMON GRASS

FROM PIENG CHOM DARBANAND AT THE IMPERIAL HOTEL, BANGKOK

I am sure you must have eaten Cantonese-style steamed fish. Cooked with a fine julienne of ginger and sliced spring onions, it is light, succulent and delicious. The Thais, influenced by the Chinese, keep to the same basic concept but add some of their own aromatic seasonings – galangal, kaffir lime leaves, fresh coriander leaves and lemon grass. Fish sauce replaces soy sauce and fresh green chillies are added if a little heat is required. No oil is called for, so this dish is perfect for dieters. If you cannot get lemon grass use 1 tablespoon finely grated lemon rind, scattering it over the fish at the same time as the lemon grass, just before steaming.

Almost any whole fish can be used, such as sole, flounder, mullet, trout or even small salmon. What *is* important is that it be very fresh. It should be gutted and its scales, gills and fins removed. In the Far East the head is always left on a steamed whole fish, but if you cannot bear to look at it you could ask your fishmonger to remove it. The fish should be of a size that can fit into your wok or steaming pan. The fish is laid out on a large serving plate (to catch the precious juices) and the plate is then balanced on a rack over boiling water, the level of which should be ¾ inch (2 cm) below the plate. The pan or wok is then covered and the fish steams, lying happily on its plate, until it is done. Any desire to lift the lid and peep inside is best resisted as precious aromas can vanish with the steam. (For suggestions on steaming equipment, see page 293.) If you do not wish to cook a whole fish, you may cook fillets or steaks by the same method.

How long do you steam the fish? This depends largely on its thickness. Steaks or fillets about ½ inch (1 cm) thick can be done in 7–10 minutes; those which are ¾–1 inch (2–2.5 cm) thick may take 10–13 minutes. A whole flat fish, such as sole, weighing 1½ lb (750 g) should take about 15 minutes while a 1½ lb (750 g) bass should be allowed 20 minutes because of its thickness. You may, of course, peep at the fish towards the very end of the cooking. Look quickly, deep down into one of the cut slits, if the fish is whole. If it is white all the way through, it is ready. For a fillet or steak, poke the flesh gently with the point of a sharp knife. If it is white all the way through, it is done.

¾ inch (2 cm) cube fresh or 6 large slices dried galangal

1 stick fresh or 1 tablespoon dried sliced lemon grass or lemon rind (see above)

1 inch (2.5 cm) cube fresh ginger

1 fresh hot green chilli (optional)

1 oz (25 g) shallots or onion

1 oz (25 g) fresh coriander leaves

1½ lb (750 g) whole fish, cleaned and scaled, or 1 lb (450 g) fish fillets or steaks (such as sole, haddock, cod, salmon or halibut)

4 teaspoons fish sauce or salt to taste

If you are using fresh galangal, peel it and cut it into fine slivers. If you are using dried galangal, soak the slices in 4 tablespoons hot water in a cup for 30 minutes. If you are using fresh lemon grass, cut off and discard the strawlike top, leaving about 6 inches (15 cm) of the bottom. Hit the bulbous bottom with a hammer or other heavy object in order to crush it lightly. If you are using dried lemon grass instead, add it to the dried galangal in the cup or soak it separately in enough water to cover. Peel the ginger and cut it into very fine slivers. Cut the green chilli into very fine rounds. Peel the shallots and cut them into fine slivers. Wash the coriander leaves, pat them dry and chop them coarsely. Set aside a generous tablespoon for garnishing; the rest is for steaming.

If you are preparing a whole fish, wash it well

4–5 fresh or dried kaffir lime
leaves

1 fresh hot red chilli or
equivalent-sized piece red
pepper

and pat it dry. With a sharp knife, cut deep slightly diagonal slits across the body on both sides of the fish. These slits should be made 1½ inches (4 cm) apart and go three quarters of the way down to the bone. If you are using dried galangal and lemon grass, drain them, reserving the soaking liquid. On an oval or rectangular plate large enough to hold the fish and fit inside your steaming pan, scatter a third of the galangal (fresh or dried), a third of the dried lemon grass (if you are using it) and a third each of the green chilli, shallots and coriander which you have reserved for steaming. Place the fish (whole, fillets or steaks) over these seasonings. Top with the remaining galangal, lemon grass, ginger, green chilli, shallots and coriander reserved for steaming. Pour the fish sauce and the liquid from the soaked spices (if any) over the fish. Top the fish with kaffir lime leaves, which, if fresh, should first be torn in two and the central vein removed.

Set some water to heat in a wok or steamer, remembering that it should be about ¾ inch (2 cm) below the plate holding the fish. Place a rack inside. When the water comes to a rolling boil, put on long oven mittens to protect you from the steam and carefully lower the plate of fish on to the rack. Cover. Let the steam build up over a high heat for 2 minutes. Turn the heat to medium-high and cook for another 5–18 minutes (see the introduction to this recipe) or until the fish is just done.

Meanwhile, cut the red chilli into fine long slivers. Lift the fish plate carefully out of the pan, again wearing oven mittens. Hold the plate level so that the precious juices do not spill over the edge. Sprinkle the fish with the red chilli slivers and the green coriander leaves reserved for garnishing. Serve at once.

SERVES 2–4

CÁ LÓC HẤP   VIETNAM

STEAMED FISH WITH GINGER AND COCONUT MILK

FROM THE ĐẶC SẢN RESTAURANT IN HỒ CHÍ MINH CITY

Here is another steamed fish with deliciously contrasting tastes. There is oyster sauce and coconut milk, fried garlic and fresh ginger, spring onions and mushrooms, all lending their flavours to the fish.. You may, of course, eat the fish with plain rice, but to eat it the traditional Vietnamese way you will need:

1 A plate containing cucumber slices, sprigs of fresh mint, basil and green coriander as well as whole lettuce leaves.

2 A plate holding sheets of rice paper (see page 270) cut in half and a bowl of water. (If you cannot get rice paper, use lettuce leaves alone to wrap the fish.)

3 Fish Sauce Seasoned with Vinegar (page 229).

To eat, you put a lettuce leaf on to a piece of rice paper. It should protrude on one side. Then, with chopsticks, take pieces of fish and cucumber and sprigs of herbs and put them on the lettuce. Wrap up or roll up the bundle and dip it into the sauce. If you find the rice paper a little too dry and crunchy for your taste, you can dip each sheet into a bowl of cold water immediately before assembling the 'package'. This will make the rice paper more malleable.

For general steaming directions see page 293.

1½ lb (750 g) whole fish (such as sole, or small salmon trout, cod, haddock or mullet) scaled and cleaned

½ teaspoon salt

Freshly ground black pepper

1 teaspoon dark brown sugar

3 cloves garlic

3½ oz (90 g) onions

Vegetable oil for shallow-frying

1 inch (2.5 cm) cube fresh ginger

2 spring onions

4 medium-sized mushrooms

Wash the fish and pat it dry. Using a sharp knife, cut deep slightly diagonal slits across the body of the fish on both sides, about 1½ inches (4 cm) apart. Put the fish on an oval or rectangular plate of a size that will fit into your steaming utensil. Rub the fish inside and outside with the salt, pepper and sugar. Peel the garlic and cut it into fine slivers. Peel and finely slice the onions.

Put about ½ inch (1 cm) of oil in a frying-pan and set it over a medium-low heat. While you are waiting for the oil to get hot, set a sieve over a bowl and place it near the hob. Spread some kitchen paper on a large plate and place that nearby also. When the oil is hot, put in the garlic slivers. Stir

1½ tablespoons oyster sauce

6 tablespoons coconut milk
(see page 263)

4–5 tablespoons Roasted
Peanuts (see page 236),
crushed

and fry until they are golden. Empty the oil and garlic into the sieve. Spread the drained garlic over part of the kitchen paper. Put the oil in the bowl back into your frying-pan and heat it again on a medium heat. Set the sieve back on the bowl. When the oil is hot, put in the onion slices. Stir and fry until they are golden-brown and crisp. Empty them into the sieve; then, when they are well drained, spread them on the unused part of the kitchen paper.

Peel the ginger and cut it into fine slices. Stacking a few slices together at a time, cut the ginger into fine slivers. Cut the spring onions crossways into very fine rounds along their entire length. Slice the mushrooms thinly.

Combine the oyster sauce with 2 tablespoons of the coconut milk and pour the mixture evenly over the fish. Scatter the ginger, spring onions and mushrooms as well as the fried garlic and half the fried onions over the top.

If steaming is a technique which is new to you, follow the instructions on page 293. Bring some water to the boil in a wok or steamer, remembering that it should be ¾ inch (2 cm) below the plate. Place the fish plate on the rack in the steamer. Cover and let the steam build up over a high heat for 2 minutes. Turn the heat down to medium-high and steam for another 18 minutes or until the fish is just done. Remove the cover and spoon some of the sauce from the fish into a bowl. Carefully lift the fish plate out of the steamer. Add the remaining 4 tablespoons coconut milk to the sauce in the bowl. Mix well and pour it over the fish. Scatter the crushed peanuts and the remaining fried onions over the fish and serve.

SERVES 3–4

FISH POACHED IN AROMATIC TAMARIND BROTH

FROM PIENG CHOM DARBANAND AT THE IMPERIAL HOTEL, BANGKOK

When I want a light meal, I have this poached fish with plain rice and then follow it with a green salad. The Thais, of course, serve this soupy dish as a main course along with rich coconut-based curries, stir-fried meats, rice and salads.

You could buy almost any filleted fish that you fancy. Moderately priced fillets, such as those from cod, halibut and haddock, are perfectly suited to this dish, though you could also use sole, bass or turbot. It is important to buy *thick* fillets or the thicker end of large fillets as they hold their shape best; about 1 inch (2.5 cm) is a suitable thickness.

1 oz (25 g) shallots or onion

1½ inch (4 cm) cube fresh ginger

About 2 oz (50 g) fresh coriander (preferably with roots still attached)

1 teaspoon shrimp or anchovy paste

1¼ pints (750 ml) chicken stock

1 tablespoon tamarind paste (see page 272) or 2 teaspoons lime juice

1 teaspoon dark brown sugar

¼–½ teaspoon salt

1 lb (450 g) thick white fish fillets

1 spring onion

Peel the shallots and chop them coarsely. Peel the ginger and chop two thirds of it coarsely. Cut the remaining third into very fine julienne strips – as thin as you can manage – and set these aside. Cut the roots off the coriander and chop them coarsely. In an electric blender combine the chopped coriander roots, the chopped shallots, the chopped ginger, shrimp paste and 3 tablespoons water. Blend until you have a purée.

Put the stock into a medium-sized frying-pan. Add the purée from the blender as well as the tamarind paste (or lime juice), sugar and salt. Bring to a simmer, and simmer gently for 5 minutes. Taste and adjust the seasoning, if necessary.

Meanwhile, cut the fish into 3–4 inch (7.5–10 cm) squares. Cut the spring onion crossways into very fine rounds. Put the fish in a single layer into the poaching liquid. Bring the liquid to a simmer again. Cook gently for 1 minute. Turn the fish pieces over carefully. Cook gently for another 5–8 minutes, basting the top of the fish frequently, until it is cooked through. With a wide fish slice, pick up the fish pieces carefully and put in a wide serving bowl. Pour the poaching liquid over the fish. Scatter the sliced spring onion and the reserved julienned ginger over the top and serve.

SERVES 3–4

CÁ KHO   VIETNAM

FISH BRAISED IN TEA

Oily fish, such as mackerel and sardines, are amazingly good when they are braised over a long period. Their flesh turns meltingly tender but does not fall apart, while the braising juices add extra flavour. Teabags are needed here. It is best to use a plain, dark tea that has not been made too aromatic with added seasonings.

This mackerel is served at room temperature or cold with some of its juices poured over it. You may eat it with a green salad that contains fresh herbs such as basil, coriander and mint. You may also serve this fish in much the same way that you might serve tinned sardines – on toast with sliced tomatoes, or arranged over salad greens as a first course.

1½ lb (750 g) mackerel, cleaned, gills removed

1 inch (2.5 cm) cube fresh ginger

1 tablespoon Chinese dark soy sauce

2 tablespoons fish sauce or 1 tablespoon soy sauce mixed with 1 tablespoon water and ¼ teaspoon sugar

2 teabags

1 tablespoon sugar

Cut the mackerel crossways into 3 inch (7.5 cm) sections. The head may be left on the fish or discarded. Wash the mackerel pieces and put them into a medium-sized pan. Cover with about 1¾ pints (1 litre) water and add all the other ingredients. (The ginger does not need to be peeled.) Bring to the boil. Turn the heat down to medium-low and simmer, uncovered, for 1½ hours. You should now have about 5 fl oz (150 ml) of sauce left at the bottom. Leave the fish to cool in the sauce. When you are ready to serve, lift the fish out of its liquid. Skin it, if you like, and open the pieces like a book, removing the centre bone. Pour just a little sauce over the top.

SERVES 4 AS A FIRST COURSE OR 2 AS A MAIN COURSE

GULAI IKAN INDONESIA

WEST SUMATRAN FISH CURRY WITH COCONUT MILK

FROM THE SANUAR FAMILY IN PANDAI SIKAT

This dish calls for rather a lot of coconut milk so I nearly always use a good tinned variety. It does behave slightly differently from fresh milk and I have therefore had to change Mrs Sanuar's recipe slightly. I do hope that this will meet with her approval, as she sits in her beautifully carved *minangkabau* house, with its roof curving up at the ends like a water-buffalo's horns.

For this recipe you need steaks from a firm-fleshed white fish such as cod, haddock or bass. Salmon, though not white, would be wonderful, if expensive. The Sanuars use a large goldfish from their very own tank and either cook it whole or, rather casually, chop in half. The souring agent used in Western Sumatra was not regular tamarind but *asem candis*, something that I knew already from India as *kokum*. This is the dried sour skin of a mangosteen-like fruit. It is generally added whole or in segments to a dish where it slowly imparts its sourness. If you can obtain this seasoning, put in about 3 pieces when you add the fish. Tamarind paste or lime juice make a good substitute.

2¹⁄₁₀ pints (1.2 litres) coconut milk

8–12 dried hot red chillies

2 sticks fresh or 2 tablespoons dried sliced lemon grass

1½ inch (4 cm) cube fresh or 5–6 slices dried galangal

½ oz (15 g) candlenuts or cashew nuts

4 oz (100 g) red pepper

4 oz (100 g) shallots or onions

1 inch (2.5 cm) cube fresh ginger

3 cloves garlic

½ teaspoon ground turmeric

1 teaspoon paprika

2 lb (1 kg) fish steaks about 1 inch (2.5 cm) thick

Leave the coconut milk to stand for a while until the cream has risen to the top.

Crumble the red chillies into a small bowl. Add the dried lemon grass and dried galangal, if you are using them, and the nuts. Add enough water just to cover and leave to soak for 1 hour. If you are using fresh lemon grass, cut about 6 inches (15 cm) off each stick, measuring from the bottom, and discard the rest. Crush the bulbous bottoms lightly with a hammer or other heavy object and set aside. If you are using fresh galangal, peel and coarsely chop it.

Remove the seeds from the red pepper and chop it coarsely. Peel the shallots, ginger and garlic and chop them coarsely. In an electric blender combine the soaked ingredients and their soaking liquid, the fresh galangal (if you are using it), the red

1½ teaspoons salt

2½ tablespoons lime or lemon juice

4 tablespoons vegetable oil

4–5 fresh kaffir lime leaves or 3 × ½ inch (7.5 × 1 cm) piece lemon rind

10 fresh curry leaves or 3 dried bay leaves

15–20 fresh mint leaves

8–10 cherry or very small tomatoes

pepper, shallots, ginger, garlic, turmeric and paprika. Blend thoroughly, adding another 1–2 tablespoons water if it seems necessary.

Rub the fish steaks with ½ teaspoon of the salt and 1 tablespoon of the lime juice. Set aside. Thick coconut cream should have risen to the top of the coconut milk. Spoon it off and set it aside. Add enough water to the remaining thin coconut milk to make it up to about 2½ pints (1.5 litres).

Put the oil in a large, preferably non-stick frying-pan and set it over a medium-high heat. When the oil is hot, put in the paste from the blender. Stir and fry until the paste turns dark red and separates from the oil. (Turn the heat down a little, if necessary, while you do this.) Put in the thin coconut milk-water combination and the 2 whole sticks fresh lemon grass, if you are using it. Bring to the boil, scraping up any hardened juices stuck to the bottom of the pan. Turn the heat to low and simmer gently for 15 minutes. Remove the lemon grass and set it aside. Empty the contents of the pan into a sieve set over a bowl and push the sauce through. Return all but 4 tablespoons of the sieved sauce to the frying-pan and bring it to a simmer. Put the lemon grass sticks back in along with the lime leaves (or lemon rind), curry leaves, mint, the remaining 1½ tablespoons lime juice and the remaining 1 teaspoon salt. Stir. Now lay the fish steaks in a single layer in the pan and bring its contents to a simmer again over a medium-low heat. Cook gently for about 10 minutes or until the fish is done, spooning the hot sauce over the steaks frequently.

Put the thick coconut cream into a bowl and stir it well. Slowly add the 4 tablespoons of reserved sauce and mix it in. Pour this over the fish. Halve the tomatoes and add them to the pan. Cook until everything is just heated through, then serve.

SERVES 4

GRILLED MACKEREL (OR SALMON) WITH SWEET SOY SAUCE

You may cook mackerel or salmon fillets in this way – or even whole eels that have been split open. All you need is Sweet Glazing Sauce and some skewers. The Japanese like to skewer their fish before it is grilled. The reason is simple, and practical enough: it is much easier to turn the fish over with the help of skewers. If you want both sides browned and glistening with the glaze of the sauce, there is no better way to do it. And it is the only way to make the skin crisp.

There are a few pointers here which might prove useful. In order to prevent the fish from falling off the skewers while it is being cooked, the skewering must always be done against the grain. Push the skewers into the flesh just under the skin. Also, let the skewers fan out so that the handles are all close together but the tips are quite separated. This way you will be able to hold all the handles with one hand when the fish needs to be turned.

The Japanese also like to salt fatty fish before setting it to grill. This draws out excess water and firms up the flesh. You may grill this fish over charcoal outdoors or cook it indoors under your kitchen grill.

2 tablespoons coarse sea salt

1½–2 lb (750 g–1 kg) unskinned mackerel or salmon fillets

Sweet Glazing Sauce (see page 235), cooled

A little vegetable oil

Ginger Shreds in Sweet Vinegar (see page 235)

From the height of about 1 foot (30 cm), sprinkle half the salt on one side of the fish pieces. (This ensures an even sprinkling of salt.) Turn the fish over and do the same on the other side. Set aside for 15 minutes and then wash the salt off. Pat the fish dry and put it into a large bowl. Pour the Sweet Glazing Sauce over it. Mix well so that the sauce covers both sides of the fish. Leave it to marinate for 1 hour.

Pre-heat an indoor kitchen grill or an outdoor charcoal grill. If you can control the heat, keep it at medium-high. Lift the fish pieces out of the marinade. (Save the marinade sauce.) Put between 3 and 5 skewers into each piece of fish, depending on its size, going against the grain and keeping the skewers just under the skin (see page 186).

Lightly oil the grill rack so that the fish will not stick to it. Arrange the grill rack so that it is about 5 inches (13 cm) from the heat source. Grill the fish, skin side down, until it is medium-brown. Turn the fish over carefully and grill it until the second side is light brown. Brush this second side with some of the remaining marinade and continue to grill until the fish is glazed and brown. Turn the fish over very carefully, brush with the marinade and grill until this side is glazed and brown. To serve, lift the fish very carefully on to a plate and hand the Ginger Shreds round separately.

SERVES 4

SAENGSUN CHIGAE   KOREA

FISH, SHELLFISH AND BEAN CURD STEW

This is one of my family's favourite stews. It has a bit of everything in it and is deliciously spicy to boot. You can put in almost any fish that you like. Rather like a *bouillabaisse*, the ideal combination includes a whole white-fleshed fish cut crossways into three or four pieces (including the head if you wish), a few molluscs (such as clams or mussels), chunks of bean curd (which happily absorbs the good sauce), dried mushrooms, sliced courgettes and just a few slices of beef for a more complex flavour.

There is one seasoning ingredient in it, however, that is hard to find but very easy to improvise. It is Hot Fermented Bean Paste (*kochu chang*) and contains, among other things, fermented soya bean powder and chilli powder. To make a rough equivalent at home I combine Japanese-style *miso* or fermented soya bean paste – red or brown miso is available in most health food shops – with chilli powder and a little sugar (see page 230). Hot Fermented Bean Paste is *very* hot. *My* paste is relatively mild, though you could add more chilli powder to it for a more fiery dish.

It might interest you to know that the water used in this stew in Korea is that which is saved from the second washing of raw rice. Because it is not from the first washing, it is clean. It adds a little flavour and the starch in the water helps to thicken the sauce just very slightly.

The pots used for cooking these stews (or *chigaes*) are made of heavy clay and are taken directly from the fire to the table. They retain their heat for a long time, so the stew stays hot. I use a heavy casserole dish instead. This stew is generally served with rice.

10 dried Chinese mushrooms or fresh mushrooms

4 oz (100 g) lean tender beef

6 oz (175 g) courgettes

2 cloves garlic

1 tablespoon Japanese soy sauce (shoyu)

1 teaspoon sesame oil

4 tablespoons Hot Fermented Bean Paste (see page 230)

4 spring onions

1 oz (25 g) green pepper

1 oz (25 g) red pepper

8 small clams

10–11 oz (275–300 g) bean curd

1½ lb (750 g) whole white fish (such as mullet, trout or small haddock or cod), scaled, cleaned and cut crossways into 3–4 pieces, or 1 lb (450 g) fish steaks

2 teaspoons vegetable oil

Few celery leaves to garnish

Soak the dried mushrooms in about 10 fl oz (300 ml) hot water and set aside for 30 minutes or until they are soft. Cut off the hard stems and slice the caps into 3–4 pieces. If you are using fresh mushrooms, first trim the ends of the stalks and wipe the caps with damp kitchen paper. Thickly slice the mushrooms. Cut the beef into very thin slices, about 1 × 2 inches (2.5 × 5 cm). Trim the courgettes and cut them crossways into ⅓ inch (0.75 cm) thick rounds. Peel the garlic and chop it finely. In a bowl combine the mushrooms, beef, courgettes, garlic, soy sauce, sesame oil and Hot Fermented Bean Paste. Mix and set aside.

Cut the spring onions into 2 inch (5 cm) lengths. Cut the peppers into ½ inch (1 cm) squares. Scrub the clams well with a stiff brush under cold running water. Cut the bean curd into 1 inch (2.5 cm) cubes. Wash the fish and pat dry.

In a large, wide, flameproof casserole that can be brought to the table, heat the oil over a medium-high heat. When it is hot, put in the meat mixture. Stir and fry for 2 minutes. Pour in 1½ pints (900 ml) water and bring to a simmer, scraping off all the cooked meat juices stuck to the bottom of the casserole. Put in the fish pieces, spring onions and peppers. Bring to a simmer. Cover and simmer for 5 minutes. Add the bean curd and clams, scattering them about and submerging them in the liquid as gently as possible. Bring to a simmer again. Cover and cook on medium-low heat for another 5 minutes or until the clams open.

Meanwhile, coarsely chop the celery leaves. Scatter them over the stew and serve.

SERVES 4

PRAWN AND VEGETABLE FRITTERS

The Japanese may have learned the technique of making deep-fried fritters from Portuguese missionaries in the late sixteenth century, but by now they have made this dish their own. Only the freshest fish and vegetables are used, the batter is exceedingly light, and the dipping sauce a glorious, almost drinkable mixture of stock, soy sauce, sweet *sake* and grated white radish.

In Japan the best way to eat *tempura* is at a *tempura* bar. You sit at a counter behind which the chefs work right before your eyes. One item at a time is dipped in batter, fried and placed in your paper-lined basket. You eat it immediately while it is still crunchy and hot, dipping it quickly either into its dipping sauce or into the tiny bowls of salt and lemon juice which also sit on the counter. Warm *sake* or cold beer flow freely.

On one of my visits to Osaka, Professor Shizuo Tsuji, one of Japan's leading food authorities, arranged for me to have what he regarded as the best *tempura* in Japan. That the restaurant was in another town did not worry him at all. He had me driven to Kobe, but only after making sure that a certain fresh prawn from the local seas had not already been sold out. He sent two of his leading chefs, Mr Hatta and Mr Saito, with me to extend his hospitality and to make sure that all my questions would be answered.

I had had *tempura* all over Japan – in Tokyo, where the batter is golden yellow; in the markets of Kyoto, where they like to build up the batter in a more-than-generous layer around the food (according to Professor Tsuji, 'The common man goes for the crunch more than for the food it covers'); in Osaka, which is famed for its pale, almost white, batter; and now I was to try it in Kobe.

The *tempura* here just could not be improved upon. The wild prawn we were served are sold live. This restaurant has first choice in the market, the prawns being selected for their size and colour. They had a very fresh sea flavour. We also had rolled white fish (*kisu*) fillets, minnows (all lumped into a ball), a moss-eating trout (*ayu*), octopus pieces, sea eels, baby prawns and vegetables such as baby aubergines, lotus root slices, mushroom caps and green chillies. We ended with a *miso* soup, rice and pickles, to be followed by an exotic (and expensive) fruit, sweet prickly pears from Columbia.

Tempura, for the average person, is a simpler affair: one or two prawns (they are very expensive in Japan), a few green beans and a few slices of sweet potato, aubergine and lotus root. A small Japanese salad is generally served beforehand and soup, rice and pickles at the end. All in all, it is very satisfying and good.

While I consider prawns essential, you can add almost any other seasonal vegetable or leaf. Kyoto specialises in serving red maple leaves in the autumn. You might serve mint in the summer. Among the vegetables that can be dipped in batter and fried you have a choice of cauliflower, potatoes, green pepper, asparagus, mushrooms, sliced onions and broccoli.

The batter must be mixed only at the last moment, though all the ingredients for it may be measured and kept in readiness some time beforehand. It is important that the batter be left lumpy and not be overmixed. The flour and water are measured by volume here. After you have fried a batch of tempura, clean the oil of all debris using a slotted spoon. (In Japan this debris – little droplets of batter – is usually saved. It is then rinsed off and put into soup as tiny dumplings.)

If you are using *dashi-no-moto* instead of Japanese Soup Stock, use 2 tablespoons soy sauce in the dipping sauce.

12 uncooked unpeeled prawns
3 oz (75 g) green pepper
About 16 green beans
About ½ medium sweet potato
3 oz (75 g) onions
8 medium mushrooms
8 fl oz (250 ml) Japanese Soup Stock (see page 66) or light unsalted chicken stock
2½ tablespoons Japanese soy sauce (shoyu)
3 tablespoons *sake*
2 teaspoons sugar
3½ oz (90 g) white radish (mooli)
Salt
6 tablespoons lemon juice
Vegetable oil for deep-frying
1 egg yolk
8 fl oz (250 ml) ice-cold water
8 fl oz (250 ml) plain white flour plus extra for dusting

Prepare all the foods that are to be fried. Peel the prawns but leave their tails on. The tails have a little water in them which must be pushed out. To do this, cut the very tip off each tail and then press the water out by pulling the blunt side of a knife along the tail. De-vein the prawns. Make a few strokes crossways on the underbelly of each prawn so that it does not curl up. Cut the green pepper lengthways into ½ inch (1 cm) wide strips. Trim the green beans, but leave them whole. Peel the sweet potato and cut it into slices, each about ⅛ inch (0.3 cm) thick. Put the slices in a bowl of water. Peel the onions and cut them in half lengthways. Lay the onion halves on your work-surface, cut side down. Push cocktail sticks vertically into the onion halves along their entire length at ¼ inch (0.5 cm) intervals so that they go all the way through. Cut the onion halves into slices downwards between the cocktail sticks. The sticks will hold the onions slices together.

Next make the dipping sauce. Combine the stock, soy sauce, *sake* and sugar in a small pan and

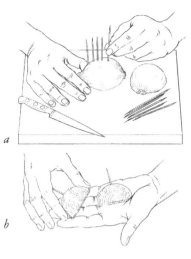

Inserting toothpicks into an onion

a) *Peel the onion and cut it in half, lengthways. Place the onion halves on your work surface cut side down and stick toothpicks along the length at ¼ inch (5 mm) intervals. Ensure that they are pushed all the way through the onion.*

b) *Cut the onion crossways between the toothpicks. The toothpicks will hold the onion slices together.*

simmer gently for 1 minute or until the sugar dissolves. Divide the sauce among 4 bowls and keep them warm. Peel the radish and grate it finely. Put one small hillock of grated radish on to each of 4 tiny saucers or into 4 tiny bowls. Prepare also a tiny bowl of salt and a tiny bowl of lemon juice for each diner.

Set the oil to heat in a wok or deep-fat fryer to a temperature of 350–370°F (180–190°C). Drain the sweet potato and pat all the foods dry.

Make the batter. In a large bowl beat the egg yolk lightly and add the cold water to it. Mix lightly. Sift the 8 fl oz (250 ml) flour and then dump it all at once into the bowl with the egg yolk and water. Stir lightly with a fork or chopsticks to mix. Do not overmix. The batter should be lumpy and floury-looking.

Put the dusting flour on a plate. Dip the pepper strips first in the dusting flour, shaking off any excess, then dip them in the batter. Fry as many pieces as your wok or deep-fat fryer will hold easily in one layer for 2–3 minutes, turning once or twice, until the batter is golden. Remove with a slotted spoon. Drain once on kitchen paper and serve. Fry all the vegetables in this way, removing the debris from the oil with a slotted spoon between each batch. Stir the batter lightly every now and then to keep it from separating. Fry the prawns last.

Diners usually put some or all of the grated radish into the dipping sauce. They dip the food into the sauce or into the lemon juice and salt before eating.

SERVES 4

XIAN LUSUN CHAD XIAQIU   HONG KONG

PRAWNS WITH ASPARAGUS

FROM WILLY MARK

I serve this elegant Cantonese dish both as a main course and, in small portions, as a first course.

8 oz (225 g) uncooked unpeeled prawns

1 small egg white

2½ teaspoons cornflour

2 teaspoons sesame oil

Salt

8 oz (225 g) fresh asparagus (untrimmed weight)

3 tablespoons vegetable oil

¾ inch (2 cm) cube fresh ginger

1 clove garlic

1½ teaspoons oyster sauce

1 teaspoon Chinese light soy sauce

2 teaspoons Chinese rice wine or dry sherry

¼ teaspoon sugar

Peel and de-vein the prawns. Wash well, pat them dry and put them in a small bowl. Beat the egg white lightly and add that to the bowl along with 2 teaspoons of the cornflour, 1 teaspoon of the sesame oil and a pinch of salt. Mix well, cover and set aside for 30 minutes or longer, refrigerating if necessary.

Trim and discard the woody bottom ends of the asparagus spears. Peel the lower third of the spears and then cut them slightly diagonally along their entire length into 1½ inch (4 cm) long pieces. Bring about 1¼ pints (750 ml) water to a rolling boil in a medium-sized pan. Add ½ teaspoon salt and 1 tablespoon of the vegetable oil to the water. Stir. Put in the asparagus. Boil rapidly for 2–3 minutes or until the asparagus is just done but is still crisp and bright green. Drain and rinse under cold running water. Drain again and set aside.

Peel the ginger and garlic and chop each finely. Keep them separate. In a small bowl combine the oyster sauce, soy sauce, the remaining 1 teaspoon sesame oil, the rice wine, sugar and 2 tablespoons water. In a cup, mix the remaining ½ teaspoon cornflour with 1 tablespoon water.

Just before you are ready to eat, put the remaining 4 tablespoons vegetable oil in a wok or large frying-pan and set it over a high heat. When the oil is hot, put in the prawns. Stir and fry for about 3 minutes or until they just turn opaque. Remove the prawns with a slotted spoon and set them aside. Remove all but 1 tablespoon of the oil from the wok and heat over a medium heat again. When it is hot, put in the ginger. Stir once and add the garlic. Stir once or twice and put in the prawns and asparagus. Stir once or twice and add the oyster sauce mixture. Stir a few times and take the wok off the heat. Give the cornflour mixture a good stir, pour it into the centre of the wok and stir to mix. Put the wok back on a low heat and cook briefly until the sauce has thickened, stirring as you do so. Serve immediately.

SERVES 3–4 AS A MAIN COURSE OR 6 AS A FIRST COURSE

GAMBAS PICANTES   PHILIPPINES

Piquant Prawns

FROM THE NIELSON TOWER RESTAURANT IN MANILA

Glenda Barretto, a very fine cook herself, has used her entrepreneurial skills in opening of some of Manila's most distinguished restaurants. The Nielson Tower is one of them. From 1937 to 1947 it was an airport terminal. Today it is the haunt of the city's movers and shakers in a different way – it feeds them. This dish, Spanish in its origins as are a great many other Filipino dishes, is served in the restaurant as an appetiser. I often serve it as a main course with rice and a simple vegetable. If you prefer a milder flavour, substitute 1½ oz (40g) finely chopped green pepper for the chillies.

1 lb (450 g) uncooked
   unpeeled prawns
1 teaspoon paprika
5 cloves garlic
1–2 fresh hot green chillies
4 tablespoons olive oil
½ teaspoon salt
Freshly ground black pepper

Peel and de-vein the prawns. Wash them, pat them dry and put them in a bowl. Add the paprika and toss. Peel the garlic and chop it finely. Chop the chillies finely. Put the oil in a wok or large frying-pan and set it over a high heat. When the oil is hot, put in the garlic. Stir-fry for 30 seconds or until the garlic turns golden. Put in the prawns and green chillies. Stir-fry over a high heat for 2–3 minutes or until the prawns turn opaque all the way through. Add the salt and pepper. Toss again and serve.

SERVES 4 AS A MAIN COURSE OR 6 AS A FIRST COURSE

GULAI LABU · MALAYSIA

SPICY PRAWN AND CUCUMBER CURRY

FROM HASNA ABU BAKAR IN PENANG

This curry is actually made with bottle gaud – a pale green vegetable shaped like a bowling pin. You can easily use cucumber instead as its taste is similar when cooked. The origins of this Malay dish probably lie in India – the use of ground coriander and fennel seeds as well as the final popping of seasonings in hot oil all testify to that. What I find utterly fascinating here is the use of white pepper. The original recipe calls for 1 tablespoon finely ground white pepper. This may sound unusual, and excessive, in the West. But if you travel in the regions where pepper has grown for thousands of years, such as Kerala in South India where black pepper may well have originated, you will find that the use of such large amounts is not at all uncommon. It makes the dish decidedly peppery. What must be kept in mind is that red chillies arrived in this part of the world only in the late fifteenth century.

If you cannot get ground fennel seeds, simply grind whole seeds in a clean coffee grinder.

12 oz (350 g) uncooked unpeeled prawns

10 oz (275 g) cucumber

4 oz (100 g) shallots or onions

6 cloves garlic

2 tablespoons ground coriander seeds

1 tablespoon ground fennel seeds

1 teaspoon ground white pepper or to taste

1 tablespoon ground cumin seeds

1 teaspoon ground turmeric

3–4 dried hot red chillies

¾–1 teaspoon salt

1 teaspoon sugar

14 fl oz (400 ml) thick coconut milk (see page 263)

Peel and de-vein the prawns. Wash them and pat them dry. Peel the cucumber and cut it crossways into ½ inch (1 cm) thick rounds. Peel 3 oz (75 g) of the shallots and chop them very finely. Peel and finely slice the remaining shallots. Peel the garlic cloves. Chop 4 of them very finely and cut the other 2 into fine slivers. Combine the sliced shallots and slivered garlic and set these aside.

In a medium-sized pan combine the chopped shallots, chopped garlic, ground coriander, ground fennel, white pepper, ground cumin, turmeric and 15 fl oz (450 ml) water. Crumble in the red chillies. Stir and bring to the boil. Boil, uncovered, on a highish heat for about 5 minutes. Add the cucumber rounds and bring to a simmer. Cover and simmer gently for 5 minutes. Then add the prawns, salt and sugar. Bring to a simmer again and simmer gently for about 1 minute, stirring the prawns around in the sauce. Give the

4 tablespoons vegetable oil

1 teaspoon whole fennel seeds

coconut milk a good stir and pour it in. Bring the mixture to the boil, then lower the heat and simmer for 1 minute, stirring now and then.

Put the oil in a very small pan or small frying-pan and set it over a medium-high heat. When the oil is hot, put in the slivered shallots and garlic. Stir and fry until they turn a golden colour. Add the whole fennel seeds. Stir once and quickly pour the contents of the pan (oil and seasonings) into the pan containing the curry. Cover the curry pan immediately to trap all the aromas.

SERVES 4–6

YAM PLA MUK   THAILAND

SQUID SALAD

Squid is such an underused seafood. It is cheap and I happen to love it, so I cook it in as many different ways as I can. This is an easy salad that can be served as a main course in the summer and as an appetiser in the winter.

2 lb (1 kg) squid, cleaned (see page 291)

3 oz (75 g) shallots or onions

4 tablespoons lime juice

3 tablespoons fish sauce or salt to taste

1 teaspoon sugar

¼ teaspoon chilli powder

6–8 tablespoons fresh coriander leaves

FOR THE GARNISHES:

3–4 lettuce leaves

5 oz (150 g) cucumber

8–10 cherry or very small tomatoes

Cut the tubelike bodies of the squid crossways into ¼ inch (0.5 cm) wide rings. Wash these rings and the tentacles and then put them in a pan with 4 tablespoons water. Bring to the boil, cover, and simmer for about 3 minutes or until the pieces of squid turn opaque. Drain them and put them in a bowl.

Peel and finely slice the shallots. Add these to the squid along with the lime juice, fish sauce, sugar, chilli powder and coriander leaves. Toss well. Check the seasoning.

Just before serving, arrange the lettuce leaves on a serving plate. Peel the cucumber and slice it into thin rounds. Cut the tomatoes in half vertically. Put the squid salad on top of the lettuce and surround with the cucumber slices and tomato halves.

SERVES 4–6 AS A MAIN COURSE OR 8 AS A FIRST COURSE

SOTONG MASAK KICAP   MALAYSIA

SQUID IN BLACK SAUCE

FROM THE SRI MELAKA RESTAURANT AT THE HYATT SAUJANA HOTEL IN KUALA LUMPUR

The ingredients used in this recipe are simple and humble, but the dish, another Nonya classic, is exquisite. (Nonyas are women of mixed Chinese and Malay ancestry, born in the Straits settlements of Penang, Malacca or Singapore.) The black sauce used here is thick, smooth, very slightly sweet and made with mashed fermented soya beans. I find bottled black bean sauce to be fairly similar. If you cannot obtain it, use 1½ tablespoons tinned or dried fermented black beans, washed and mashed, mixed with 1 tablespoon oyster sauce.

9–10 oz (250–275 g) onions

1 lb (450 g) squid, cleaned (see page 291)

4 tablespoons vegetable oil

2 tablespoons bottled black bean sauce

1 tablespoon Chinese light soy sauce

1½ teaspoons ground white pepper

FOR THE GARNISHES:

1 green section spring onion, cut into rings

1 oz (25 g) fresh coriander leaves (optional)

Few rings cut from a fresh hot red chilli (optional)

Peel the onions and cut them in half lengthways. Cut each half crossways into ⅛ inch (0.3 cm) thick slices. Wash the squid and pat it dry. Cut the tubular bodies of the squid crossways into ¾ inch (2 cm) wide rings. The tentacles may be left clumped together or separated into 2–3 clumps.

Put the oil in a frying-pan and set it over a medium-high heat. When the oil is hot, put in the onions. Stir and fry them for about 4 minutes or until they are soft. Put in the squid, black bean sauce, soy sauce and white pepper. Stir and cook on the same heat for about 3 minutes or until the squid is opaque. Empty the contents of the pan into a serving dish. Garnish with the chopped green section of a spring onion and, if liked, coriander leaves and hot red chilli rings.

SERVES 4

ADOBONG PUSIT   PHILIPPINES

SQUID WITH TOMATOES

FROM THE HOME OF DOCTORA FE ESLEYER IN BACOLOD CITY, NEGROS

This easy dish, very Spanish in its heritage, is generally eaten with rice in the
Philippines. I often serve it with pasta or enjoy it all by itself with a salad on
the side when I want to eat lightly. It never ceases to amaze me that something
as good should still be so cheap to make. Perhaps I should not speak too
loudly!

I have used tinned tomatoes in this recipe as they are always available and are
usually redder and riper than anything I can get in the market. If you have
access to good fresh tomatoes, use 7½–8 oz (215–225 g). Just drop them into
boiling water for 15 seconds so that you can peel them easily.

1 lb (450 g) squid, cleaned (see
page 291)

4 cloves garlic

2 oz (50 g) onion

6 tinned plum tomatoes,
lightly drained

3 tablespoons olive oil

1 teaspoon vinegar

¾ teaspoon salt

Wash the squid and pat it dry. Cut the tubular
bodies crossways into ½ inch (1 cm) wide rings.
Cut the tentacles area into 2 or 3 pieces. Peel the
garlic and chop it finely. Peel the onion and chop it
finely. Chop the tomatoes coarsely.

Put the oil in a medium-sized pan over a
medium-high heat. When the oil is hot, put in the
garlic. Stir once or twice and add the onions. Turn
the heat to medium. Stir and cook for 1 minute.
Then put in the tomatoes. Stir and cook on a
medium-high heat for 2–3 minutes or until you
have a thickish sauce. Turn the heat to high and
put in the squid, vinegar and salt. Stir and cook
just until the squid turns opaque – a matter of
minutes.

SERVES 3–4

VEGETABLES AND SALADS

PACHERI TERONG   MALAYSIA

AUBERGINE IN A THICK, HOT, SWEET AND SOUR CHILLI SAUCE

FROM MRS ZAIDAH AHMED IN KUALA LUMPUR

Another dish of Indian-Malay ancestry, this hot, sweet and sour *pacheri* may be made with fresh pineapple cubes as well.

7 oz (200 g) onions

1 inch (2.5 cm) cube fresh ginger

2 teaspoons whole cumin seeds

2 teaspoons ground coriander seeds

3–5 dried hot red chillies

4 whole cloves

2 inch (5 cm) stick cinnamon

1 lb (450 g) aubergines

6 tablespoons vegetable oil

1 tablespoon paprika

3–4 tablespoons tamarind paste or 3 tablespoons lime juice mixed with 2 tablespoons dark brown sugar

1–2 tablespoons dark brown sugar

1½–2 teaspoons salt

Peel and finely slice the onions. Peel the ginger and cut it into fine shreds. Put the cumin, ground coriander, dried chillies, cloves and cinnamon into a clean coffee grinder or other spice grinder. Grind as finely as possible. Cut the aubergines into 1 inch (2.5 cm) cubes, leaving the skin on.

Put the oil in a large, preferably non-stick frying-pan or large wok and set it over a medium-high heat. When the oil is hot, put in the sliced onions and the ginger. Stir and fry for about 4 minutes or until the seasonings have a dryish look but have not browned. Add the spices from the spice grinder. Stir for 1 minute. Quickly put in 10 fl oz (300 ml) water and turn the heat down a little. Add the paprika, tamarind (or lime juice and sugar), sugar and salt. Stir to mix. Put in the cubed aubergines and bring to a simmer. Cover and cook gently for 20–30 minutes, stirring now and then, until the aubergines are tender. Remove the lid, turn up the heat and cook most of the remaining liquid away. You should have just a thick sauce clinging to the aubergine pieces.

SERVES 4

CÀ TÍM NƯỚNG   VIETNAM

Smoky Aubergines in a Lime Sauce

This is a superb dish, inspired in every way. Aubergines, all smoky from being charred over a flame, are smothered with stir-fried pork and then submerged in a delicious lime sauce. You may roast the aubergines outdoors over charcoal in the summer, over an open fire indoors during the winter or under your kitchen grill at any time of year. I find that the most convenient way is directly on top of a gas burner. When buying the aubergines, make sure that they have their green sepals and a short length of stalk still attached. This makes the cooking easier and the presentation prettier.

2 aubergines each 7–8 oz (220–225 g)

4 tablespoons Fish Sauce Seasoned with Lime Juice (see page 228)

2½ oz (65 g) onion

1 clove garlic

1 spring onion

1 tablespoon vegetable oil

4 oz (100 g) lean pork, minced

¼ teaspoon salt

Freshly ground black pepper

Do not trim the aubergines. Prick them lightly with a fork to prevent them from bursting during cooking. Line a burner on a gas cooker with aluminium foil, leaving an opening for the gas. (Line two burners if you wish to cook both aubergines simultaneously.) Hold one aubergine by its stem end and stand it upright, directly on top of a medium-low flame. Let the bottom char. Now lay the aubergine down on top of the flame and let one side char. Keep turning the aubergine until all of it is charred and roasted and the entire vegetable has gone limp. You may need to hold it with a pair of tongs towards the end. Cook the other aubergine in the same way.

Peel the charred skin off the aubergines, picking them up carefully by the stem now and then, holding them under cold running water to wash away small bits of skin. The aubergines should stay intact though they will be somewhat flattened. If small portions do get loose, the aubergines can easily be reassembled. Put the aubergines side by side into a serving dish that has a slight depth to it as there will be a little sauce later. Pat them dry with kitchen paper. (You can prepare the dish up to this point a day in advance. Cover and refrigerate the aubergines. The following day, bring them to room temperature before proceeding with the next step.)

Make the Fish Sauce Seasoned with Lime Juice. Peel the onion and garlic and chop them finely. Cut the spring onion crossways into very fine rings.

Put the oil in a frying-pan and set it over a medium-high heat. When the oil is hot, put in the onion and garlic. Stir once or twice and add the pork, salt and lots of black pepper. Stir and fry for about 5 minutes or until the meat is cooked through, breaking up any lumps as you do so. Put in the spring onion and stir for 10 seconds. Spread the pork over the aubergines. Pour the Fish Sauce Seasoned with Lime Juice over the top and serve.

SERVES 4

SHENGBIAN CANDOU   HONG KONG

BRAISED BROAD BEANS

FROM ANDY'S KITCHEN RESTAURANT IN CAUSEWAY BAY

You can make this Shanghai-style dish with fresh or frozen broad beans. Here the hard outer skin around each individual bean is not peeled away before cooking. Instead, it is popped open by the diner, just before being devoured.

1 spring onion

10 oz (275 g) fresh broad beans (shelled weight) or frozen broad beans

3 tablespoons vegetable oil

½ teaspoon salt

5 fl oz (150 ml) chicken stock

½ teaspoon sugar

1 tablespoon sesame oil

Cut the spring onion crossways into very thin rounds. Wash the broad beans and, if they are frozen, de-frost them completely in a bowl of luke-warm water. Drain thoroughly. Put the oil in a wok or large frying-pan and set it over a high heat. When the oil is hot, put in the broad beans. Stir briskly for about 30 seconds and then add the salt, stock and sugar. Cover and cook on a high heat for 6–7 minutes or until the beans are just tender. Remove the lid and boil away all the liquid. Add the spring onion and sesame oil. Toss and serve.

SERVES 3–4

TUMIS BUNCHIS

INDONESIA

GREEN BEANS AND CARROTS WITH GINGER AND CHILLIES

FROM THE HOUSEHOLD OF USMAN AND ROSALINA BEKA, JAKARTA

When little girls start learning how to cook in Indonesia, this is frequently one of the dishes they start with. A *tumis* is a stir-fried dish with just a little liquid in it. The beans (in Indonesia long beans are used) are usually combined with bean curd or bean sprouts. If you wish to use either of these, you will need about 1½ cakes of pressed bean curd or about 8 oz (225 g) fresh bean sprouts. Add them to the dish at the same time as the beans. The bean curd should be cut into pieces about the same size as the beans. I have used carrots instead, only because they are more easily available and because the West has so few imaginative carrot dishes. If you cannot get fresh galangal, just do without it.

1 lb (450 g) green beans

2 medium carrots

3–4 fresh hot green chillies

1 inch (2.5 cm) cube fresh ginger

1 inch (2.5 cm) cube fresh galangal (optional)

4–6 cloves garlic

2 oz (50 g) shallots or onions

3 tablespoons vegetable oil

8–10 fresh or dried curry leaves or 2 bay leaves

¾ teaspoon salt

Trim the beans and cut them into 1 inch (2.5 cm) pieces. Peel the carrots and cut them crossways into 2 inch (5 cm) lengths. Cut each piece lengthways into quarters and then halve these.

Finely chop the green chillies. Peel the ginger and cut it into paper-thin slices. Stack a few slices together at a time and cut them into minute dice. If you have fresh galangal, peel and dice it just as you have the ginger. Peel the garlic and shallots and chop them finely.

Set a wok over a high heat. When it is hot, swirl in the oil. When the oil is hot, put in the chillies, ginger, galangal, garlic, shallots and curry (or bay) leaves. Stir and fry briefly. As soon as the spices start to brown, put in the green beans, carrots and salt. Stir and fry for a minute. Put in 6 fl oz (175 ml) water and cover. Turn the heat to medium and cook for about 5 minutes or until the vegetables are just tender.

SERVES 4

MOO PAD PRIK SAI TUA FAK YAO   THAILAND

STIR-FRIED GREEN BEANS WITH PORK AND CHILLIES

Versions of this dish are to be found in many parts of South-East Asia. I met an official in Hanoi who often lunches on this in his office. In the Sichuan province of China, beans are cooked with similar seasonings, but soy sauce is used instead of fish sauce. This particular recipe comes from a long-toothed lady with a food stall ensconced right in the middle of the Weekend Market in Bangkok. She served it to me for lunch along with a plate of plain rice. It was a simple but quite memorable meal.

You may make these beans as hot as you like by increasing the number of chillies. In Thailand fresh hot red chillies are used and they not only contrast stunningly in flavour with the green beans and brown pork, but add bright flecks of colour as well. I tend to use green chillies as they are easier to find at my grocer's. If you like, you can throw in a small amount of finely diced red pepper in the last five minutes of cooking, just for the colour. In Thailand long beans are preferred. If you cannot obtain them, use ordinary string beans.

1¼ lb (500 g) green beans

12–16 cloves garlic

6–9 fresh hot green or red chillies

5 tablespoons vegetable oil

10 oz (275 g) lean pork, minced

½ teaspoon paprika

1 teaspoon dark brown sugar

3 tablespoons fish sauce or salt to taste

Wash and trim the beans. Cut them crossways into ¼–⅓ inch (0.5–0.75 cm) rounds. Peel the garlic and chop it finely. Cut the chillies crossways into very thin slices.

Put the oil in a wok and set it over a medium-high heat. When the oil is hot, put in the garlic and green chillies. Stir and fry until the garlic turns golden, then add the pork. Stir and fry, breaking up any lumps, until the pork has losts its raw look. Put in the beans, paprika, sugar, fish sauce and 10 fl oz (300 ml) water. Stir and cook on a medium-high heat for about 8–10 minutes or until the beans are tender and most of the water has been absorbed.

SERVES 4

JAPAN

GREEN BEANS WITH SESAME DRESSING

FROM THE TAWARAYA INN IN KYOTO

You may choose from a variety of green beans to make this dish. French *haricots verts* should be trimmed and cut into 1½ inch (4 cm) lengths; all other green beans, the rounded and flat varieties, may be either sliced diagonally or first cut into 2 inch (5 cm) lengths and then into thin slivers.

This dish may be served as an appetiser or as an accompanying vegetable with any meat or fish. It may be made ahead of time and refrigerated. Take it out of the refrigerator at least 20 minutes before serving.

12 oz (350 g) green beans

1 tablespoon salt

10 fl oz (300 ml) Japanese Soup Stock (see page 66) or chicken stock at room temperature, lightly salted to taste

2½ tablespoons sesame seeds

About 1½ tablespoons Japanese soy sauce (shoyu)

1 tablespoon *mirin* or 1½ teaspoons sugar dissolved in 1½ teaspoons of the above stock

Trim the beans and cut as suggested above. Bring a large pan of water to a rolling boil. Add about 1 tablespoon salt to it and put in the beans. Boil rapidly for 2–5 minutes or until the beans are just tender but still crisp. Drain and quickly plunge them into cold water to set the colour. Drain again and put the beans into a bowl. Pour the stock over them and set aside for 30 minutes or longer.

Now prepare the dressing. Put the sesame seeds in a small cast-iron frying-pan set over a medium-high heat. Stir the seeds about for a few minutes until they are roasted and give out a nutty aroma. Reserve about ½ tablespoon of the seeds for garnishing the dish. Grind the rest in a clean coffee grinder, then empty them into a bowl. Add the soy sauce, *mirin* and 1 tablespoon stock taken from the soaking beans. (If you are using sugar and stock instead of *mirin*, just take another 1½ teaspoons of stock from the beans.) Mix well.

Drain the beans thoroughly. (Save the stock for soup or another dish.) Put them into a bowl, add the dressing and mix. To serve, Japanese-style, pile the beans in a little hillock in the centre of each of 4 small bowls or plates. Sprinkle the reserved roasted sesame seeds over the top of each serving.

SERVES 4

KERABU TAWGEH   MALAYSIA

BEAN SPROUTS WITH A SPICY COCONUT DRESSING

FROM AMINAHBI AT RESTORAN MINAH IN PENANG

Here is a very simple refreshing vegetable dish-cum-salad. It has an unusual dressing of lime juice, tomatoes and roasted coconut. If you cannot get fresh coconut, use unsweetened desiccated coconut and roast it *before* soaking it in hot water.

3 tablespoons uncooked rice

4 oz (100 g) fresh coconut, grated (see page 262) or 2 oz (50 g) unsweetened desiccated coconut

3 oz (75 g) red pepper

2 teaspoons shrimp or anchovy paste (optional)

3 tablespoons lime or lemon juice

2 tinned peeled plum tomatoes, lightly drained

¼ teaspoon chilli powder or to taste

1½ teaspoons salt

1½ teaspoons sugar

¾ inch (2 cm) cube fresh ginger

2½ oz (65 g) onions

1 lb (450 g) fresh bean sprouts

6 oz (175 g) cabbage

FOR THE GARNISHES (ALL OPTIONAL):

6 cherry or very small tomatoes

2 spring onions

Few tablespoons celery leaves

5–6 fresh hot green chillies

Set a small cast-iron frying-pan over a medium heat. When it is hot, put in the rice. Stir the rice around until it is golden and roasted. Empty the rice on to a plate. Put the coconut into the same frying-pan. Stir and fry it until it is golden-brown in parts. Empty it on to a separate plate; or, if you are using desiccated coconut, put it in a small bowl with 4 fl oz (120 ml) hot water and leave it to soak for 30 minutes. It will absorb most of the liquid. Put the rice into the container of a clean coffee grinder and grind until it is powdery.

De-seed the red pepper and dice it coarsely. Combine the red pepper, shrimp paste (if you are using it), lime juice, tinned tomatoes, chilli powder, salt and sugar in a blender. Blend until smooth.

Peel the ginger and grate it finely. Peel and finely slice the onions. Break off the threadlike tails at the end of each bean sprout, if you feel up to it. Cut the cabbage into fine long shreds.

Set a large pan of water over a high heat. When it comes to a rolling boil, drop in the bean sprouts and cabbage. Let the water return to the boil. Boil for about 1 minute or until the cabbage is barely limp. Drain and rinse under cold running water. Drain thoroughly again.

Prepare the garnishes, if you are including them. Cut the small tomatoes vertically in half.

Cut the spring onions crossways into fine rings. Finely chop the celery leaves. Just before serving, put the bean sprout-cabbage mixture into a bowl. Add the ground rice, roasted coconut, grated ginger and sliced onions. Mix well. Add the sauce from the blender and stir it in. Put the mixture into a serving dish. Sprinkle the spring onions and celery leaves over the top. Garnish the edges with the tomato halves and whole green chillies.

SERVES 4–6

HOBAK NAMUL   KOREA

STIR-FRIED COURGETTES WITH SESAME SEEDS

This superb, gently flavoured dish may be served with almost any Asian meal as well as with roasted and grilled meats. It is good even with sausages and hamburgers.

2 lb (1 kg) medium courgettes

2 teaspoons salt

4 cloves garlic

1 spring onion

3 tablespoons vegetable oil

1 tablespoon sesame oil

2½ tablespoons roasted sesame seeds (see page 270)

Trim the courgettes and cut them in half lengthways. Then cut the halves crossways into ¼ inch (0.5 cm) thick slices and put the slices into a large bowl. Sprinkle 1½ teaspoons of the salt over them, mix well and set aside for 30–40 minutes. Drain thoroughly and pat dry. Meanwhile, peel the garlic and chop it finely. Cut the spring onion into very fine rounds along its entire length.

Set a wok over a high heat. When it is hot, put in the vegetable oil. When the oil has heated, put in the garlic. Stir once or twice or until the garlic begins to colour. Add the courgettes. Stir and fry for 4–5 minutes or until the courgettes are just done. Put in the remaining ½ teaspoon salt, the spring onion and sesame oil. Stir once or twice. Add the roasted sesame seeds. Stir once and serve. This dish may also be served cold as a salad.

SERVES 6

BẦU XÀO   VIETNAM

COURGETTES WITH PORK AND PRAWNS

When I asked a government official in Hanoi what he had had for his lunch that day, he said that he had brought it from home and that it consisted of green beans stir-fried with a little pork and some rice. Vegetables are nearly always cooked with pork or seafood, or both, in Vietnam. The amount of flesh is not necessarily large, but just enough to flavour the vegetables. For this recipe, I buy one large thin-cut pork chop and then take the meat off the bone.

1¼ lb (500 g) courgettes

½ teaspoon salt

4 oz (100 g) uncooked unpeeled prawns

4 oz (100 g) lean pork

2½ oz (65 g) onions

1 clove garlic

7–8 tablespoons fresh coriander leaves

1 spring onion

2 tablespoons vegetable oil

Freshly ground black pepper

2 tablespoons fish sauce or salt to taste

Trim the courgettes and cut them into quarters lengthways. Cut away and discard most of the seeded area. Now cut the courgette shells into fingers that are roughly 2½ inches (6 cm) long, ½ inch (1 cm) thick and ¼ inch (0.5 cm) wide. Put these into a bowl. Add the salt and toss. Set aside for 30 minutes. Then wash the courgettes under cold running water and pat them as dry as possible.

Peel and de-vein the prawns and split them in half lengthways. Hit each half with the flat side of a large knife to discourage its tendency to curl up. Cut the pork into ⅛ inch (0.3 cm) thick slices that are about 2½ inches (6 cm) long and about ¼–½ inch (0.5–1 cm) wide. Peel the onions and garlic and chop them finely. Chop the coriander leaves coarsely. Cut the spring onion into fine rings along its entire length, including the green section.

Put the oil in a large frying-pan or wok and set it over a high heat. When the oil is hot, put in the garlic and onion. Stir and fry for a minute. Add the pork and prawns. Stir and cook for 2 minutes. Then put in the courgettes, black pepper and fish sauce. Stir and fry for about 3 minutes. Add the coriander and spring onion. Stir and cook for 30 seconds. Serve hot.

SERVES 4

GUDANGAN   INDONESIA

CAULIFLOWER AND CARROTS WITH A COCONUT DRESSING

This Javanese dish, eaten with slight variations throughout much of Indonesia, consists of nothing more than blanched mixed vegetables (they could be greens of various sorts or long beans or bean sprouts) which are tossed with an exquisite dressing that includes lime juice, coconut and red pepper. It is an inspired mixture. You may serve it hot, at room temperature or cold, though I feel that it is best to mix the dressing in while the vegetables are still hot.

If you cannot get fresh coconut, use 1 oz (25 g) unsweetened desiccated coconut soaked in 4 tablespoons hot water for 30 minutes. The water will be absorbed by the coconut.

2 lb (1 kg) whole cauliflower (untrimmed weight) or 15 oz (425 g) cauliflower florets

4 oz (100 g) carrots

2 oz (50 g) red pepper

1 clove garlic

4 teaspoons lime or lemon juice

1 teaspoon dark brown sugar

¼ teaspoon chilli powder

4¼ teaspoons salt

2 oz (50 g) fresh coconut, very finely grated (see page 262) or desiccated coconut (see above)

Trim the cauliflower and cut it into slim delicate florets – no head should be wider than 1 inch (2.5 cm) or thicker than ½ inch (1 cm), and no stem longer than 2 inches (5 cm). Trim and peel the carrots. Cut them crossways into 2 inch (5 cm) lengths. Quarter the thick end of each carrot lengthways and cut the thinner portions in half lengthways.

Coarsely chop the red pepper, discarding the seeds. Peel and chop the garlic. In an electric blender combine the red pepper, garlic, lime juice, sugar, chilli powder and ¼ teaspoon salt. Blend until smooth. Taste the dressing; you may wish to add a little more salt.

Just before you are ready to eat, bring 8 pints (4.5 litres) water to a rolling boil in a large pan. Throw in 4 teaspoons salt and stir it in. Put in the cauliflower and carrots and boil rapidly for several minutes or until the vegetables are just tender but still retain a hint of crispness. Drain them quickly and put them into a serving bowl. Toss the vegetables first with the dressing and then with the coconut. Serve immediately.

SERVES 4

PAK BUNG LOY FA   THAILAND

Greens with Garlic and Oyster Sauce or 'Flying' Greens

It all started, apparently, in the northern town of Phitsanulok with a simple stir-fried dish of swamp morning glory. These greens, also known as swamp cabbage and water spinach (*pak bung* and *kangkung*), grow in or near water, are cheap, nourishing and utterly delicious, and are routinely eaten throughout South-East Asia.

One day, or so this recent legend goes, a young chef in an open-air restaurant, having stir-fried the dish in a wok, tossed the dish into the air a few times before transferring it to a serving plate. He noticed that he had an audience. He threw it higher the next time, then higher and higher until he made an act out of it. Soon he was not content with throwing the greens 20 feet into the air and catching them. He decided to throw them across the street where an acrobatic second chef ran to catch them on a serving plate. Of course, a few strands did end up on telephone wires and in trees, but the dining audience was hooked! Nowadays members of the same family do their 'act' in Chiang Mai and Pattaya as well, to great acclaim.

The greens taste good even if they are not air-borne before being eaten. Most of us cannot get swamp morning glory, but luckily any greens will do – young spring greens, spinach, Swiss chard, the Chinese *choi sam* and *gai lan*.

In Chiang Mai, where I saw these greens being prepared, the ingredients were combined on a plate and then emptied into a very hot wok encircled by billowing flames. Because most of us cannot expect to get this sort of intense heat in our kitchens at home, I put the ingredients in in my own slower order.

12 oz (350 g) spring greens (trimmed weight)

3 cloves garlic

2 tablespoons any meat, poultry or vegetable stock or water

1 tablespoon oyster sauce

2 teaspoons crushed yellow bean sauce or soy sauce

3 tablespoons vegetable oil

Separate the leaves of the greens and trim them. Bring a large pan of water to a rolling boil. Drop in the greens and boil them at a high temperature for a few minutes or until they are just tender. Drain immediately and plunge them into cold water to fix the colour. Drain thoroughly.

Peel the garlic and chop it finely. Combine the stock, oyster sauce and yellow bean sauce.

Set a wok over a high heat. When it is hot, put in the oil and let it heat. Then put in the garlic.

Stir quickly once or twice or until the garlic is light brown, then add the greens. Stir them about for a brief minute. Add the stock mixture and stir and cook, still on a high heat, for another minute or so. Pour out the liquid, if there is any, into a serving dish. Give the greens another stir and then lift them out, laying them over the liquid in the dish.

SERVES 4

SITSARO GUISADO   PHILIPPINES

MANGE-TOUT STIR-FRIED WITH PRAWNS

FROM TITO REY'S RESTAURANT IN MANILA

Many vegetables in the Philippines are cooked with just a few chopped prawns or cockles or bits of pork in order to flavour them gently. This exquisite dish fits just as successfully into Western meals as it does into Eastern ones.

12 oz (350 g) mange-tout

3 cloves garlic

1 oz (25 g) onion

About 4 medium uncooked unpeeled prawns

3 tablespoons olive oil

½ teaspoon salt

4 tablespoons stock (pork, chicken and pork, chicken or duck)

Freshly ground black pepper

Snap the stem off each mange-tout and then drag it along the 'backbone' of the pod in order to string it. Peel the garlic and chop it finely. Peel the onion and chop it finely too. Peel and de-vein the prawns. Wash them and pat them dry. Cut them crossways into ¼ inch (0.5 cm) pieces.

Put the oil in a large wok or frying-pan and set it over a medium-high heat. When the oil is hot, put in the garlic and onion. Stir for about 30 seconds or until the garlic and onion turn golden. Add the prawns. Stir for 30 seconds and then put in the mange-tout. Stir for another 30 seconds. Add the salt and stir to mix. Put in the stock and cover immediately. Cook on a medium-high heat for about 1½ minutes or until the vegetables are just done. Sprinkle the black pepper over the top, mix and serve.

SERVES 4

SALA LOBAK INDONESIA

CABBAGE STIR-FRIED WITH RED PEPPER PASTE

I discovered this absolutely delicious dish in the remote hills of Western Sumatra. Even though there was an array of fine foods laid out on the floor-cloth – curries of beef, chicken and fish – all hands went first to the cabbage and it was, indeed, the dish that was finished first.

There are two points of interest here. First, only the dark outer leaves of cabbage were cooked. I can think of no better way to use up a portion of a vegetable that is normally thrown away. If you are slightly short of the required weight of dark leaves, as I often am, use some of the inner cabbage as well. The mixture is exceedingly pleasant. Second, a small flat piece of dried fish was fried and added to the seasoning. I use a small amount of shrimp or anchovy paste instead.

You may serve this dish with any Eastern meal. It also goes particularly well with roast pork, roast lamb and various chops and cutlets.

1 lb (450 g) dark outer cabbage leaves or cabbage greens or spring greens

4 oz (100 g) red pepper

2 oz (50 g) shallots or onions

2 large cloves garlic

½ teaspoon shrimp or anchovy paste (optional)

¼ teaspoon chilli powder

6 tablespoons vegetable oil

½ teaspoon salt

Wash the cabbage leaves. Stacking several of them together, cut them crossways into long, fine, ⅛ inch (0.3 cm) wide shreds. Remove the seeds from the red pepper and chop it coarsely. Peel the shallots and garlic and chop them coarsely. Combine the red pepper, shallots, garlic, shrimp paste, chilli powder and 3 tablespoons water in an electric blender. Blend until a coarse paste results – it should not be too smooth.

Set a wok over a high heat. When it is hot, put in the oil. Once the oil has heated, put in the spice paste. Stir and fry for about 5 minutes or until the oil separates and the mixture has a dark red appearance. Add the cabbage and salt and stir for 30 seconds. Cover tightly, turn the heat to medium-low and cook for 8–10 minutes or until the cabbage is just done. (No water should be needed, but check after 5–6 minutes.)

SERVES 4

Prawn and vegetable fritters (page 163)

Grilled mackerel with sweet soy sauce (page 160) and
Ginger shreds in sweet vinegar (page 235)

Stir-fried green beans with pork and chillies (page 176)

Top: *Mange-tout stir-fried with prawns (page 183);*
bottom: *Smoky aubergines in a lime sauce (page 173)*

Rice with seafood, chicken and sausages (page 210)

Bottom: *Noodles in broth with poached egg and vegetables (page 222); top: Rice noodles in a coconut curry soup (page 220)*

Bottom: *Candied walnut halves (page 255)*; top:
Caramel custard Filipino-style (page 248)

Fresh Fruit (page 244) — see key opposite.

LIANG BAN YANGCAI   HONG KONG

SALAD OF CARROTS, CELERY, CUCUMBER AND HAM

FROM BERNADETTE AU-YEUNG

This Shanghai-style salad is normally made with the addition of vermicelli-like strands of vegetable gelatine known as agar-agar. Most health food shops stock agar-agar, but unfortunately they sell only a powdered version. Since the supply of the stranded version is limited to Chinese and Asian grocers, I have excluded it here. If you can find it, cut about ⅓ oz (12 g) into 2 inch (5 cm) lengths with a pair of scissors and then soak it for 30 minutes in 15 fl oz (450 ml) water. Drain, pat it dry and add it to the salad ingredients. The dressing should, in any case, be mixed in only at the last minute.

4 oz (100 g) carrots

2½ oz (65 g) celery

5½ oz (165 g) cucumber

1 oz (25 g) lean ham

1 tablespoon Chinese light soy sauce

1 tablespoon distilled white vinegar

1 tablespoon sesame oil

¼ teaspoon sugar

Peel the carrots and cut them into fine, 2 inch (5 cm) long julienne strips. Cut the celery crossways into 2 inch (5 cm) lengths and then cut the segments lengthways into fine julienne strips. Fill a medium-sized pan with water and bring it to a rolling boil. Drop in the carrots and celery and leave them for 30–40 seconds. (The water may not even come to the boil again during this time.) Drain the vegetables and immediately run cold water over them. Drain them again and put them into a bowl.

Peel the cucumber, cut it into fine, 2 inch (5 cm) long julienne strips and add it to the bowl of vegetables. Cut the ham into fine, 2 inch (5 cm) long julienne strips as well. Wrap it in cling-film and refrigerate if necessary.

Mix the soy sauce, vinegar, sesame oil and sugar in a small bowl and set aside. Just before serving, combine the vegetables and ham. Stir the dressing, pour it over the salad and toss to mix.

SERVES 4

Key to colour plate opposite
See pages 244–8 for identification of fruit.

NỘM SU HÀO   VIETNAM

KOHLRABI OR BROCCOLI STEM SALAD

FROM LƯU THANH NHÀN IN HANOI

This very popular and delicious salad is served at most weddings in north Vietnam. It calls for kohlrabi, a vegetable which is probably still unfamiliar to many Westerners. When I was a child growing up in India, we, the four girls, insisted that our father grow it in our vegetable garden. We loved it with a passion and devoured it raw while it was still young and tender. I did not care for it in its cooked version then, though I have since completely changed my mind and now love it in all its forms.

Kohlrabi belongs to the cabbage family. You have probably seen it in Indian or South-East Asian grocers' shops. It consists of a pale green or purple turnip-shaped ball from which grow long edible leaves. Only the ball itself is required for this recipe (some shops sell only the ball). If you cannot obtain it, use the larger stems from heads of broccoli. Peel them before cutting them into julienne strips. You will need 8 oz (225 g) peeled stems. The taste of the two is almost identical. When cutting kohlrabi, you will notice that almost a quarter of the bottom end is fibrous and very hard. This may be cut away entirely and discarded.

14 oz (400 g) whole kohlrabi with leaves (peeled weight 8 oz/225 g) or broccoli stems (see above)

2 oz (50 g) carrot

Salt

4 teaspoons distilled white vinegar

1 teaspoon sugar

⅛ teaspoon chilli powder

10–12 fresh mint leaves

2–3 tablespoons fresh coriander leaves

1 fresh hot red or green chilli (optional)

1½ oz (40 g) Roasted Peanuts (see page 236)

Peel the kohlrabi and cut it lengthways into ¹⁄₁₆ inch (0.15 cm) thick slices. Stacking a few slices at a time together, cut it lengthways again into ¹⁄₁₆ inch (0.15 cm) thick julienne strips. Peel the carrot and cut it crossways into 1½–2 inch (4–5 cm) long segments. (They should be the same length as the kohlrabi pieces.) Cut these segments into ¹⁄₁₆ inch (0.15 cm) thick julienne strips.

Put the kohlrabi and carrot into a bowl. Add 1 teaspoon salt and mix thoroughly with your hands. Set aside for 10–15 minutes. The kohlrabi will begin to sweat. Squeeze out as much moisture as you can and pat dry. Wipe the bowl dry and put the vegetables back in it. Add the vinegar, sugar, chilli powder and another ¼ teaspoon or so of salt. Toss and mix. Taste the salad and adjust the seasoning if necessary. Tear up the mint leaves and put them, along with the coriander leaves, into the salad. Toss to mix.

Cut the chilli into fine shreds. Chop the peanuts coarsely. Just before serving, put the peanuts into the salad and toss. Garnish the top of the salad with the chilli shreds.

SERVES 4

KINOKO NO AEMONO   JAPAN

Mushrooms in a Spring Onion Dressing

The mushrooms remain raw in this recipe so it is best to get very fresh unblemished ones. If you cannot obtain Japanese rice vinegar, use 3 tablespoons distilled white vinegar mixed with 1 tablespoon water and ¼ teaspoon sugar.

14 oz (400 g) large fresh mushrooms (preferably with 2 inch (5 cm) caps)

5 spring onions

2 tablespoons Japanese soy sauce (shoyu)

4 tablespoons Japanese rice vinegar

3 tablespoons *sake*

½ teaspoon salt

Wipe the mushrooms with a damp cloth. If they are large, quarter them. If they are smaller, halve them. Cut the spring onions crossways into very fine rounds along their entire length, including the green section. Then chop these rounds finely.

Put the mushrooms and onions in a bowl. Add all the other ingredients and toss. Let the mushrooms sit in their dressing for 5 minutes and then toss again. Wait for another 5 minutes and toss once more. The mushrooms are now ready to be served.

SERVES 4

PEPES JAMUR INDONESIA

SPICED MUSHROOMS IN A PACKET

I was driving through Jogyakarta's university area with Sri Owen, the noted Indonesian food specialist, when she brought the car to an abrupt halt. She pointed to a lone vendor on a bicycle, saying, 'There, there he is,' and hopped out, only to return with several banana leaf packets of some of the tastiest mushrooms I had ever eaten. Fresh straw mushrooms, which I am very partial to anyway, had been tossed with a spicy coconut mixture, wrapped up in banana leaves and steamed. Fresh straw mushrooms may not be available to us in the West (I keep hoping that this will change soon), but I find that ordinary white mushrooms make a good substitute in this recipe. Instead of steaming them, I have baked my mushroom packets. If you cannot get fresh coconut soak 1 oz (25 g) unsweetened desiccated coconut in 4 tablespoons boiling water for 30 minutes. Most of the water will become absorbed.

2 oz (50 g) fresh coconut, very finely grated (see page 262) or desiccated coconut (see above)

1 large clove garlic

2 tablespoons lime or lemon juice

1–2 fresh hot green or red chillies

½ teaspoon shrimp or anchovy paste

⅛ teaspoon chilli powder

¾ teaspoon salt

8 oz (225 g) fresh mushrooms

If you are using unsweetened desiccated coconut, soak it in 4 tablespoons boiling water for 30 minutes. Peel the garlic and crush it or put it through a press. Add it to the lime juice. Chop the chillies very finely. Combine the garlic-lime juice mixture, chillies, shrimp paste, coconut, chilli powder and salt in a large bowl and mix well.

Pre-heat the oven to gas mark 4, 350°F (180°C). Wipe the mushrooms with a damp cloth and cut them into ¼ inch (0.5 cm) thick slices. Put the mushrooms into the bowl with the spices. Toss well. Prepare a large piece of aluminium foil about 18 inches (45 cm) long. Empty the tossed mushrooms and all the spices right in the centre of it. Fold the foil over the mushrooms from the top and the bottom and then from the sides to make a neat packet. Place the packet in the oven and bake for 30 minutes. Open carefully and empty the mushrooms into a serving bowl.

SERVES 4

Seasoned Spinach

Even though this recipe comes from Korea, a very similar dish is eaten in Japan as well. Both are offered at room temperature in relatively small quantities and serve as appetisers. The Koreans tend to put the entire amount on to a single plate while the Japanese divide it up into individual portions and serve it mounded up into tiny hillocks.

10 oz (275 g) fresh spinach

Salt

1½ tablespoons sesame seeds

1½ tablespoons Japanese soy sauce (shoyu)

1 teaspoon sugar

1 tablespoon sesame oil

Trim the spinach, separate the leaves, and wash them well. Bring a large pan of lightly salted water to a rolling boil and drop in the spinach. Boil it rapidly until the leaves have wilted. Drain well and immediately plunge the spinach into cold water to set the colour. Drain and squeeze out as much water as possible. Cut the spinach into 2 inch (5 cm) lengths.

Now make the dressing. Put the sesame seeds into a small cast-iron frying-pan set over a medium-high heat. Stir the seeds about for a few minutes until they are roasted and give out a nutty aroma. Empty the seeds into a clean coffee grinder or mortar and grind them coarsely. Put the ground seeds into a bowl. Add the soy sauce, sugar and sesame oil and mix together. Pour the dressing over the spinach and mix well. Taste to check whether the seasoning is as you like it. Add more soy sauce if you think you need it and mix again.

SERVES 4

PAD PAK BUNG   THAILAND

SPINACH WITH GARLIC AND FISH SAUCE

Here is a simple and delicious way to cook spinach in the Thai style.

1¾ lb (750 g) fresh spinach

3 cloves garlic

5 tablespoons vegetable oil (preferably groundnut)

4–5 teaspoons fish sauce or salt to taste

Pull the spinach leaves apart and wash them well. Drain. Bring a large pan of water to a rolling boil. Drop in the spinach. Bring the water to the boil again, and boil rapidly for 2 minutes or until the spinach is just done. Drain and rinse under cold running water to fix the bright green colour. Drain again.

Peel the garlic and chop it finely. Put the oil in a wok or large frying-pan and set it over a medium-high heat. When the oil is hot, put in the garlic. Stir a few times or until the garlic turns golden. Add the spinach. Stir and fry for 3 minutes. Add the fish sauce or salt, a little at a time, stirring and tasting as you go. Cook for another minute, stirring frequently.

SERVES 4–6

GADO-GADO   INDONESIA

SALAD OF ASSORTED VEGETABLES WITH A DELICIOUS PEANUT DRESSING

My family's idea of a perfect lunch is *gado-gado*. It is light and meatless, which suits us in the middle of the day. It also happens to be mouth-wateringly good and totally satisfying in a way many so-called 'light' salads are not.

This Indonesian favourite may be described as a composed salad: vegetables of various humble sorts (cabbage, cauliflower, green beans, bean sprouts, carrots, potatoes, cucumbers), as well as hard-boiled eggs, are all neatly laid out on individual plates. Then a kind of cooked vinaigrette, rich with crushed peanuts, is poured over the top. The result is as magical as it is nutritious.

Even though I have suggested what vegetables to include in this recipe, you may change them or their quantities according to what you have available. It is the perfect way to use up the odd few carrots or the remaining quarter of a cabbage!

All the parts of this salad may be prepared several hours ahead of time. It can also be assembled in advance and covered with cling-film until you are ready to eat. The dressing should, however, be poured on at the last minute. In Indonesia Prawn Wafers (*krupuk udang*, page 63) are always served on the side. You may do without them if you wish.

9 oz (250 g) potatoes
  (preferably new)

3 eggs

4 oz (100 g) green beans

3 oz (75 g) carrots

5 oz (150 g) cauliflower

4 oz (100 g) cabbage

4 oz (100 g) bean sprouts

5 oz (150 g) cucumber

2 teaspoons salt

FOR THE PEANUT DRESSING:

4 oz (100 g) Roasted Peanuts
  (see page 236)

2 cloves garlic

1 oz (25 g) shallots or onion

2 tablespoons vegetable oil

½ teaspoon chilli powder

½ teaspoon salt

2 teaspoons dark brown sugar

Freshly ground black pepper

4–5 teaspoons lime or lemon
  juice

Set the potatoes to boil. When they are done, cool but do not refrigerate them. Peel them and cut them into ¼ inch (0.5 cm) thick slices. Hard-boil the eggs. Shell them and cut them lengthways into quarters.

Keep all the raw vegetables separate as you prepare them. Trim the green beans and cut them into 2 inch (5 cm) lengths. Trim and peel the carrots. Cut them crossways into 2 inch (5 cm) sections and then halve or quarter the sections lengthways so that the carrots match the beans in size. Cut the cauliflower into small delicate florets. Cut the cabbage into fine long shreds. Break off the threadlike tails of the bean sprouts and rinse them well in a bowl of water. Drain. Peel the cucumber and cut it crossways into round slices.

Set a bowl near the stove with a sieve balanced on it. Also set out several plates to hold the different vegetables as they are cooked.

Bring 3½ pints (2 litres) water to a rolling boil in a medium-sized pan. Add 2 teaspoons salt to it and stir. Put the green beans and the carrots together into the boiling water. Let the water come to a rolling boil again and boil rapidly for about 3 minutes or until the vegetables are just cooked through. Empty the contents of the pan, vegetables and water, into the sieve. Lift up the sieve and drain the vegetables. Rinse the vegetables under cold running water and put them on to a plate. Pour the water in the bowl back into the pan and bring it to a rolling boil again. Put the cauliflower into the pan. Let the water return to the boil. Boil the cauliflower rapidly for about 1½ minutes or until it is just tender but retains a hint of crispness. Empty the contents of the pan into the sieve, lift up the sieve and drain the cauliflower. Rinse the cauliflower under cold running water and put it on to a plate. Cook the cabbage and bean sprouts in the same way, boiling the cabbage for about 1 minute and the bean sprouts for 30 seconds. Drain each and refresh under cold running water. Squeeze any excess moisture from the cabbage and bean sprouts and then separate the strands before putting them on to separate plates.

Now make the dressing. Put the peanuts into a clean coffee grinder and grind them as finely as possible. Peel the garlic and shallots and chop them finely. Put the oil in a smallish pan over a medium heat. When it is hot, put in the garlic and shallots. Stir and fry for about 1 minute or until the garlic and shallots have turned a medium brown. Put in 15 fl oz (450 ml) water, the chilli powder, salt, sugar and ground peanuts. Stir and bring to the boil. Turn the heat to medium-low and simmer for 15–20 minutes or until the sauce has thickened. It should be no thicker than a creamy salad dressing. Stir now and then to break up any lumps.

Remove the cooked dressing from the heat and let it cool a little. Add the black pepper, beat in the lime juice and taste to check whether the seasoning is as you like it. Arrange the potatoes, eggs, green beans and carrots, cauliflower, cabbage, bean sprouts and cucumber side by side on 4 individual plates. Just before serving, pour about a quarter of the dressing evenly over each serving.

SERVES 4 AS A MAIN COURSE OR 8 AS A FIRST COURSE OR SALAD

SPICY YELLOW SPLIT PEAS

FROM PUAN RASHIDAH IN KUALA LUMPUR

This was originally a South Indian dish, as its Tamil name attests. It has changed, just very slightly, as it moved through Malaysia. Here, even though the traditional Indian *toovar dal* is preferred, it is harder to find and more expensive. Hence yellow split peas are commonly used instead. This dish may be served with rice or with a bread such as *pitta* or *chappatis*.

10½ oz (280 g) yellow split peas

2 × 2 inch (5 cm) sticks cinnamon

4–8 dried hot red chillies

½ teaspoon ground turmeric

8 oz (225 g) potatoes

1 large clove garlic

½ inch (1 cm) cube fresh ginger

1½ teaspoons salt

7 fl oz (200 ml) coconut milk (see page 263)

1½ oz (40 g) onion

1 teaspoon whole mustard seeds (black or yellow)

½ teaspoon whole fennel seeds

6–8 fresh or dried curry leaves (optional)

4 tablespoons vegetable oil or *ghee*

Wash the peas, drain them and put them in a heavy-bottomed pan. Add the cinnamon, half the red chillies, the turmeric and 1½ pints (900 ml) water. Bring to a simmer. Cover loosely, leaving the lid slightly ajar, and simmer gently for about 45 minutes or until the peas are almost tender.

Meanwhile, peel the potatoes and cut them into pieces about ½ inch (1 cm) thick and about ¾ inch (2 cm) long. Peel the garlic and ginger and cut them into very fine strips. When the peas have cooked for 45 minutes, add the potatoes, garlic, ginger, salt and 4 fl oz (120 ml) water. Bring to a gentle simmer and cook, covered, for about 20 minutes, stirring now and then to prevent sticking. Stir the coconut milk and pour it in. Stir to mix and bring to a simmer. Cover and turn off the heat. Keep in a warm place.

Peel and finely slice the onion. Combine the mustard seeds, fennel seeds, remaining chillies and curry leaves in a small bowl. Heat the oil or *ghee* in a small frying-pan. When it is hot, put in the onion. Stir and fry until the onion turns a medium brown colour. Add the whole seasonings which you have mixed in the small bowl. Stir once or twice. Lift the lid of the pan containing the peas and pour in the entire contents of the frying-pan. Cover immediately to hold in the aromas.

SERVES 4–6

HAOYOU DOUFU   HONG KONG

BEAN CURD WITH OYSTER SAUCE

This dish is made with fried bean curd. Bean curd turns spongy when fried and is better able to absorb sauces.

6–8 dried Chinese mushrooms or large fresh mushroom caps

1 lb (450 g) firm bean curd

Oil for deep-frying

3 tablespoons oyster sauce

1 teaspoon Chinese light soy sauce

2 teaspoons Chinese dark soy sauce

2 teaspoons sugar

4 fl oz (120 ml) plus 1 tablespoon chicken stock

1 teaspoon cornflour

1 clove garlic

4½ oz (120 g) fresh peas (shelled weight) or frozen peas, de-frosted

1 tablespoon sesame oil

Cover the dried mushrooms with warm water and leave to soak for 30 minutes or until soft. Remove them from the water and cut off the hard stems.

Cut the bean curd into slices about ½ × 1½ × 2 inches (0.5 × 3.5 × 5 cm). Spread these between 2 layers of kitchen paper to dry them off.

Put the oil in a wok or deep-fat fryer over a medium-high heat. (It should be about 2 inches (5 cm) deep in the centre of the wok if you are using one.) When the oil is hot, fry the bean curd until golden brown on both sides. Remove it and leave to drain on a plate lined with kitchen paper.

Combine the oyster sauce, light and dark soy sauces, sugar and 4 fl oz (120 ml) chicken stock in a small bowl. Stir to mix. Combine the cornflour and the remaining 1 tablespoon chicken stock in a small cup. Peel the garlic and chop it finely.

Put 2 tablespoons oil in a wok or large frying-pan and set it over a high heat. When the oil is hot, put in the garlic. Stir and fry it for 30 seconds. Put in the Chinese mushrooms or fresh mushroom caps and continue to stir and fry for about 1 minute. Now add the bean curd. Toss it gently with the mushrooms. Put in the oyster sauce mixture. Cover, turn the heat to low and simmer very gently for 8 minutes. Then add the peas. Simmer, covered, for another 2 minutes. Remove the lid and take the wok off the heat. Stir the cornflour mixture and pour it in. Put the wok back on the heat and add the sesame oil. Stir gently and cook on a low heat until the sauce has thickened.

SERVES 4–6

RICE, NOODLES AND PANCAKES

PLAIN LONG-GRAIN RICE

In this recipe and all those following in which rice is used, you will see that
the rice is measured by volume rather than by weight. I prefer to do it this way
because the ratio of rice to cooking liquid is crucial and this method makes for
greater accuracy.

15 fl oz (450 ml) long-grain
rice

Put the rice in a bowl and fill the bowl with water.
Rub the rice gently with your hands. When the
water turns milky, pour it off. Do this several
times in quick succession until the water runs
clear. Now fill the bowl with fresh water and let
the rice soak for 30 minutes. Drain.

Put the drained rice into a heavy medium-sized
pan. Add 1 pint (600 ml) water and bring to the
boil. Cover with a tight-fitting lid. (If your lid is
not the tight-fitting kind, cover the pan first with
aluminium foil, crimping the edges, and then
cover with the lid.) Turn the heat to very low and
cook for 25 minutes. If left covered in a warm
place, this rice will retain its heat for a good hour.

SERVES 4–6

GOHAN, PAB   JAPAN, KOREA

PLAIN JAPANESE AND KOREAN RICE

The rice in Japan and Korea is a fat short-grain variety which develops a most pleasing stickiness when it is cooked. The grains not only adhere to each other, thus making them easy to pick up with chopsticks in small lumps, but they can also be easily rolled into ovals and rounds, all the better to be devoured with neat slivers of raw fish or roasted sesame seeds.

The brand to look for in Asian grocers' shops is *Kokuho Rose*. If you cannot find it, use a Thai or American long-grain rice and cook it according to the recipe for Plain Long-Grain Rice on page 203. Aromatic rices, such as *basmati*, are quite unsuitable for Japanese and Korean meals.

If you wish to cook more or less rice than suggested in the recipe below, remember that the proportion of rice to water, in volume, is 1:1¼. The cooking time remains exactly the same.

15 fl oz (450 ml) Japanese rice

Put the rice in a bowl and add water to cover it generously. Swish the rice around gently with your hand, kneading it lightly as you do so. Pour off the water when it has turned milky. Do this several times in quick succession, until the water remains almost clear. Drain the rice through a sieve. Leave the rice in the sieve for 30 minutes–1 hour to allow it to absorb the moisture that clings to it.

Put the rice into a heavy-bottomed pan. Add 19 fl oz (550 ml) water and bring to the boil. Cover, turn the heat to very low and cook for 20 minutes. Turn the heat to high for 30 seconds and then turn it off. Let the pan sit, covered and undisturbed, for another 10–15 minutes.

SERVES 4–6

$\mathcal{G}$LUTINOUS RICE

Glutinous rice is also known as sticky rice and sweet rice. The grains are short and white and, when cooked, they turn translucent and slightly glutinous. Throughout much of the Far East this rice is used for both sweets and stuffings. In the region around northern Thailand, however, it is the staple grain. At each meal it is served from a large basket. Each diner forms the rice into a little ball, combines that ball with a bit of meat and a bit of vegetable and then pops the morsel into his or her mouth. The two easiest ways to cook this rice are by steaming and by using a double-boiler. Here is the double-boiler method.

15 fl oz (450 ml) glutinous rice	Wash the rice in several changes of water and drain it. Put it in a bowl, cover with plenty of water and leave it to soak for 6 hours. Drain, wash again, and drain thoroughly.
	Heat some water in the bottom of a double-boiler. When it starts to boil, fit in the top of the double-boiler and into it put the rice and enough water to bring the level to ½ inch (1 cm) above the rice. When the water with the rice begins to boil, cover the pan and cook on a medium heat for 25 minutes.

SERVES 4–6

KAYAKU GOHAN   JAPAN

$\mathcal{M}$IXED RICE

ADAPTED FROM A RECIPE OF THE ÉCOLE TECHNIQUE HÔTELIÈRE TSUJI IN OSAKA
This delightful mixture of rice, chicken and vegetables may be served all by itself with accompanying salads (and beer!) or, if you leave the chicken out, it may be served with all manner of simply grilled meats and fish. You may substitute any cubed white fish fillets for the chicken, in which case do not bother with the blanching. The rice will probably develop a slightly brown crustiness at the bottom: this is as it should be.

15 fl oz (450 ml) Japanese rice

2 chicken thighs or 1 whole leg

1 small carrot

4 green beans

1 large or 2 small mushrooms

19 fl oz (550 ml) Japanese Soup Stock (see page 66) or chicken stock

3 tablespoons Japanese soy sauce (shoyu)

2 tablespoons *mirin* (or 1 tablespoon sugar well dissolved in 1 tablespoon *sake* or water)

About 15 mange-tout

Salt

2 tablespoons *sake* (optional)

Put the rice in a bowl and add water to cover it generously. Swish the rice around gently with your hand. Pour off the water when it turns milky. Do this several times in quick succession, until the water remains almost clear. Drain the rice through a sieve and leave it in the sieve for 30 minutes– 1 hour to allow it to absorb the moisture that clings to it.

Meanwhile, bone the chicken (follow the instructions on page 289). Skin the meat and cut it into ¼ inch (0.5 cm) dice. Drop the meat into a pan of boiling water for 10–15 seconds. Drain it quickly, rinse it briefly under cold running water, and then drain thoroughly.

Peel the carrot and cut it into 1 inch (2.5 cm) lengths. Cut these lengths into fine julienne strips. Trim the green beans and cut into 1 inch (2.5 cm) lengths. Cut these lengths into fine julienne strips. Wipe the mushroom with a damp cloth and cut it into thin slices. Cut the slices into fine strips.

Combine the rice, chicken, carrot, green beans, mushroom, stock, soy sauce and *mirin* in a heavy-bottomed pan. Bring the mixture to the boil. Cover tightly, turn the heat to very low and leave to cook for 20 minutes.

While the rice cooks, string the mange-tout and cut them into 1 inch (2.5 cm) lengths. Cut the lengths into fine strips. Throw the mange-tout into a pan of lightly salted boiling water. Boil rapidly for 15–20 seconds. Drain, rinse under cold running water and drain again.

When the rice has been cooking for 20 minutes, lift the lid and quickly put in the mange-tout and *sake*. Cover the pan immediately with a clean teatowel and then with the lid. Take the pan off the heat and set it aside for 10–15 minutes before serving, so that any excess moisture in the rice can be absorbed by the teatowel.

SERVES 4–6

NASI GORENG ISTIMEWA INDONESIA

SPECIAL FRIED RICE WITH BEEF AND PRAWNS

This fried rice, served with Prawn Wafers (page 63) and Red Pepper Sauce (page 231) or Red Pepper Sauce with Shrimp Paste (page 233), can be a meal in itself. In Indonesia hot chillies and cucumbers, cut prettily to resemble tropical flora, decorate the rice plate like bunting, as do Egg Strips (page 237) and Crisply Fried Shallot Flakes (page 240). You may, if you like, chose a simpler garnish of chopped hard-boiled eggs and finely sliced spring onions sprinked over the rice and halved cherry or other small tomatoes and cucumber slices arranged around the edges. Cooked prawns may be used in this dish if uncooked ones are unavailable; if they are small, increase the quantity recommended.

It is a good idea to cook the rice itself well ahead of time so that it has time to cool off completely before you stir-fry it. For the best flavour, the rice should be stir-fried with all the other ingredients just before eating.

10 fl oz (300 ml) long-grain rice

4 oz (100 g) red pepper

1 oz (25 g) shallots or onion

1 teaspoon shrimp or anchovy paste

1 teaspoon salt

¼ teaspoon chilli powder

4 oz (100 g) lean beef steak

4 uncooked unpeeled prawns

2 cabbage leaves

4 tablespoons vegetable oil

Wash the rice in several changes of water, then drain it. Cover it generously with water and leave it to soak for 30 minutes. Drain again. Put the rice into a heavy-bottomed pan. Add 13 fl oz (375 ml) water and bring it to the boil. Cover tightly, turn the heat to very low and cook for 25 minutes. Switch off the heat. Keep the pan covered and let the rice come to room temperature.

Coarsely chop the red pepper, removing all the seeds. Peel and coarsely chop the shallots. Combine the red pepper, shallots, shrimp paste, salt and chilli powder in an electric blender. Blend until a smooth paste results.

Cut the steak across the grain into very thin slices. Cut the slices crossways into ¼ inch (0.5 cm) wide strips. Peel and de-vein the prawns. Cut them crossways into ¼ inch (0.5 cm) wide segments. Cover both and set aside, refrigerating if necessary. Cut the cabbage leaves into very fine long shreds.

Just before you are ready to serve, set a wok over a medium-high heat. When it is hot, put in the oil. When the oil has heated, pour in the spice paste. Stir and fry for 3–4 minutes or until the spice paste turns dark red and the oil separates. Add the beef and prawns. Stir and fry for 1 minute. Add the cabbage. Stir and fry for another minute. Now put in all the rice, breaking up any lumps with the back of a slotted spoon. Stir and fry for 4–6 minutes or until the rice has heated through. Garnish as suggested above, and serve.

SERVES 4

NASI ULAM   MALAYSIA

Perfumed Rice with Vegetables Nonya-Style

FROM THE HYATT SAUJANA HOTEL IN KUALA LUMPUR

This unusual rice dish is first perfumed with fresh herbs, then flavoured with a little fish and finally topped with crunchy raw vegetables. It is exquisite, both in taste and appearance. Rather like fried rice, to which it is a very superior cousin, it may be eaten with other foods or all by itself. Use any tender green beans other than runner beans; in Malaysia long green beans would be used.

If you have an Asian grocer near you, try to obtain fresh lemon grass and fresh kaffir lime leaves as the dry ones just cannot be used in this dish. However, if you cannot get the fresh herbs, all is not lost. Western herbs, such as basil, chervil and summer savory, may be substituted. The aromas are different but they do make the rice very interesting.

In Malaysia, where the climate is generally balmy, this rice is served at room temperature. I prefer to serve it hot or warm.

4–5 fresh kaffir lime leaves or 1½ tablespoons grated lemon rind

1 stick fresh lemon grass or 15 fresh basil leaves, torn into small pieces

2½ oz (65 g) cucumber

Cut the centre vein out of the kaffir lime leaves and then cut the leaves crossways into the thinnest hairlike strips. Trim the lemon grass, discarding its very hard bottom tip and its strawlike top. Cut the rest (which should be about 6 inches (15 cm) long) crossways into very, very thin rounds.

2½ oz (65 g) tender green or long beans (*not* runner beans)

3 medium shallots or ½ small onion

2 oz (50 g) uncooked unpeeled prawns

4 tablespoons vegetable oil

Salt

15 fl oz (450 ml) long-grain rice

Combine with the lime leaves and cover. Peel the cucumber and cut it into ⅛ inch (0.3 cm) dice. If the cucumber has large seeds, discard them and use only the outer seedless section. Trim the ends of the beans and then cut them crossways into ⅛ inch (0.3 cm) pieces. Combine the beans with the cucumber and cover. Peel the shallots and cut them into paper-thin slices. Peel and de-vein the prawns and then cut them crossways into ¼ inch (0.5 cm) segments.

Line a plate with kitchen paper. Put the oil in a frying-pan and set it over a medium heat. When the oil is hot, put in the shallots. Stir and fry until they turn medium brown and crisp. Remove them with a slotted spoon and spread them out over the kitchen paper to drain. Put the cut prawns into the same oil. Stir and fry for about 1 minute or until the prawns are cooked through. Remove them with a slotted spoon and put them into a bowl. Sprinkle the prawns very lightly with salt, toss them and then cover. Save the oil in the pan.

Wash the rice in several changes of water. Drain. Cover well with water, soak for 30 minutes, and then drain again. About 30 minutes–1 hour before you intend to eat, combine the rice, 1 pint (600 ml) water and 1 teaspoon salt in a medium-sized, heavy-bottomed pan. Bring the water to the boil, cover, turn the heat to *very* low and cook for 25 minutes. If you are not eating at once, cover the rice and keep it warm.

Just before serving, empty all the rice into a serving bowl, breaking up any lumps with the back of a slotted spoon. Put in the prawns, the reserved oil in which they were cooked, the kaffir lime leaves and the lemon grass. If you are using basil leaves and lemon rind, add these now. Toss to mix. Scatter the cucumber and beans over the top followed by the fried shallots and serve.

SERVES 4–6

RICE WITH SEAFOOD, CHICKEN AND SAUSAGES

WITH HELP FROM RUBY ROA

One of the glories of Spain, this dish now also decks the tables at fiestas and banquets all over the Philippines. While the main ingredients, rice and a touch of saffron, remain the same (the less affluent use colouring from caper-shaped Mexican *achuete* seeds instead), all other ingredients are left to the whim, and pocket, of the cook. In the poorer *barrios*, chicken, green peas and tomatoes suffice, while in the mansions of the rich, *paellas* come with prawns, squid, clams and mussels peeping invitingly out of the rice.

Traditionally a *paella* was cooked on a *paellera*, and in some homes it still is. A *paellera* is a very large, round tray. Rice is cooked in it rather in the manner of an Italian *risotto* with frequent additions of hot stock and much stirring. Raw, partially cooked and fully cooked meats and seafood are embedded in the rice at frequent intervals and in a sequence that only practised chefs have mastered. All ingredients must be ready at the same time.

Since most of us do not have *paelleras*, here is a delicious *paella* that is cooked in a saucepan. You do need a large, wide, heavy pan with a tight-fitting lid. If you are unsure of the fit of the lid, cover the pan first with aluminium foil.

2 sweet or hot Italian or Spanish sausages (such as *chorizo*), weighing in total about 6 oz (175 g)

2 whole chicken legs, each cut into 3–4 pieces

Salt

Freshly ground black pepper

6 tablespoons olive oil

8 fresh clams

8 fresh mussels

Generous pinch saffron threads

About 15 fl oz (450 ml) chicken stock

12 uncooked unpeeled prawns

3 oz (75 g) red pepper

Prick the sausages with a fork and put them into a frying-pan with 5 fl oz (150 ml) water. Bring to the boil. Cover, turn the heat to medium and cook for 5 minutes. Uncover and continue to cook until the water boils away. Brown the sausages in the fat which they have exuded. Let them cool, then cut them into ¼ inch (0.5 cm) slices.

Dust the chicken lightly with salt and pepper. Put the olive oil in a clean frying-pan and set it over a medium heat. When the oil is hot, put in the chicken pieces and fry them for about 10 minutes or until they are brown on both sides. Remove them with a slotted spoon. Save the oil.

Clean the clams and mussels with a stiff brush under cold running water, pulling off any beards that

3 oz (75 g) green pepper

3½ oz (90 g) onions

3 cloves garlic

6 oz (175 g) fresh peas (shelled weight) or frozen peas

1¼ pints (750 ml) long-grain rice

may still be attached to the mussels. Put the clams and mussels into a pan with 1¼ pints (750 ml) water and bring to the boil. Cover the pan and simmer vigorously over a medium heat for about 5 minutes or until the molluscs open. Remove them as they open and wash them quickly under cold running water if they seem to be gritty. Cool, cover and set aside. Save the cooking liquid. Strain the liquid through a clean cloth and put it in a large measuring jug or bowl. Add the saffron and enough chicken stock to make up 1¾ pints (1 litre).

Peel and de-vein the prawns. Wash them and pat them dry. De-seed the red and green peppers and cut them lengthways into ¼ inch (0.5 cm) wide strips. Peel and thinly slice the onions. Peel and finely chop the garlic.

If the peas are fresh, boil them in 1 pint (600 ml) water until they are just tender. Drain and refresh them under cold running water. Drain again and set them aside. If the peas are frozen, cook them for just 1 minute. Drain them, refresh under cold running water and drain them again.

In a large, wide, heavy pan put 5 tablespoons of the oil used for frying the chicken and set it over a medium-high heat. When the oil is hot, put in the onions and garlic. Fry for about 2½ minutes or until they are soft. Add the peppers. Stir and cook for another 2½ minutes. Now add the rice. Stir and fry for 2 minutes, turning the heat down a little if the rice seems to stick. Add the saffron-flavoured clam-mussel liquor, the sausages, the chicken and 1 teaspoon salt. Bring to the boil. Cover, turn the heat to very low and cook for 20 minutes. Lift the lid and quickly bury the prawns in the rice and scatter the peas over the top. Cover the pan again and cook for another 5 minutes. Lift the lid and quickly put in the clams and mussels. Cover and cook for another 2 minutes.

SERVES 6

NASI TOMAT   MALAYSIA

TOMATO RICE

FROM AMINAHBI AT RESTORAN MINAH IN PENANG

Like many Malaysians, Aminahbi is of mixed Malay and Indian ancestry. Her exquisite food acknowledges her dual heritage with pride, as this recipe shows. When rice is cooked in thick liquid, there is a tendency for the grains on top to remain slightly underdone. The solution is to turn the rice over half-way through the cooking. This has to be done rather fast as the minimum amount of steam should be allowed to escape.

15 fl oz (450 ml) long-grain rice

4 tinned peeled plum tomatoes, lightly drained

4 tablespoons plain yoghurt

2 oz (50 g) shallots or onions

1 inch (2.5 cm) cube fresh ginger

8–10 fresh mint leaves

3 tablespoons vegetable oil

½ teaspoon whole cumin seeds

5 whole cloves

5–6 whole cardamom pods

2 inch (5 cm) stick cinnamon

1 whole star anise

1½ teaspoons salt

Wash the rice in several changes of water. Drain and put it in a bowl. Cover it generously with water and leave it to soak for 30 minutes. Drain. Meanwhile, mash the tomatoes to a pulp. Put the yoghurt in a measuring cup and beat it with a fork until it is smooth and creamy. Add the tomatoes and enough water to make up 1 pint (600 ml). Mix. Peel the shallots and cut into fine slices. Peel the ginger and cut it into very thin slices and then into minute dice. Chop the mint leaves coarsely.

Put the oil in a medium-sized heavy pan and set it over a medium heat. When the oil is hot, put in the cumin, cloves, cardamom, cinnamon and star anise. Stir once or twice and add the shallots. Stir and fry until the shallots are reddish-brown. Put in the ginger and stir once. Add the rice and stir for 2 minutes, turning the heat down a little if the rice starts to stick to the bottom of the pan. Put in the tomato-yoghurt mixture, the salt and the mint. Bring to the boil. Cover well, first with aluminium foil and then with a lid. Turn the heat down to very low and cook for 15 minutes. Lift the lid, gently toss the rice with a slotted spoon so that the top layer is well buried at the bottom, cover again and continue cooking for another 15 minutes or until the rice is done.

SERVES 4–6

GANJA BUCHIN   KOREA

Potato Pancakes

Koreans eat these scrumptious, slightly glutinous pancakes as a snack with a spicy dipping sauce. They can also be served as part of a meal. I often serve them at brunch or at breakfast along with scrambled eggs. Once the potatoes have been grated and the batter mixed, you need to proceed apace and cook all the pancakes, for the batter tends to darken if not used straight away. Use 2 frying-pans at once if necessary. If you wish to make more than 8 pancakes, make another batch of fresh batter.

Korean Dipping Sauce (see page 230)
8 oz (225 g) potatoes
1 oz (25 g) onion
1 egg
1½ tablespoons cornflour
¼ teaspoon salt
3–4 tablespoons vegetable oil

Make the Korean Dipping Sauce. Peel the potatoes and put them into a bowl of water. Peel the onion and chop it very finely. Beat the egg and set it aside. Measure out the cornflour and mix it with the salt. Just before eating, grate the potatoes finely so that they turn into pulp. Add the onion, egg and the cornflour-salt mixture to them. Mix well.

Put just enough oil into 2 large frying-pans to coat the bottom and set each over a medium heat. When the oil is hot, drop 1 rounded tablespoon batter into a corner of a frying-pan, spreading it out with the back of a spoon until the pancake is about 3 inches (7.5 cm) in diameter. You should be able to fit 4 pancakes into 1 large frying-pan. Cook each pancake for 2–3 minutes on the first side, or until it turns reddish-brown. Turn the pancakes over and cook on the second side for another 2–3 minutes, or until that side develops reddish spots. Serve hot with the Korean Dipping Sauce.

MAKES 8 SMALL PANCAKES AND SERVES 2–4

BON BON JIHAN BANMIAN   HONG KONG

COLD SESAME NOODLES WITH CHICKEN AND VEGETABLES

FROM BERNADETTE AU YEUNG

The noodles in this dish can be cooked in advance, rinsed in cold water and then tossed with a little sesame oil. All the other parts of the dish can be prepared ahead of time as well. All you need to do at the last minute is mix everything together in a large bowl. It is, as a result, a perfect party dish. I have served it both as a first course and as a main dish.

8 oz (225 g) fresh or dried egg noodles (preferably fresh Chinese)

1 tablespoon sesame oil

4 oz (100 g) chicken breast, skinned and boned

Salt

2 oz (50 g) carrot

2 oz (50 g) celery

2 spring onions

4 oz (100 g) cucumber

FOR THE SAUCE:

4 tablespoons sesame paste

2 tablespoons sesame oil

2 teaspoons Chilli Oil (see page 227)

2 tablespoons Chinese light soy sauce

1 tablespoon distilled white vinegar

1 teaspoon sugar

⅛–¼ teaspoon chilli powder (optional)

5 tablespoons chicken stock

Bring a large pan of water to a rolling boil. Drop in the noodles and cook for 3–5 minutes or until they are just done. Drain. Rinse with cold water and drain again. Put them into a bowl, add the 1 tablespoon sesame oil and toss. Cover well with clingfilm and set aside, refrigerating if necessary.

Cut the piece of chicken breast lengthways into ¾ inch (2 cm) wide strips. Put the chicken strips in a medium-sized pan along with ¼ teaspoon salt and enough water just to cover the meat. Slowly bring to a simmer. Continue to simmer gently for 2–4 minutes or until the meat turns white all the way through. Drain the meat and allow it to cool. (Save the stock for use in this recipe or another dish.) Using both your hands, pull the cooked chicken into fine long shreds. Put the shredded chicken into a bowl.

Peel the carrot and cut it into 2 inch (5 cm) long, very fine julienne strips. Cut the celery and spring onions crossways into 2 inch (5 cm) long sections and then cut the sections lengthways into very fine strips. Bring a medium-sized pan of water to a rolling boil. Drop in the carrot and celery. Bring to the boil again and cook rapidly for 40 seconds. Drop in the spring onions and boil for another 10 seconds. Drain the vegetables and rinse them under cold running water. Drain again and pat dry. Put the vegetables in the bowl with the chicken, keeping aside just a few pieces for garnishing the finished dish. Peel the cucumber and cut it crossways into 2 inch (5 cm) chunks. Cut these chunks lengthways into fine julienne strips. Put most of these strips into the bowl with the chicken, saving a few for garnishing. Cover the chicken bowl with cling-film and refrigerate, if necessary. Wrap the vegetables reserved for garnishing in a piece of cling-film and set aside.

Now make the sauce. Put the sesame paste in a bowl and stir it well. Slowly add all the other sauce ingredients, mixing as you go. (You could do this in a blender if you wish.) Set aside. Just before you are ready to serve, put the noodles in a bowl. Add the chicken and vegetables. Stir the sauce and pour it over the top. Toss well and taste to check whether the seasoning is as you like it. Transfer to a serving dish or individual plates. Top with the vegetables reserved for garnishing.

SERVES 3 AS A MAIN COURSE OR 6 AS A FIRST COURSE

CHAPCHAE   KOREA

CELLOPHANE NOODLES WITH BEEF AND VEGETABLES

Also called transparent bean thread noodles, pea starch noodles and bean
sticks, cellophane noodles are made from mung beans. They can be put into
soups and combined with almost any meat and vegetable. Here is a Korean way
of preparing them:

2 oz (50 g) cellophane noodles

4 spring onions

4 cloves garlic

5 oz (150 g) tender beef steak

4 teaspoons plus 1 tablespoon
soy sauce (preferably
Japanese – shoyu)

4 teaspoons sugar

Freshly ground black pepper

1 tablespoon plus 1 teaspoon
sesame oil

5 dried Chinese mushrooms

1 medium carrot

1 small courgette

5 oz (150 g) fresh spinach

5 tablespoons vegetable oil

Salt

1 tablespoon roasted sesame
seeds (see page 270)

Put the cellophane noodles in a bowl. Pour warm
water over them and let them soak for 30 minutes–
1 hour or until they are soft. Drain them and cut
them into 3 inch (7.5 cm) lengths. Cut the spring
onions into 3 inch (7.5 cm) lengths. Cut each piece
lengthways into 2–3 strips. Peel the garlic and
chop it finely.

Cut the beef against the grain into very thin
slices. Cut these slices, also against the grain, into
thin julienne strips, each around 3 inches (7.5 cm)
long. In a small bowl combine the beef with 4
teaspoons of the soy sauce, 2 teaspoons of the
sugar, 1 tablespoon of the spring onions, 1
teaspoon of the garlic, some black pepper and 1
tablespoon of the sesame oil. Toss to mix.

Soak the dried mushrooms in enough hot water
to cover for 30 minutes or until they are soft. Lift
them out of the water and cut off their hard stems.
Slice the caps into ⅛ inch (0.3 cm) thick strips.
Peel the carrot and cut it into 3 inch (7.5 cm)
lengths. Cut each section lengthways into thin
slices and then into fine julienne strips. Trim the
courgette and cut it lengthways into quarters. Cut
away the seeded sections and then cut the lengths
into 3 inch (7.5 cm) segments. Cut each segment
into long julienne strips. Wash the spinach
thoroughly and discard any tough stems. Drop the
spinach into a pan of boiling water. Boil for

1 minute or until the spinach has wilted. Drain and rinse under cold running water. Squeeze out as much water as possible and then separate the leaves. Combine the carrot, courgette, spinach and remaining spring onions in a bowl.

Put 3 tablespoons of the vegetable oil in a wok or very large frying-pan over a high heat. When the oil is hot, put in the remaining garlic. Stir and fry for 30 seconds. Empty the bowl of vegetables into the wok. Stir and fry for 3–4 minutes or until they are tender-crisp. Salt and pepper lightly. Toss. Take the vegetables out of the wok and put them back into the bowl. Put the remaining 2 tablespoons vegetable oil into the wok. When the oil is hot, put in the meat and sliced mushrooms. Stir and fry for 1–2 minutes or until the meat is just cooked through. Remove the meat and mushrooms with a slotted spoon, leaving the juices, if any, behind.

Turn the heat to low, add 2 fl oz (50 ml) water to the wok along with the remaining 1 tablespoon soy sauce and 2 teaspoons sugar. Mix, then turn the heat to medium. Put in the cellophane noodles. Cook for about 2 minutes or until the noodles are heated through and tender. Empty the noodles and liquid into a serving bowl. Add the meat and mushrooms, the vegetables, the remaining 1 teaspoon sesame oil and the roasted sesame seeds. Toss and serve.

SERVES 4

PHO^z   VIETNAM

RICE NOODLES IN SOUP WITH BEEF

FROM NGUYỄN VĂN Y IN HANOI

In Vietnam *phở^z*, a soupy dish which derives its name from the fresh rice
noodles that are in it, is a meal in itself. Millions of Vietnamese eat it for
breakfast at the crack of dawn as they sit hunched in small restaurants, their
chopsticks digging in with gusto. It is quite a sight. In Hanoi I saw huge
cauldrons of all-purpose stock boiling away in the fronts of restaurants. A peep
inside revealed beef and pork bones, chicken carcasses, chunks of fresh root
ginger and onions. As orders came in – and at dawn they come fast – slithery
white noodles were dipped in hot water to be heated and then divided into
several bowls at the same time. They were topped with slices of cooked chicken
or, for those who could afford it, beef, which is preferred rare. A veritable
salad of fresh green herbs and seasonings, rich in vitamins, went in next: mints,
coriander, spring onions and hot green chillies. Finally, a healthy ladle of the
stock wilted the greens and released their varying aromas.

That was not all. At the table were more seasonings in the form of sauces –
fish sauce, a sauce of hot red chillies and a third one of vinegar and chillies.
There were lime wedges, too, for those who wanted them.

I am told by Vietnamese who have left Vietnam that true *phở^z* is made only
with beef and beef stock and that the use of chicken is a change brought about
by harder times. Here I give the more traditional recipe. Incidentally, even
though *phở^z* is a much loved breakfast food, it is also eaten for lunch and
dinner and as a snack.

The *phở^z* (pronounced 'far') noodle is hard to find in the West except in cities
with large Far Eastern or Chinese populations. Use any fresh flat rice noodle, if
you can find it. Just heat it briefly in boiling water. Dried *phở^z* noodles, usually
sold as *banh phở^z*, are available at many Chinese and Thai grocers' shops. They
need to be soaked in water for 2 hours and then cooked very briefly in boiling
water. If you cannot find any rice noodles, use flat egg noodles as a last resort,
cooking them just before you intend to eat.

---

10 oz (275 g) dried flat rice
  noodles (preferably *banh
  phở^z*) or flat egg noodles
8 oz (225 g) tender beef steak,
  about 1 inch (2.5 cm) thick

If you are using dried rice noodles, soak them in
water for 2 hours or more. Drain them before
cooking. Cut the raw beef steak into paper-thin
slices 1 inch (2.5 cm) wide and 2 inches (5 cm)
long. (It helps if the meat is partially frozen.) Cut

2–3 fresh hot red or green
chillies

1 spring onion

6 tablespoons fresh coriander
leaves

6 tablespoons small fresh mint
leaves

1 lime

Red Pepper Sauce (see page
231)

1 small bowl fish sauce

Seasoned Vinegar (see page
236)

2½ pints (1.5 litres) Beef Stock
(see page 65) plus about ⅓
of the beef brisket used in
making it, wrapped tightly
and refrigerated

the chillies crossways into very thin slices and arrange them at one end of a large plate. Cut the spring onion into very fine rounds along its entire length, including the green section. Heap it up on the plate beside the chilli slices. Wash and dry the coriander leaves, snipping off their coarse stalks. Put the coriander near the onion. Do the same with the mint and put it near the coriander. Cover the plate with cling-film. Cut the lime into wedges. Put the Red Pepper Sauce, fish sauce and the Seasoned Vinegar in separate bowls and set these on the dining table. Put the lime wedges in another small bowl and put it on the table. Cut the cold brisket against the grain into thin slices 1 inch (2.5 cm) wide and 2 inches (5 cm) long.

Heat a large pan of water and drop the drained noodles into it. They will cook very fast – perhaps even in 1 minute – so keep testing them. When they are done, drain the noodles again and rinse them under cold running water. Leave the noodles in a bowl of cold water until they are needed.

Just before serving, heat the stock and keep it warm. To heat the noodles, drain them and then either plunge them into hot water for a few seconds or put them into a microwave oven for 1 minute. (Fresh rice noodles need only to be dropped into boiling water for just a few seconds and then drained. If you are using egg noodles, cook them according to the instructions on the packet.) Divide the noodles among 4–6 individual serving bowls. Arrange a layer of cooked brisket slices over the noodles. On top of the brisket arrange a layer of the raw beef slices. Sprinkle some chilli and onion slices, coriander and mint over the sliced steak. Ladle some hot stock over all this and serve. The diners season the dish themselves with sauces and freshly squeezed lime juice.

SERVES 4–6

CURRY MEE   MALAYSIA

RICE NOODLES IN A COCONUT CURRY SOUP

FROM THE MING COURT HOTEL IN KUALA LUMPUR

High tea in England was never quite like this one served in Malaysia! At the Ming Court Hotel in Kuala Lumpur, early evening finds tables in the lobby groaning with cakes and pastries, mango sweetmeats, stir-fried noodles and curried soups. The ritual of tea drinking has been reclaimed, albeit in its Anglicised form, by the former colony. With the beverage (and even without it) can be had not just the delicacies of the former rulers but also an array of Eastern snacks that no Malay would dream of doing without.

Rice Noodles in a Coconut Curry Soup is one of them. I think it is the finest curry soup I have ever eaten. Filled with slithery rice noodles, this coconut-enriched soup is permeated with the very Malay aromas of lemon grass and galangal. Even though there are many parts to this dish, it is easy to make.

10 oz (275 g) dried flat rice noodles (preferably *banh pho*) or flat egg noodles

1 stick fresh or 3 tablespoons dried sliced lemon grass

1 inch (2.5 cm) cube fresh or 8 large slices dried galangal

4 oz (100 g) onions

4 cloves garlic

1 inch (2.5 cm) cube fresh ginger

6 oz (175 g) red pepper

1 tablespoon paprika

1½ tablespoons shrimp or anchovy paste

½ teaspoon ground turmeric

¼–½ teaspoon chilli powder

8 tablespoons vegetable oil

2 pints (1.1 litres) chicken stock

10 fl oz (300 ml) thick coconut milk (see page 263)

If you are using dried rice noodles, soak them in water for 2 hours or more. If you are using fresh lemon grass, slice it crossways into very thin rounds, starting at the bulbous bottom end and going up about 6 inches (15 cm). Discard the strawlike top. If you are using dried sliced lemon grass, soak it in 6 fl oz (175 ml) hot water for 30 minutes. If you are using fresh galangal, peel it and chop it coarsely. If you are using dried sliced galangal, put it into hot water (with the dried lemon grass, if applicable) and soak it for 30 minutes.

Peel the onions and chop them coarsely. Peel the garlic. Peel the ginger and chop it coarsely. Remove the seeds from the red pepper and chop it coarsely. In an electric blender combine the lemon grass (fresh or dried), the galangal (fresh or dried), any soaking liquid, the onion, garlic, ginger, red pepper, paprika, shrimp paste, turmeric and chilli powder. Blend until smooth, adding a few table-

Salt

Freshly ground black pepper

4½ oz (120 g) chicken breast, skinned and boned

3 oz (75 g) fresh bean sprouts

1 stick celery (preferably from the middle of the bunch)

4 tablespoons Crisply Fried Shallot Flakes (see page 240; optional)

Lime wedges to serve

spoons of water if needed to achieve a pastelike consistency.

Put the oil in a wide heavy pan and set it over a medium-high heat. When the oil is hot put in the paste from the blender. Stir and fry for about 15 minutes or until the paste is dark red and reduced, and the oil separates from it. Add the stock, stir and bring to the boil. Turn the heat to low and simmer for 15 minutes. Strain this soup, pushing out as much liquid as you can. Stir the coconut milk well. If you have made it from fresh coconut, use only the thick milk which rises to the top. Add the coconut milk to the liquid, stir and bring to a simmer. Add salt and black pepper to taste. The soup is now ready; set it aside until later.

Put the chicken breast in a frying-pan with water just to cover. Add a generous pinch of salt and bring it slowly to the boil. Turn the heat to low and simmer for 3–5 minutes, turning the breast around a few times until the meat is white all the way through. Lift the chicken out of the liquid and shred the meat. Cover and set aside.

Pluck off the threadlike ends of the bean sprouts and put them in a bowl of cold water. Chop the celery into minute dice. Cover and set aside.

Just before you are ready to serve, set the soup on a low heat. Bring a large pan of water to a rolling boil. If you are using dried rice noodles drain them and drop them into the boiling water and cook them until they are just done. This may take only 1 minute, so watch them carefully. If you are using egg noodles instead of rice noodles, cook them according to the instructions on the packet. Drain the noodles and divide them among the individual serving bowls. Ladle the hot soup over the noodles. Top with some chicken, bean sprouts, diced celery and Crisply Fried Shallot Flakes. Offer lime wedges on the side.

SERVES 4 AS A LIGHT MEAL OR SNACK, OR 6 AS A SOUP COURSE

SANSAI UDON   JAPAN

NOODLES IN BROTH WITH POACHED EGG AND VEGETABLES

WITH HELP FROM KEIKO OKAMOTO

Noodles are to Japan what hamburgers are to America and pork pies and pasties are to England. They are available everywhere and can be simple or elegant, cheap or expensive, just as you please. Whole restaurants are devoted to them. The Japanese love their noodles and are just as content to have them quite plain and icy cold in the summer with a light dipping sauce as they are to have them topped with an elaborate assortment of vegetables, meats, fish and eggs.

Japan, like all Far Eastern countries, has many types of noodles. *Udon* are thick wheat noodles that are obtainable flat or rounded. What follows is my effort to reproduce a dish served to me on a spring day by Keiko Okamoto, the wife of a prestigious potter living in the tea-growing Uji district just outside Kyoto. Most of the vegetables she used grew wild in the hills around her. Each had been cooked separately and then arranged over the noodles at the last minute. My vegetables, I am afraid are rather more prosaic, but the dish remains delightful – and very healthy, to boot.

Noodle dishes of this type are entire meals in themselves (this, with the addition of tea to drink, was our lunch), hence they are served in rather large, deep, individual bowls. Needless to say, our bowls had been hand-crafted by the master potter himself and were objects of great beauty. The only 'cutlery' we had was chopsticks. You are supposed to pick up the noodles with chopsticks and then suck them in with a deep intake of breath which cools them off. Loud noises made in the process are considered normal and are indicative of pleasure. All solids are picked up with the chopsticks. To drink the broth, chopsticks are left on chopstick rests and the bowl is picked up with both hands and brought directly to the mouth.

As far as poaching the eggs is concerned, I have never seen it done more casually or more successfully than it was by Keiko. She just put some water in a frying-pan and it had barely come to a simmer when she cracked 4 eggs into it. Then, before the eggs were fully set, she loosely covered the pan and turned off the heat, leaving them to stand until they were done. The eggs were perfect – as mine are now that I do them this way.

Try to find Japanese *udon* noodles if you can, as there is no real substitute for them. (Many health food shops carry a wholewheat version.) If you cannot get them, use either Italian *linguine* or flat egg noodles, cooking them according to the instructions on the packet only just before you are ready to serve. After you have drained your *linguine* or egg noodles, toss them with about 8 fl oz (250 ml) stock just to prevent them from sticking to each other as you arrange the vegetables over them.

If you are using ready-prepared *dashi-no-moto* instead of Japanese Soup Stock, omit the salt in this recipe entirely or add only a very small amount, tasting as you go.

Carrots as Both Food and Garnish (see page 242)

Green Beans as Both Food and Garnish (see page 243)

Mushrooms as Both Food and Garnish (see page 241)

Bamboo Shoot Tips as Both Food and Garnish (see page 242)

Asparagus as Both Food and Garnish (see page 241; optional)

3½ pints (2 litres) Japanese Soup Stock (see page 66) or light unsalted chicken stock

3 tablespoons sugar

4 tablespoons *sake*

6 tablespoons Japanese soy sauce (shoyu)

1½–2 teaspoons salt

14 oz (400 g) Japanese *udon* noodles or *linguine* or flat egg noodles

4 eggs

Japanese seven-spice seasoning (*shichimi*) or Sesame Seed Seasoning (see page 270)

Cook the carrots, green beans, mushrooms, bamboo shoot tips and asparagus (if you are using it) according to their individual recipes. Each cooks very fast and you may make them even a day in advance and then cover and refrigerate them in their own liquid. Let them come to room temperature before you arrange them over the noodles so that they do not cool off the stock too much.

Prepare the Japanese Soup Stock. Add the sugar, *sake*, soy sauce and salt to it. Put it into a pan and simmer it very gently for 5 minutes. This too can be made a day ahead, covered and refrigerated. Heat it just before you are ready to eat.

Now cook the noodles. If you are using dried Japanese *udon* noodles, bring a very large pan of water to a rolling boil. Do *not* salt it. Now drop in the noodles. When the water comes to the boil again, put in an extra 8 fl oz (250 ml) cold water. Repeat this 3–4 times, each time waiting for the water to come to the boil again. Keep testing the noodles. When they are just done (there should be no hard core left in the centre), drain them and rinse them under cold running water, rubbing them with your hands to remove all the starch. Leave them in a colander until you are ready to eat, at which time you will need to put them into a large pan of boiling water for a few seconds to heat them through. Drain them quickly.

Poach the eggs just before you are ready to eat

and when everything else is heated and ready. Put about ¾ inch (2 cm) water in a medium-sized frying-pan. Bring it to a very low simmer. Break the 4 eggs into it so that they sit side by side. Let the water simmer very gently until the egg whites are almost set. Now turn off the heat and place a loose cover over the pan. As soon as the whites of the eggs have set, remove the cover. (This does not take very long.)

Assemble the dish quickly now. Divide the noodles between 4 large individual bowls. Lift the vegetables out of their liquid and arrange them over the noodles, laying them prettily side by side. Pour the hot stock over the top, dividing it among the 4 bowls. Place a poached egg in the centre of each bowl. Serve at once. The seven-spice mixture (or Sesame Seed Seasoning) is generally sprinked over the top. Each diner breaks the egg yolk with chopsticks, allowing it to mix with the broth.

SERVES 4

SUANLA ZHA JIANGMIAN   HONG KONG

NOODLES WITH PORK IN HOT AND SOUR SOUP

FROM THE WING LAI YUEN RESTAURANT IN HONG KONG

This spicy Sichuan speciality, which I enjoyed in a very humble restaurant on Hong Kong's Diamond Hill, is not quite a soup, though you may certainly serve it as one. It is really a meal in itself, especially when served with a Chinese-style vegetable on the side. All the different parts of the soup may be prepared in advance. You should assemble the soup just before you are to eat it.

FOR THE NOODLES:

8 oz (225 g) fresh or dried egg noodles (preferably fresh Chinese)

1 tablespoon sesame oil

First prepare the noodles. Bring a large pan of water to a rolling boil. Drop in the noodles and cook for 3–5 minutes or until they are just done. Drain them and put them in a bowl. Add the sesame oil and toss. Let the noodles cool slightly

FOR THE PORK:

3 spring onions

2 cloves garlic

1 tablespoon vegetable oil

8 oz (225 g) lean pork, minced

1½ tablespoons hoisin sauce

1 teaspoon chilli bean sauce or
    ¼–½ teaspoon chilli
    powder

1 teaspoon Chilli Oil (see page
    227)

1 teaspoon sugar

1 tablespoon Chinese dark soy
    sauce

5 fl oz (150 ml) chicken stock,
    chicken and pork stock or
    water

FOR THE SOUP:

16 fl oz (475 ml) chicken or
    chicken and pork stock

3 tablespoons sesame paste

1–2 teaspoons Chilli Oil (see
    page 227)

1 tablespoon distilled white
    vinegar

4 teaspoons Chinese light soy
    sauce

FOR THE GARNISH:

1 spring onion

and then cover with cling-film. Set aside, refrigerating if necessary.

Now prepare the pork. Cut the spring onions crossways into very fine slices along their entire length, including the green section. Peel the garlic and chop it finely. Put the oil in a wok or frying-pan and set it over a high heat. When the oil is hot, put in the garlic and spring onions and stir for 1 minute. Put in the pork and stir and fry, breaking up the lumps, until the meat has lost all signs of pinkness. Add the hoisin sauce, chilli bean sauce, Chilli Oil, sugar and dark soy sauce. Stir and fry for 30 seconds. Add the stock, cover and simmer for 10 minutes.

Next prepare the soup. Combine all the ingredients for the soup in a pan. (Stir the sesame paste well before adding it.) Mix well, taste and adjust the seasoning if necessary.

Finally, prepare the garnish. Cut the spring onion crossways into very fine slices along its entire length, including the green section.

To serve, set a large pan of water to boil and place a colander in the sink. Heat the pork and the soup in separate pans. When the soup is boiling, divide it among individual soup bowls. Plunge the noodles into the boiling water for 10–20 seconds to heat them through. Drain them in the colander and then divide them among the soup bowls, piling them up in the centre of the soup so that their 'peaks' are well above it. Top the noodles with the pork, again dividing it among the bowls. Sprinkle the spring onion over the very top and serve.

SERVES 2 AS A MEAL OR 4 AS A SOUP

DIPS, SAUCES, GARNISHES & PICKLES

TONKATSU SOSU   JAPAN

EAST-WEST SAUCE

This sauce is a mixture of Eastern and Western ingredients. It contains, among
other things, tomato ketchup and Worcestershire sauce. We must remember,
though, that ketchup is an Asian word for an Asian sauce and that tomato
ketchup may well have been an attempt to replicate the kind of sweet and sour
sauces found all over the Far East. Also, Worcestershire sauce, which is used in
this recipe, has ingredients like tamarind in it. Tamarind is very much an
Eastern ingredient. This may well be a case of an idea for a sauce travelling
from the East to the West and then back to the East in a new incarnation.

East-West sauce is served with Breaded Pork Cutlets (see page 104). You can,
however, use it with any meat, fried chicken or fried fish. Since this sauce is
prepared commercially in Japan where it is known as *tonkatsu sosu*, I never
could get an exact recipe for it. However, by tasting it again and again I have
come up with a good approximation, which I give below.

½ teaspoon mustard powder
4 tablespoons tomato ketchup
4 teaspoons *sake*
4 teaspoons Japanese soy sauce
(shoyu)
4 teaspoons Worcestershire
sauce
4 teaspoons sugar
4 teaspoons distilled white
vinegar
¼ teaspoon ground allspice
Dash ground cloves

Put the mustard powder in a smallish bowl. Add 4
teaspoons hot water and mix thoroughly. Add all
the remaining ingredients and mix.

SERVES 4–6

LAJIAO YOU   HONG KONG

CHILLI OIL

Orange-coloured chilli oil is offered as a seasoning on the tables of most restaurants in Hong Kong. A few drops, or more liberal doses, are dribbled on to any foods that need extra 'heat'. It is also a common seasoning in Chinese kitchens serving Sichuan-style food. You can buy it ready-made at Chinese grocers' shops, but it is easy enough to make at home. I find that it needs to be strained a couple of times if I want it to be really clear.

5 fl oz (150 ml) vegetable oil
  (preferably groundnut)
1 tablespoon chilli powder

Put the oil in a small pan and set it over a medium-high heat. When the oil is hot, remove it from the heat and put in the chilli powder. Mix and leave to cool, then strain the oil through a clean cloth. It is now ready to be used. You may, however, let it sit for a few hours and strain it a second time. If you have an empty bottle or jar in your cruet set, you could use it for your chilli oil.

MAKES ABOUT 5 FL OZ (150 ML)

NAM PLA PRIK   THAILAND

FISH SAUCE SEASONED WITH LIME JUICE AND CHILLI

You may put this sauce on the table when you are serving any Thai meal.

1 fresh hot green or red chilli
4 tablespoons fish sauce
2 tablespoons lime or lemon
  juice

Cut the chilli crossways into very fine rounds. Put it in a small bowl. Add the fish sauce and the lime or lemon juice. Stir to mix.

SERVES 4

NƯỚC CHẤM THÔNG DỤNG   VIETNAM

ISH SAUCE WITH VINEGAR AND LIME JUICE

This is a wonderful dipping sauce to use with spring rolls and grilled or boiled meats.

5 tablespoons fish sauce

3 tablespoons distilled white vinegar

1½–2 tablespons lime or lemon juice

2 tablespoons sugar

1–2 fresh hot green or red chillies

Combine the fish sauce with 3 tablespoons water, the vinegar, lime or lemon juice and sugar in a jug. Mix well. Slice the chillies crossways as thinly as possible and add them too. Divide the sauce equally among 4 small bowls and serve.

SERVES 4

NƯỚC MẮM TỎI ỚT   VIETNAM

ISH SAUCE SEASONED WITH LIME JUICE

FROM BICHE LOMBATIÈRE

I am told that the popularity of a restaurant often rests with the quality of this ever-present sauce.

1 clove garlic

4 tablespoons fish sauce

4 tablespoons lime or lemon juice

3 tablespoons sugar or less to taste

3–4 fresh hot red or green chillies

Peel and crush the garlic. Combine it with the fish sauce, lime or lemon juice, sugar and 4 table-spoons water. Mix well and pour into 4 individual bowls. Cut the chillies crossways into very thin rounds and divide them among the bowls.

SERVES 4

NƯỚC CHẤM VIETNAM

FISH SAUCE SEASONED WITH VINEGAR

When serving this sauce, give each diner an individual bowlful. This recipe is enough for 4 small bowls.

8 tablespoons fish sauce

6 tablespoons distilled white vinegar

1 tablespoon sugar

3–4 fresh hot green or red chillies

Combine the fish sauce, vinegar and sugar. Mix thoroughly. Cut the chillies into fine rounds and put them into the sauce.

SERVES 4

YANG NYUM JANG KOREA

KOREAN DIPPING SAUCE

This all-purpose sauce may be served with plain heated bean curd, with chicken patties and with potato pancakes.

1 small clove garlic

1 spring onion

4 tablespoons soy sauce (preferably Japanese – shoyu)

2 tablespoons distilled white vinegar

1 tablespoon sesame oil

1 teaspoon sugar

1 teaspoon roasted sesame seeds (see page 270)

¼ teaspoon chilli powder (optional)

Peel the garlic and crush it to a pulp. Cut the spring onion crossways into very thin rounds (you only need 1 tablespoon of this). Combine the garlic, 1 tablespoon sliced spring onion, the soy sauce, vinegar, sesame oil, sugar, sesame seeds and chilli powder in a small serving bowl and mix well.

SERVES 4

KOCHU CHANG   KOREA

Hot Fermented Bean Paste

Every household in Korea has a tall earthenware jar of Hot Fermented Bean Paste (*kochu chang*) sitting serenely in a courtyard, on a balcony or in some other convenient nook. It is an essential seasoning and is one of the several bean pastes used with great frequency throughout Korea. It serves as a cross between a chutney and a spice.

Its method of preparation is elaborate and long, calling for barley or glutinous rice powder to be mixed with malt, cooked slowly into a thick paste and then mixed with fermented soya bean powder, chilli powder and salt. The resulting paste is red in colour (because of the chillies) and very thick. It is added to dipping sauces, to meats that are just about to be stir-fried, and to stews. Dollops of it are also served as a kind of salty sweet and hot chutney.

Kochu chang is available only in Korean shops. It can, however, be approximated at home with ingredients available to most of us. It is best to buy brown or reddish miso for this recipe. This, when mixed with chilli powder, paprika and a little sugar, tastes and looks very much like real *kochu chang*.

4 tablespoons brown or red
   miso
1½ tablespoons paprika
1 teaspoon chilli powder
1 tablespoon sugar

Combine all the ingredients and mix well.

MAKES 4–5 TABLESPOONS

NƯỚC HÀNG   VIETNAM

CARAMEL WATER

This is used in Vietnam to add colour and extra flavour to foods.

3 tablespoons sugar

Put the sugar in a small cast-iron frying-pan and let it warm up, without stirring, over a low heat. The sugar will begin to caramelise. Tilt the pan slowly back and forth to move the sugar, but do not stir it. When all the sugar has turned brownish, slowly pour in 5 fl oz (150 ml) warm water. It will bubble vigorously, so be careful. Stir and mix. Pour the sauce into a bowl. Add another 5 fl oz (150 ml) boiling water and mix. Allow to cool and then store in a covered jar in the refrigerator.

MAKES ABOUT 10 FL OZ (300 ML)

VIETNAM, THAILAND, MALAYSIA AND INDONESIA

RED PEPPER SAUCE

In Vietnam this sauce is made by pounding red chillies and salt in a mortar, cooking the mixture and then passing it through a sieve. Some countries do not bother with the cooking and straining. Others add a little sugar and vinegar. My method is very simple: I let a blender do all the work.

2–3 dried hot red chillies
4 oz (100 g) red pepper
¼ teaspoon sugar
½ teaspoon distilled white vinegar
¼ teaspoon salt or to taste

Put 3 tablespoons water in a small cup and crumble the dried red chillies into it. Soak for 30 minutes. Coarsely chop the red pepper, discarding all the seeds. Combine the soaking chillies and their liquid with all the other ingredients in an electric blender. Blend until smooth.

SERVES 4

NAM PRIK KAENG DANG THAILAND

RED CURRY PASTE

FROM PIENG CHOM DARBANAND AT THE IMPERIAL HOTEL, BANGKOK

This curry paste recipe makes about 8 tablespoons, enough for 2 dishes each serving 4 people. You can freeze any of the paste that you do not use immediately.

7 large or 10 medium-sized dried hot red chillies

2 inch (5 cm) cube fresh or 4–6 slices dried galangal or 2 inch (5 cm) cube fresh ginger

2–3 pieces dried or 3 × ½ inch (7.5 × 1 cm) piece fresh kaffir lime rind (optional)

1 stick fresh or 2 tablespoons dried sliced lemon grass

3 cloves garlic

About 4–5 roots fresh coriander

6 shallots or ½ medium onion

1½ teaspoons shrimp or anchovy paste

2 teaspoons paprika

½ teaspoon ground coriander seeds

½ teaspoon ground cumin seeds

¼ teaspoon ground turmeric

¹⁄₁₆ teaspoon ground cinnamon

¹⁄₁₆ teaspoon ground cardamom seeds

½ teaspoon salt

Remove and discard the seeds from the red chillies. Combine the chillies and the dried galangal, dried kaffir lime rind and dried lemon grass (if you are using them) in a small bowl. Cover with about 6 fl oz (175 ml) water and set aside for 40 minutes–1 hour.

If you are using fresh galangal (or ginger), peel and coarsely chop it. If you are using fresh lemon grass, cut it crossways into very fine slices, going up about 6 inches (15 cm) from the root end. Discard the strawlike top. Peel the garlic. Wash the coriander roots well and pat them dry.

Combine the soaked seasonings and their soaking liquid – or their fresh counterparts, where applicable – with all the remaining ingredients in an electric blender. Blend well.

MAKES ABOUT 8 TABLESPOONS

SAMBAL TERASI   INDONESIA

RED PEPPER SAUCE WITH SHRIMP PASTE

This spicy relish (or *sambal*) may be served with all Indonesian meals. It will keep for at least a week in the refrigerator. Store it in a tightly lidded jar.

8 oz (225 g) red pepper

2 teaspoons shrimp or anchovy paste

½ teaspoon salt

½ teaspoon chilli powder

4 tablespoons vegetable oil

1 teaspoon dark brown sugar

2½ tablespoons lime or lemon juice

Dice the red pepper coarsely, discarding all the seeds. Put the red pepper, shrimp paste, salt and chilli powder in an electric blender. Blend until smooth.

Set a wok over a medium-high heat. When it is hot, put in the oil. When the oil has heated, put in the paste from the blender. Stir and fry for about 5 minutes, turning down the heat a little if necessary, until the paste turns dark red and the oil separates. Add the sugar and stir to mix. Take the paste off the heat and put it into a bowl. Beat in the lime or lemon juice. Taste and adjust the seasoning if necessary.

MAKES ABOUT 8 FL OZ (250 ML)

NAM PRIK NUM   THAILAND

QUICK SPICY RELISH

FROM THE HOME OF KRUAMAS WOODTIKARN IN CHIANG MAI

This relish is so good that you will want to eat it with everything – including crisps. It is found only in northern Thailand. In fact Thai visitors from the south buy kilos of it to take back home. It *is* hot, so small portions are recommended.

6 shallots

3 cloves garlic

6 fresh hot green chillies

½–1 teaspoon shrimp or anchovy paste

6 cherry or very small tomatoes

1 tablespoon fish sauce or salt to taste

1 tablespoon lime or lemon juice

Pre-heat the grill. Peel the shallots and garlic. On a grill rack lined with aluminium foil, spread out the shallots, garlic and green chillies in a single layer. Make a patty of the shrimp paste, if you are using it, and place it on the rack as well. (If you are using anchovy paste, set it aside for the time being.) Put the rack under the grill and let everything brown lightly. (This will happen quite quickly.) Turn everything over and brown the other side. Now either chop up everything you have grilled or put it all into an electric blender and blend briefly until you have a coarse paste. Empty the paste into a bowl. Chop the tomatoes into small pieces and add them (as well as the anchovy paste, if you are using it), the fish sauce (or salt) and the lime or lemon juice to the bowl. Mix. Taste to check the seasoning and adjust if necessary.

SERVES 4–6

HARI SHOGA   JAPAN

GINGER SHREDS IN SWEET VINEGAR

Even though this is a Japanese relish, I keep it on hand to serve with Western-style roast lamb and grilled chicken.

2 inch (5 cm) cube fresh ginger
4 tablespoons distilled white vinegar
4 tablespoons sugar
¼ teaspoon salt

Peel the ginger and cut it crossways into very thin slices. Stacking a few slices at a time together, cut them into very fine julienne strips. Combine the vinegar, sugar and salt in a bowl and mix well until the sugar is dissolved. Put in the ginger and stir. Set aside for at least 10–15 minutes. Lift the ginger shreds out of the liquid before serving.

SERVES 4

TERIYAKI NO TARE   JAPAN

SWEET GLAZING SAUCE

This Sweet Glazing (or *teriyaki*) Sauce, sweet and salty at the same time, is generally made with equal parts of Japanese rice wine (*sake*), soy sauce, *mirin* (a sweetened syrupy *sake*) and a little sugar. I have substituted sugar for the hard-to-find *mirin*. If you do manage to obtain it, add 5 fl oz (150 ml) of it to the soy-*sake* mixture and reduce the sugar to 2 teaspoons.

Generally speaking, *teriyaki* sauce is brushed on to grilled foods such as fish, chicken and beef when they are slightly more than half-cooked. It gives them a glorious glaze, as well as the sweet and salty *teriyaki* flavour. You may, if you like, add a little juice from grated fresh ginger to the sauce as well.

5 fl oz (150 ml) Japanese soy sauce (shoyu)
5 fl oz (150 ml) *sake*
6 tablespoons sugar

Combine the soy sauce, *sake* and sugar in a small pan and bring to the boil. Lower the heat to medium and simmer for about 5 minutes or until the sauce turns very slightly syrupy. (If the sauce is to be used as a marinade as well, it should be allowed to cool off first.)

SERVES 4

Seasoned Vinegar

This seasoning is found in all the Asian countries where the Chinese have lived or settled – Hong Kong, Vietnam, the Philippines, Malaysia, Thailand and Indonesia. Of course, the actual vinegar varies not only from country to country but often from village to village. Diners usually add just a few drops of the hot vinegar to their food. If they want to, they can also take a few chilli slices from the vinegar.

2 fresh hot green or red chillies

4 tablespoons distilled white vinegar

Cut the chillies crossways into very thin rounds. Put the vinegar into a very small bowl. Add the chillies and let them steep for 30 minutes.

SERVES 4

Roasted Peanuts

Crushed roasted peanuts are a common seasoning throughout most of South-East Asia. They add a nutty taste, a crunchy texture and protein to a dish.

Raw peanuts are sold in every market in this region, usually still covered with their red inner skins. To roast them at home, put them into an ungreased, well heated, cast-iron wok or frying-pan over a medium heat. Stir the peanuts around until they are roasted, reducing the heat if necessary. The red skins will turn crisp and papery. When the peanuts have cooled rub them with both hands and blow the skins away. To crush them, lightly or finely as required, either whirr them for a few seconds in a clean coffee grinder or, if only a few tablespoons are needed, chop them up with a large knife.

EGG STRIPS

These strips are a popular garnish for rice and noodles in many parts of South-East Asia. They are also used in salads and soups.

3 eggs
1 teaspoon sugar
⅛ teaspoon salt
About 2 teaspoons vegetable oil

Break the eggs into a bowl and add 1 tablespoon water. Beat, but not to a froth. Add the sugar and salt and beat lightly to mix. Brush a 7–8 inch (18–20 cm) non-stick frying-pan with about ½ teaspoon of the oil and set it on a medium heat. When it is hot, pour in a quarter of the egg mixture. Tilt the pan around so that the egg flows evenly to the edges. Let the mixture set, which it will do quite quickly. Turn the pancake over carefully and cook the second side until it is just firm (a matter of seconds). Remove the pancake to a plate and cover it with wax paper. Make 3 more pancakes in this way, putting them on top of each other with a layer of wax paper in between. Allow them to cool, then roll them up one at a time and cut them crossways at ⅛ inch (0.3 cm) intervals. Put the resulting strips into a covered container and store in the refrigerator if you are not going to use them immediately.

MAKES ABOUT 1½ TEACUPS

*C*ABBAGE PICKLE

It is not surprising that *kimchee* is used in Korean rituals and rites. After all, there is not a single meal, from breakfast until dinner, when it is not served. According to the Kimchee Museum in Seoul, there are at least 160 varieties of this pickle. It can be made from radish, cucumber and even from fresh ginseng, but the most common *kimchee* remains the one made from cabbage.

Koreans use a long fat cabbage which many call long or Peking cabbage. It looks like a very large, overweight head of Chinese leaves. A single head can weigh as much as 4½ lb (2 kg). An extended family of 10 people eats about 200 heads of this pickled cabbage in 3–4 months.

Around late November, when the cabbage and red chilli crops are ready, whole villages fall to the task of making their supply of winter *kimchee*. On the first day, cartloads of cabbages are trimmed, washed and left overnight in salted water to wilt and soften. The next day they are washed again while another group of workers prepares the stuffing. Large white radishes are julienned, green onions and Chinese celery are cut, ginger is chopped and red chillies crushed. This mixture, along with shelled oysters, salt and tiny salted shrimps, is slapped between each leaf of the cabbages. The cabbage heads are then packed into large, Ali Baba-sized vats where they seethe, bubble and ferment until they turn deliciously sour. In the villages the vats are buried up to their necks in the earth to prevent the pickle from freezing. In city homes all vats stand like sentinels, lined up on balconies.

1 lb (450 g) half-head Chinese cabbage or leaves

Salt

1 lb (450 g) long white radish (mooli)

3 inch (7.5 cm) cube fresh ginger

8 spring onions

8–10 large cloves garlic

2 teaspoons chilli powder

1 teaspoon sugar

10 shelled oysters or 10 tinned anchovy fillets

1 tablespoon plain flour

Half the Chinese cabbage or leaves length ways. Trim the very bottom of the stalk end of the cabbage but keep the leaves attached. If the half-head is very thick, cut it in half again lengthways. (Chinese leaves, however, should be cut in half only.) Wash the cabbage well, carefully removing the dirt between each leaf.

In a large bowl, combine 2½ pints (1.5 litres) water with 3 tablespoons salt. Put the cabbage into the solution. Weigh it down with a clean heavy plate so that it does not float. Cover loosely and leave for 8 hours.

Prepare the 'stuffing'. Peel the radish and cut it

crossways into 2 inch (5 cm) chunks. Now cut each chunk lengthways into ⅛ inch (0.3 cm) thick slabs. Cut each slab into ⅛ inch (0.3 cm) thick julienne strips.

Peel the ginger and garlic and chop them coarsely. Put them into an electric blender with 3 tablespoons water. Blend until smooth. Cut the spring onions into fine rounds along their entire length, including the green section.

In a large bowl combine the radish, ginger-garlic paste, spring onions, chilli powder, sugar and oysters. If you are using anchovy fillets, wipe off the oil and chop them finely before adding them. Mix. Add 1 tablespoon salt and mix again. Put the flour in a small pan and slowly add 12 fl oz (350 ml) water, mixing as you go. Bring this water to a simmer. Simmer gently until slightly thickened.

Remove the cabbage from the salt water and rinse thoroughly several times. Keep the leaves attached. Drain. Starting with the outside leaves, put some stuffing in between each cabbage leaf. Tuck the largest leaf under so that it will hold the 'package' together. Continue in this way until you have stuffed all the cabbage sections. Fit the cabbage packages tightly inside a clean, wide-mouthed, 3½ pint (2 litre) crock or jar. Pour the flour water over the top. Make sure that there is some room on top for the fermenting pickle to expand. Cover and set aside for 3–7 days, depending upon the weather; the hotter it is, the quicker the cabbage will pickle. Taste the pickle now and then to see if it has turned sufficiently sour. Once the pickle is ready, it should be refrigerated.

To serve, remove just as much of the cabbage from the liquid as you need and put it in a small bowl. In Korea the liquid is used to flavour stews and soups.

MAKES ENOUGH TO FILL A 3½ PINT (2 LITRE) JAR

CRISPLY FRIED SHALLOT (OR ONION) FLAKES

A young lady in Padang, Indonesia, told me with great authority that shallot flakes turn much crisper if they are soaked in lightly salted water before being fried. Theories abound: this one makes sense, however, as salt draws out some of the moisture. I think that starting the frying at a medium-hot rather than a very hot temperature also helps.

In much of South-East Asia shallots are cheap and used rather as onions are used in the West. Crisply Fried Shallot Flakes serve both as a garnish and as a seasoning. Often they are fried in bulk and kept in tightly lidded jars to be used as needed. If you cannot obtain shallots, use onions. Cut them in half lengthways and then crossways into very fine half-rings. Fry them just as you would the shallots. (Small amounts of shallots, intended for use the same day, may be fried without first being soaked in salted water.)

7 oz (200 g) shallots or onions
Salt
Vegetable oil for deep-frying

Peel the shallots and cut them lengthways into fine slivers. Put them in a bowl. Add ½ teaspoon salt and toss lightly. Cover with 15 fl oz (450 ml) water and leave for 30 minutes. Drain them well and pat them dry.

Put about 2 inches (5 cm) oil in a wok set over a medium heat, or heat the recommended quantity of oil in a deep-fat fryer to 375°F (190°C). When the oil is hot, put in the shallots. Stir and fry for 1 minute. Turn the heat down to medium-low, or the deep-fat fryer to 325°F (160°C). If you are using a wok, keep stirring and frying until the shallots are reddish-brown and crisp. Remove them with a slotted spoon and spread them out on kitchen paper to drain. When they are cool and crisp, store them in a tightly lidded jar until needed.

MAKES ENOUGH TO FILL A 12 FL OZ (350 ML) JAR

Asparagus as both food and garnish

The asparagus here may be used as a garnish for meats, fish or chicken, or placed over a dish of noodles in broth. If you are using prepared *dashi-no-moto* instead of the Japanese Soup Stock, omit the salt that is added to the stock.

12 medium-thick spears asparagus (prepared weight about 4 oz/100 g)

Salt

5 fl oz (150 ml) ice-cold Japanese Soup Stock (see page 66) or light unsalted chicken stock

Trim away the woody section of each asparagus spear and then peel the lower half. Cut each spear into 2–2½ inch (4–6 cm) sections. Bring about ½ inch (1 cm) water to boil in a medium-sized frying-pan. Add ¼ teaspoon salt to it and put in the asparagus. Cover, lower the heat and cook for about 3 minutes or until the asparagus pieces are just tender. Drain and immediately plunge the asparagus pieces into the cold stock. Add ¼ teaspoon salt and mix in gently. Let the asparagus sit in the stock for at least 15 minutes.

SERVES 4

Mushrooms as both food and garnish

If you are using prepared *dashi-no-moto* instead of Japanese Soup Stock, omit the salt.

8 medium mushrooms

5 fl oz (150 ml) Japanese Soup Stock (see page 66) or light unsalted chicken stock

1 tablespoon *sake*

2 teaspoons Japanese soy sauce (shoyu)

2 teaspoons sugar

¼ teaspoon salt

Wipe the mushrooms with a damp cloth and cut them in half lengthways. Combine the stock, *sake*, soy sauce, sugar and salt in a small pan and bring it to a simmer. Put in the mushrooms and cook them for about 2½ minutes over a medium-low heat, stirring now and then. Turn off the heat and let the mushrooms cool in their liquid. Drain and serve.

SERVES 4

Bamboo Shoot Tips as both Food and Garnish

Since the bamboo shoots in this recipe need to look as good as they taste, only the tips are used. These are sometimes available in tins (the tins are labelled 'winter bamboo shoots') and come in conical shapes of various sizes. They need to be washed and then cut vertically into wedges that are about ⅛ inch (0.3 cm) thick on the outside, while their inside looks like the teeth of a comb. Tender bamboo shoot chunks can be used as a substitute. They can be cut into triangular slices about 2 inches (5 cm) long and ⅛ inch (0.3 cm) thick. Do not make this dish if you can get only sliced bamboo shoots. If you are using prepared *dashi-no-moto* instead of Japanese Soup Stock, omit the salt.

3 oz (75 g) tinned bamboo shoot tips or chunks

5 fl oz (150 ml) Japanese Soup Stock (see page 66) or light unsalted chicken stock

1 tablespoon *sake*

2 teaspoons Japanese soy sauce (shoyu)

1 tablespoon sugar

¼ teaspoon salt

Slice the bamboo shoot tips as suggested above and wash them well in water. Combine the stock, *sake*, soy sauce, sugar and salt in a small pan and bring to the boil. Drop in the bamboo shoots and simmer on a medium-low heat for 5 minutes, turning the shoots around now and then. Leave them to cool in the liquid, again turning the pieces around several times so that they pick up the colour evenly.

SERVES 4

Carrots as both Food and Garnish

Small quantities of carrots often provide a colourful accent, and a third dimension, to plates of chicken or fish in Japan. These carrots can also be arranged along with other vegetables over a bowl of noodles. You could easily double or triple the quantities given below if you wish to serve the carrots, Western-style, as an accompanying vegetable at a meal. The cooking time, however, will remain the same. If you are using prepared *dashi-no-moto* instead of Japanese Soup Stock, omit the salt.

4 oz (100 g) carrots

4 tablespoons Japanese Soup Stock (see page 66) or light unsalted chicken stock

2 teaspoons sugar

¼ teaspoon salt

Peel the carrots. Cut them crossways into 2½ inch (6 cm) segments and then cut each segment lengthways into ⅛ inch (0.3 cm) thick slices. You may leave the slices like this or cut them, again lengthways, into ⅛ inch (0.3 cm) wide julienne strips.

Combine the carrots, stock, sugar and salt in a small pan and bring to the boil. Boil for about 1 minute. The carrots should retain some crispness. Immerse the pan in a bowl of cold water to cool off the carrots quickly. When serving, lift the carrots out of their liquid and arrange as required.

SERVES 4

INGEN   JAPAN

GREEN BEANS AS BOTH FOOD AND GARNISH

When Japanese food is presented, sometimes just a few vegetables are used as a kind of garnish or arranged over noodles along with several other similarly prepared vegetables, fungi and roots. You could always increase the quantity if you wish to serve the beans at a Western-style meal. If you are using prepared *dashi-no-moto* instead of Japanese Soup Stock, omit the salt that is put into the ice-cold stock.

4 oz (100 g) green beans

1¾ teaspoons salt

4 fl oz (120 ml) ice-cold Japanese Soup Stock (see page 66) or light unsalted chicken stock

Trim the green beans and cut them into 2½ inch (6 cm) lengths. Combine 1 pint (600 ml) water and 1½ teaspoons of the salt in a pan and bring to the boil. Put in the beans and cook quickly for about 4 minutes (this depends on the size of bean) or until they are crisp but tender. Drain them and immediately drop them into the ice-cold stock. Add the remaining ¼ teaspoon salt to the stock and stir it in. Leave the beans in the liquid for at least 15 minutes or until you are ready to use them. When serving, lift the beans out of the liquid and arrange as required.

SERVES 4

DESSERTS AND DRINKS

PLATE OF FRESH FRUIT

In much of Asia meals end not with puddings and desserts, but with fruit. Sometimes it is just one glorious seasonal fruit, such as perfumed summer mangoes chilled in iced water, or it could be a collection of several fruits, all pared and cut into neat mouthfuls. In Korea these neat mouthfuls sit on a common platter set in the centre of the table. Each piece of fruit is pierced with a small 2-pronged fork so that it can be picked up with ease and nibbled at will. In Thailand, where a whole school is devoted to the art, fruit comes carved in the most elaborate floral and geometric designs; you cannot even get a simple papaya in your hotel room without some slight hint of delicate fingers at work. In Japan, where the fruit is not tropical, I was stunned by a plate that held just a whole orange and a bunch of black grapes. The orange had been peeled in one neat spiral and sectioned. It had then been re-assembled so that the fruit looked whole. Each grape, too, had been seeded and loosened inside from its coarse skin (how did they do this?). All I had to do was hold a grape to my lips and just suck in the smooth insides.

While I do not suggest that you spend all day carving fruit – enough effort is required to prepare the main meal – here are helpful hints on fruit that you may be unfamiliar with and which are now often sold in many Western shops and supermarkets. (*Superscript numbers refer to colour plate key on page 193.*)

MANGO[1]

Sweet, juicy and, at its best, smooth-textured, a mango to me is the king of fruit. There are hundreds of varieties, each with its own taste, texture and colour. Most varieties in the northern hemisphere ripen in the summer, from late April to early July, so that would be the best time to buy them. Mangoes sold by most shops are hard and under-ripe. Smell the mango at its stem end, and if it seems to have the potential of being sweet, buy it. You will be taking a bit of a chance, but if it works out once, look for the same variety again. When you get home, wrap the hard mango in newspaper and put it in a basket or an open cardboard box. Do not refrigerate it. You can ripen several mangoes together in this way, wrapping each one separately in newspaper first. In Thai villages, baskets of mangoes are left to ripen under the bed. When the perfume becomes overwhelming, the household knows that the mangoes are ready to be eaten! Examine your mangoes every day.

They should eventually yield very slightly to the touch, but should *not* have black spots on them. You may now chill the mangoes in the refrigerator, or put them to cool in a bucket of water to which you have added plenty of ice.

While there are people who believe that mangoes are best eaten with the hands, and in a bathtub, there is a neater approach for those who would like to use an implement – and stay at the table. The mango usually has two flatter sides. Cut a thick slice lengthways off each of these sides as close to the stone as you can. (Peel the remaining mango and devour it in the kitchen by yourself. This is your reward for the work you are putting in.) Put these two slices on a plate. This is one serving. The mango pulp may now be scooped decorously out of the skin with a spoon. You could also cut a cross-hatch pattern in the flesh, making rows at about ½ inch (1 cm) intervals with a sharp knife. Cut all the way down to the skin, but not through it. Now put the fingers of both your hands under the skin and push upwards. The flesh of the mango will rise up in an arch and open in a most interesting pattern. Eat it with a spoon. You could, if you like, peel the mango, slice it and cut it into dice. Serve the stone only to those who do not mind using their fingers.

a) Slice the mango down beside the stone, lengthways. Cup the mango section you have just sliced off in your hand and make a grid pattern in the flesh with a knife, taking care not to pierce the skin.

b) Turn the mango section inside out.

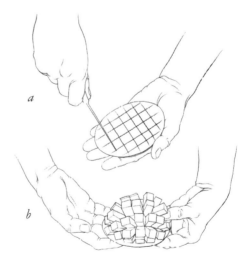

LITCHIS[2]

These, to my mind, must always be eaten in quantity. Eating one or two is like eating one or two peanuts. Litchis have a red or reddish-brown, somewhat tough, crisp skin. As you peel the egg-sized fruit, a sweet, clear juice begins to drip from it. The inside is white, translucent and glistening, not unlike the skin of a peeled squid. Pop the litchi into your mouth, but remember that there is a long stone in the centre.

Chill the litchis before serving. You may put a whole bunch of litchis in a bowl in the centre of your table and let people break off their own, peel them and eat them. Or you can peel the litchis yourself and arrange them on a plate with other cut fruit. Do not remove the stone; that is the least people can do for themselves.

RAMBUTAN[3]

This is a large red litchi with red hairlike spikes on the outside. It tastes a little like a litchi, but is much less juicy. The Thais often leave half-peeled rambutans on a fruit plate to show off their interesting skins. Rambutans also have seeds in them.

MANGOSTEEN[4]

The fruit that has won most kudos among Western travellers is perhaps the mangosteen. One ancient traveller compared it to nectar and ambrosia, saying that it 'surpassed the golden apples of the Hesperides and was, of all the fruit of the Indies, the most delicious.' I remember sitting on a park bench in Malacca and greedily devouring about a dozen of them, sticky juice dripping all over me.

In spite of its name, the mangosteen is in no way related to the mango. It is purplish or reddish-brown on the outside, the size of a tangerine and quite hard. There is a knack to cracking it open with a good twist, which I have now finally mastered, but I will suggest an easier method. Take a sharp knife and make an equatorial cut all around the fruit. Do not cut all the way through; you do not want two equal halves. Now pull the top off like a cap. Sitting propped up inside a natural cup, like a scoop of ice-cream, will be 5–8 white, juicy, translucent segments. You may eat them with a spoon. They will be sweet with just a hint of sourness, and very good. I long for one as I write this.

PASSION FRUIT[5]

From the outside, this looks like a dented egg of purplish (or sometimes yellow) colour. Split it open and you will find crunchy seeds covered with a clear, gelatinous flesh nestling in the hollow. At their best, passion fruit have a sweet and sour taste that seems to combine the flavour of limes and berries. If it is too sour, a little sugar should be sprinkled over the pulp before it is eaten. The pulp may also be strained and then served over ice-cream.

CUSTARD APPLE[6]

This is a heart-shaped fruit that seems to be covered with a green alligator skin. It must be fully ripe when it is bought, which means that it should yield easily to the touch when pressed. Serve each person a whole chilled custard apple. You can easily split it open lengthways, using nothing but your hands. The inside is filled with white, creamy, sugar-sweet buds that often harbour smooth, black seeds. Ease your spoon into the custard-like pulp. The art of eating this fruit lies in knowing how to dislodge the seeds from the pulp while the buds are still in your mouth and then delicately spitting out the seeds while retaining your dignity.

PINEAPPLE[7]

By now, I am sure, you know how to serve a pineapple. When buying one, smell it; it should smell sweet. Look at its colour – the yellower it is, the riper it will be. Feel its very top, near the leaves – it should have a little give. To prepare a pineapple, peel it, remove its 'eyes', core it and then serve it cut in wedges as they do in South-East Asia, or in round slices. It is best when it is chilled. If it is not too sweet, sugar may be added, but remember that sugar will make it syrupy, so it will not be suitable for a plate of mixed fruit.

DURIAN[8]

Dare I mention it? This is the fruit that is banned from hotels and aeroplanes because of its lingering odour. South-East Asians are always surprised when a Westerner can allow himself or herself to go near it, let alone eat it. I love it passionately and recommend it without hesitation.

It looks unprepossessing – large, green and full of murderous spikes, a football made by a dinosaur for a dinosaur. It needs to be cracked open with a hatchet wielded by a practised hand. Lying inside its five compartments are pale, off-white segments of the creamiest, smoothest texture imaginable. These segments are sweet, in flavour and texture the most heavenly blend of cream, bananas and flowing ripe brie.

In Indonesia the durian is considered to be an aphrodisiac and, the saying goes, 'When the durian comes in, the sarongs go up.' Might that induce you to try it?

STAR FRUIT[9]

When this yellowish coloured fruit is cut crossways into slices, each slice looks like a star – hence its name. Its flavour can be sour, sweet and sour, or just sweet, depending upon the type. It is exceedingly juicy. Once, when we were grilling fish outdoors in Sumatra on a particularly hot day, I remember my hostess breaking off a star fruit from a bunch that hung above us and offering it to me. 'It will quench your thirst and cool you down,' she said. As I bit into it, juice went flying in every direction. It was just as good as drinking an icy lemonade.

Slices of star fruit can be added to a plate of fruit served at the end of a meal. They can also be left on the table, along with herbs and lettuce leaves, to be nibbled upon at will during the course of a Vietnamese, Thai or Malaysian meal.

POMELO[10]

This is best described as an extra-crisp, crunchy, flaky grapefruit. Once it has been peeled, its wedge-like sections can be separated and the papery skin on each wedge pulled off with ease. This makes it ideal for fruit plates and salads. Each peeled wedge can be flaked by separating all the individual 'buds' in it. In Thailand the 'flaked' version is used in everyday salads.

PAPAYA[11]

This should be very ripe and sweet. It should yield slightly to the touch and have a nice yellowish colour on the outside. Chill it first, then cut it in half lengthways. Scoop out all the seeds. You may now cut it into long slices, or you may serve a whole half with a wedge of lime, or you may peel the papaya halves and cut them into cubes.

BANANAS[12] AND WATERMELON[13]

Sliced bananas and watermelon chunks may be added to any plate of tropical fruit that you wish to serve.

LECHE FLAN   PHILIPPINES

CARAMEL CUSTARD FILIPINO-STYLE

I have such a weakness for soothing, slithery milk desserts – especially for caramel custard. It is made particularly well in the Philippines where, as in Spain, it could be considered the national dessert. What do the Filipinos do differently? They never seem to use fresh milk, for one thing. Their love affair with tinned American products continues unabated and, I must say, in this case works to great advantage. The dessert is rich, creamy and, as one of my daughters pronounced, the best ever.

All households in the Philippines seem to agree on the use of tinned evaporated milk but seem to disagree on the number of eggs and whether they should be used whole or in part. One is apt to hear comments like, 'I make my *leche flan* with 3 eggs [and then a face is made as if to say that this custard is, well, tolerable] but you should really have my mother's. She uses 8 egg yolks. Hers is delicious.' The recipe I give below calls for 3 whole eggs and 2 egg yolks, a very happy middle ground.

In the Philippines caramel custard is served on special occasions with a topping of slivered *macapuno*, a mutant glutinous coconut. *Macapuno* in syrup is available tinned from some South-East Asian grocers. If you find it, you might wish to give it a try. If you want to invert the custard on to a serving plate to bring it to the table, you should butter the mould lightly before pouring in the liquid custard.

FOR THE CUSTARD:

3 large eggs

2 large egg yolks

3 oz (75 g) sugar

Pinch of salt

1¼ pints (750 ml) tinned evaporated milk

1½ teaspoons vanilla essence

Butter for greasing (optional)

FOR THE CARAMEL:

3 oz (75 g) sugar

Pre-heat the oven to gas mark 3, 325°F (160°C). Pour about 1 inch (2.5 cm) hot water into a roasting tin large enough to hold a custard mould of about 2 pints (1.1 litres) capacity or 4 individual moulds. Place this tin in the oven.

Put the eggs and egg yolks into a bowl. Beat them lightly, but not to a froth. Add the sugar and salt and mix in. Heat the evaporated milk until it is very hot. Slowly pour the hot milk into the bowl with the eggs, whisking vigorously as you do so. Add the vanilla and mix it in.

If you are intending to invert the custard when serving, grease the custard mould or 4 individual moulds with butter. Put the sugar for the caramel into a heavy frying-pan or other wide heavy pan, spreading it over the bottom. Heat it over a medium heat. Do not stir. As the sugar melts and turns brown, tilt the pan around so that the sugar moves a little. When all the sugar has caramelised, pour it into the custard mould (or divide it among the 4 individual moulds). Tilt the mould(s) around so that the sides are coated a little as well as the bottom. The sugar will harden: this is as it should be. Now strain in the hot liquid custard and place the mould(s) in the roasting tin of water. Cook in the oven for 1 hour–1 hour 10 minutes or until a knife inserted into the centre of the custard comes out clean and the custard seems set. Let the custard cool somewhat before inverting it, if that is what you want to do. You may serve it warm (I love it like this) or cold in the traditional way.

SERVES 4

SANKHAYA   THAILAND

COCONUT MILK CUSTARD

Instead of making custard with milk, many countries of South-East Asia use
coconut milk. The results are superb. You may, if you like, garnish the top of
each custard with desiccated coconut, sweetened or unsweetened, though I like
it quite plain with nothing to mar its smoothness.

This custard is cooked in a steamer. If you do not have one, you can
improvise. Use a wok with a rack or steaming tray with holes placed inside.
You could also use a large pan and balance a flat trivet on a tin inside it (cut out
the top and bottom of the tin). It is important that the water stays below the
trivet or steaming tray and that it is kept at a bare simmer so that the custard is
not filled with bubbles.

Tinned coconut milk, well stirred, is of the correct consistency for this
custard.

2 eggs

8 fl oz (250 ml) thick coconut
  milk (see page 263)

2½ oz (65 g) light brown sugar

Beat the eggs lightly. Stir the coconut milk well
and add it and the brown sugar to the eggs. Stir to
mix. Strain this mixture into a heavy pan or a
double-boiler set over boiling water. Cook gently,
stirring all the time with a whisk, until the mixture has thickened into a custard. Watch carefully
and do not let the eggs curdle. (If very slight curdling does occur, it can be strained out.) Strain the
custard into 4 small bowls. Cover lightly with
upturned saucers or aluminium foil and steam *very*
gently for 15–20 minutes or until the custard is
just set. Cool.

SERVES 4

WAIYOU HETAO TANG   HONG KONG

SWEET WALNUT SOUP

INSPIRED BY YUNG KEE, DESSERT SPECIALIST, OF HONG KONG

There is a neat clean restaurant in Hong Kong, freshly done up in peach and shining white formica, that specialises in desserts. Policemen, politicians and bankers in Rolls-Royces all haunt its pristine quarters and can be found there during the after-dinner hours.

One of the specialities is hot sweet soup. Machines in the back whirr busily, grinding sesame seeds to a fine paste for sweet sesame seed soup. One may order sweet red bean soup, or almond cream soup, or a sweet walnut soup. This soup may be served chilled in the summer.

2 teaspoons cornflour

3 oz (75 g) shelled walnut halves

4 fl oz (120 ml) groundnut oil

3½ tablespoons sugar

4 fl oz (120 ml) single cream

Mix the cornflour with 2 tablespoons water and set aside. Drop the walnuts into 2 pints (1.1 litres) boiling water and boil for 10 seconds. Drain the walnuts and leave them in a sieve.

Put the oil in a wok or small pan over a medium heat. Do not let the oil get very hot: the temperature should be around 325°F (160°C). Put in the walnuts and immediately take the wok or pan off the heat. Stir the walnuts for 5 seconds and then remove them with a slotted spoon. Put the walnuts in a blender, add 8 fl oz (250 ml) water and blend until smooth. Pour the walnut mixture into a clean pan. Some of the mixture will cling to the blender, so pour in another 8 fl oz (250 ml) water and blend again for a few seconds. Pour this liquid into the pan as well. Add the sugar, mix and bring to a simmer. Give the cornflour mixture a stir and add that to the pan as well. Stir and cook for 30 seconds or until the soup has thickened slightly. Add the cream and heat through. Pour into Chinese soup bowls or any other bowls of your choice and serve hot.

SERVES 4

APPLE OR GUAPPLE PIE

FROM THE EL IDEAL BAKERY IN SILAY

The El Ideal Bakery in the Negros township of Silay makes some of the best pies in the country. A crumbly guapple pie is only one of its superb offerings. What is a guapple? It is a big, round, hard guava. To prepare it, remove the seeds, coarsely chop it and then, to give it the tartness it lacks, toss it with lime juice, as well as with the more usual cinnamon and sugar. While the bottom of the pie has a regular short crust, the top is all crumb. If you can find very hard guavas, do use them for this recipe. I have used apples instead. You will need 1–2 limes to provide 1½ tablespoons finely chopped rind.

FOR THE BOTTOM CRUST:

5 oz (150 g) plain flour plus extra for dusting

1½ oz (40 g) chilled margarine

1 oz (25 g) chilled lard

About 2 tablespoons ice-cold water

FOR THE FILLING:

5 oz (150 g) sugar

¾ teaspoon ground cinnamon

1½ tablespons finely chopped lime or lemon rind

2 lb (1 kg) hard sour apples (such as Granny Smith)

1½ tablespoons cornflour

FOR THE CRUMB TOPPING:

4 oz (100 g) plain flour

7 oz (200 g) sugar

3 oz (75 g) chilled butter

First make the bottom crust. Sift the flour into a bowl. Cut the margarine and lard into small pieces and add them to the flour. Using 2 knives, or a pastry cutter, or your finger tips, cut or rub in the fat until the mixture resembles coarse bread-crumbs. Sprinkle in just enough ice-cold water – about 2 tablespoons – so that you can gather the dough into a ball. Knead lightly and quickly with the heel of your hand and then form a ball again. Spread a sheet of wax paper about 16 inches (40 cm) long on your work-surface. Put the ball of dough on it and flatten it a little. Place another sheet of wax paper on top of the dough. Now roll the dough from the centre outwards, keeping it between these sheets of paper, until you have a round that is about 10 inches (25 cm) in diameter. Lift up and remove the top sheet of paper. Now lift up the dough with the help of the lower sheet of wax paper and overturn it on top of an 8 inch (20 cm) pie plate or tin. Fit the pastry in. Trim away the uneven edges and then press down on the rim with the prongs of a fork. Refrigerate the pie plate containing the bottom crust.

Prepare a shelf in the lower third of your oven. Pre-heat the oven to gas mark 7, 425°F (220°C).

Next make the pie filling. Put the sugar and cinnamon into a large bowl. Add the finely chopped lime or lemon rind to the sugar mixture and toss. Peel, core and quarter the apples one at a time. As you cut each quarter, slice it crossways into ¼ inch (0.5 cm) thick pieces and let the pieces fall into the sugar mixture in the bowl. Toss them every now and then. When all the apples have been cut, add the cornflour to the bowl and toss again.

Now make the crumb topping. Put the flour in a bowl. Add the sugar and mix. Cut the butter into very small pieces and rub it in with your fingers. The mixture should resemble coarse breadcrumbs.

You are now ready to assemble the pie. Take the bottom crust out of the refrigerator. Put into this crust all the apples and their juice. Sprinkle the crumb topping over the apples. Put the pie in the oven on the prepared shelf and bake for 10 minutes. Turn the oven temperature down to gas mark 4, 350°F (180°C). Bake for another 45–50 minutes, or until the pie is nicely browned on the top. Serve lukewarm.

SERVES 6

BAN CHAN KUAY, SWEET MARTABAK   MALAYSIA, INDONESIA

FLUFFY PANCAKES WITH SWEET SESAME-PEANUT FILLING

WITH THE HELP OF RISNAWATI AGUS IN PADANG AND LIM SUAN HAR IN PENANG
A thick sweet pancake with crumpet-like holes, this is a very popular street snack in both Malaysia and Indonesia. Its origins probably go back to the *appam* (or 'hopper', as the British called it) of South India. I found it very interesting that a similar pancake, cooked today by Muslim fisherwoman of the southern Philippines, is still called an *appam*. In former times the yeast for this dish was provided by fermented palm toddy. Today most people seem to use either packaged yeast or baking powder.

In the streets of Padang in Western Sumatra the filling often consists of butter, sugar, crushed peanuts and, would you believe it, chocolate vermicelli! In Penang in Malaysia the chocolate is left out and roasted sesame seeds are added to the peanuts. Both versions are very good.

To make these pancakes, you need a heavy cast-iron frying-pan or an old-fashioned cast-iron crêpe pan. It should be about 6 inches (15 cm) in diameter, though a larger one would be acceptable. A lid is also required. (You can improvise with anything that fits.) These pancakes must be eaten hot. Since each pancake takes about 6 minutes to cook, I often have two pans going at the same time.

8 oz (225 g) plain flour

2 teaspoons plus 2 tablespoons castor sugar

2 teaspoons baking powder

¼ teaspoon salt

1 large egg

10 fl oz (300 ml) milk

4 teaspoons vegetable oil

1½–2 oz (40–50 g) Roasted Peanuts (see page 236)

1½ oz (40 g) unsalted butter

3 tablespoons roasted sesame seeds (see page 270)

2 tablespoons icing sugar (optional)

Sift the flour, the 2 teaspoons castor sugar, baking powder and salt into a bowl. Beat the egg lightly. Make a well in the centre of the flour and drop in the egg, milk and oil. Mix until you have a smooth batter. (You could mix all the ingredients in a blender if you like.) Cover and set aside for 2 hours or longer.

Crush the peanuts to a coarse powder in a mortar or a clean coffee grinder. Let the butter soften slightly. Put the remaining castor sugar and the roasted sesame seeds in separate bowls and keep them and the crushed peanuts near you when you start to cook.

Each pancake will require about 4 generous tablespoons of the batter. Pour that amount of water into a small cup or ladle just to get a rough idea of how much batter you will be scooping up each time. Discard this water and wipe your cup or ladle dry.

Set a cast-iron frying-pan on a medium-low heat. When it is hot, put in ½ teaspoon of the butter. Stir the batter quickly. Then pour in one measure of the batter, cover immediately and turn the heat to low. Cook for 3 minutes or until the top turns whitish and bubbles appear. Quickly spread 1 teaspoon of the butter over the pancake and top with 1 teaspoon castor sugar, followed by 1½ teaspoons sesame seeds, followed by 1 tablespoon peanuts. Cover again and cook for another 2½–3 minutes or until the pancake is done. Uncover and fold the pancake in half. Serve it as it is or dusted with 1 teaspoon icing sugar. Wipe out the frying-pan thoroughly before making the next pancake. Make all the pancakes in this way, not forgetting to stir the batter each time.

MAKES 6 PANCAKES

HOTOO TWIKIM   KOREA

CANDIED WALNUT HALVES

FROM MRS CHOI SANG IN

Fried candied walnuts are often served as after-dinner treats or snacks in both China and Korea. Here is the Korean version.

4 tablespoons sugar

4 oz (100 g) shelled walnut halves

10 fl oz (300 ml) groundnut oil

Put the sugar in a wide bowl or saucer. Bring a large pan of water to a rolling boil. Drop in the walnuts. Boil rapidly for 20 seconds. Drain the walnuts thoroughly and toss with the sugar. The sugar should cling to the nuts. Spread the walnuts out on a clean plate and let them cool off and dry for 30 minutes.

Set a strainer over a bowl. Put the oil in a wok or small frying-pan and set it on a medium-low heat; the oil should heat to about 250°F (120°C). Put in the walnuts. Stir and fry for 5–6 minutes or until the walnuts begin to glisten with a soft brown colour. Do not let them darken or they will taste bitter. Immediately pour the oil and walnuts into the strainer. Spread the walnuts out on a plate or tray, separating each one of them. Allow them to cool. Spread them on two changes of kitchen paper to absorb any remaining frying oil. Then store the walnuts in a tightly lidded jar.

SERVES 4

Peanut Candy

You need palm sugar for this candy which is made throughout South-East Asia. If you cannot get it easily, a good substitute is jaggery, sold by Indian grocers. It is sold in lump form and the best kind is crumbly and breakable, not hard as a rock.

5 oz (150 g) raw shelled unskinned peanuts

2 teaspoons groundnut oil

6 oz (175 g) palm sugar or jaggery

Set a medium-sized, preferably cast-iron frying-pan to warm up on a medium heat. Put in the peanuts. Stir and roast them for about 3 minutes or until they just begin to show signs of browning. Turn the heat down to medium-low. Continue to stir and cook for another 6–7 minutes or until the peanuts are roasted. Empty the peanuts on to a piece of kitchen paper and let them cool enough to handle. Now rub off the papery skins with the help of the kitchen paper and either blow them away or pick out the peanuts and put them in a bowl. Wipe out the frying-pan.

Brush a 7 inch (18 cm) pie tin with 1 teaspoon of the oil. Break up the palm sugar into small lumps and put it, as well as the remaining 1 teaspoon oil and 2 tablespoons water, into the frying-pan. Set it over a medium heat. When it is bubbling, turn the heat to low and let the palm sugar melt. Cook very gently for about 5 minutes for chewy candy, and about 8 minutes for hard, more brittle candy. The palm sugar will become thicker as it cooks. Take it off the heat. Put all the peanuts into the pan and immediately pour its contents into the oiled pie tin, letting the mixture spread evenly. Cool and then pull, tear or break the candy into pieces.

SERVES 4

Serving Japanese Rice Wine

Japanese habits are changing. It is now considered chic to drink whisky with a meal, and it is quite common to have beer, but *sake*, the indigenous rice wine, remains the national drink. Famed as the mythical drink of the gods in ancient times and limited to exclusive consumption by nobles and priests through the Middle Ages, today *sake* is available to the masses even in cardboard cartons that are sold out of slot machines just like Coca-Cola.

Sake is colourless, like vodka, though much less potent. Its alcoholic content can range from 15 to 17 per cent for the general market, and up to 20 per cent for some very special domestic varieties. At weddings and banquets it may be served cool, straight out of specially ordered cedar casks, rather like beer out of barrels. These days, it may also be served chilled. Chilled *sake* is being promoted quite a bit now in Japan to lure back the infidels who have been seduced by the fashionable white wines of France.

The most common way to drink *sake*, however, is not cooled or chilled, but warmed. Warming releases its aromas and allows the alcohol to enter the bloodstream with a more pronounced sense of urgency. *Sake* that has been warmed once is not considered good for drinking any more as its aromas have been dispersed. (It is, however, good for cooking.) It is for this reason that only small quantities of *sake* are warmed at a time. Servings, too, are small as the entire amount – a few thimblefuls – is supposed to be drunk at one go, before it has a chance to cool off. It is considered polite to serve one's neighbours when their glasses are empty and to let them do the same for you. It is *not* quite the done thing to serve oneself when in company. *Sake* can be drunk through every course of a Japanese meal.

Once a bottle of *sake* has been opened, it behaves rather like wine and it is best to drink it all up. You may, if you have to, keep it for 2–3 weeks in a cool place or in a refrigerator, but its life is limited.

For heating and serving this drink, *sake* bottles and cups are sold by many oriental shops. If you do not wish to buy a set, it is very easy to improvise. For drinking, use the smallest liqueur glasses in your possession. The size will probably be just right. For heating and serving, use any pretty glass or ceramic bottle of roughly 10 fl oz (300 ml) capacity. Fill it with *sake*. Half-fill a medium-sized pan with water and stand the bottle of *sake* in it. Heat the water gently. The *sake* should be very warm but not very hot. The temperature you should aim for is around 130°F (54°C). Heat several batches, one after the other, as you need them. By the way, the word for 'cheers' is *kampai*!

SALABAT PHILIPPINES

GINGER TEA

Ginger tea in some form or other is drunk nearly everywhere in the Far East. It is meant to be very good for coughs and colds and is also a digestive. In the Philippines it is often offered at breakfast and with mid-day snacks or *merienda*.

3 × 1 inch (2.5 cm) cubes fresh ginger

4–5 teaspoons honey or light brown or demerara sugar to taste

Peel the ginger and chop it coarsely. Put it into a small pan along with 1¾ pints (1 litre) water and the honey or sugar. Bring to the boil. Turn the heat to low and simmer gently for 15–20 minutes. Strain and serve. You may also serve this tea cold.

SERVES 4

KOPI JAHE INDONESIA

GINGER COFFEE

Indonesians grow their own coffee and one of the ways they drink it is very sweet, with a strong ginger flavour. It is quite easy to make such coffee at home. Whether you drink the instant version or use a filter, all you have to do is prepare a ginger broth and make your coffee with that instead of water. (Perhaps it is *not* advisable to make this coffee in one of the newer coffee machines in case the chemicals in ginger affect their inner workings.)

1 inch (2.5 cm) cube fresh ginger

Coffee, instant or ground for filtering, enough for 4 cups

Brown, demerara or white sugar to taste

Peel the ginger and dice it coarsely. Put it into a pan with about 4¼ teacups water. Bring the water to the boil, turn the heat to low and simmer gently for 15 minutes. Strain. If you are making instant coffee, put about 1 teaspoon coffee (or whatever amount you like) into each cup and pour the hot ginger broth over it. Stir it to mix. If you are using a filter, measure out just enough coffee for 4 people and put it into the filter. Pour the hot ginger broth over the coffee and let it filter through. Hand the sugar round separately when you serve the coffee.

SERVES 4

INGREDIENTS

Far Eastern cuisines depend for their distinctive flavours on some special ingredients. It is worth making the effort to seek these out from specialist grocers. Some ethnic grocers operate a mail order service (see page 299 for details). For the recipes in this book I have suggested substitutes for those ingredients which may be harder to find; in such cases the authentic ingredient is always given first, followed by the suggested substitute.

AGAR-AGAR This is a vegetarian gelatine made from a seaweed. It is available from Japanese, Korean and Chinese grocers in powder, flakes and sticks. The sticks, which look like uneven clear noodles, can be melted and used just like ordinary gelatine but this book only requires them to be used in salads. To do this, you should first soak them in cold water until they are soft but retain a nice crunch. Drain them and then cut them into any size you desire. They may now be added to any salad and dressed.

ANCHOVY PASTE This is the best substitute I can think of for the various types of shrimp paste used in South-East Asia. Most of the better supermarkets, delicatessens and certainly all speciality food shops sell it.

BAMBOO SHOOTS Unfortunately, we cannot usually get fresh bamboo shoots in the West and must make do with tinned ones. Good tinned bamboo shoots should be creamy white and crisp with a clean refreshing taste. Among the better brands available here is Companion, whose winter bamboo shoots in water are generally of excellent quality. You can buy tinned bamboo shoots in rather large hunks which may then be cut up into cubes of the desired size, or you can sometimes buy the cone-shaped and very tender bamboo shoot tips which are usually cut into comb-like wedges. Some tinned bamboo shoots come ready sliced. Try to get the chunks instead if possible.

All bamboo shoots that come out of a tin have a faint tinny taste. They should be washed in fresh water and drained before use. Any bamboo shoots that are unused may be covered with clean water and stored in a lidded jar in the refrigerator. In order to keep the bamboo shoots fresh, the water should be changed every day.

BASIL Many different types of fresh basil are used in South-East Asia. Each country – sometimes each province within a country – has different names for the basils. There is sweet basil (*bai horapha* in Thailand); holy basil with thin purplish leaves (*bai kaprow* in Thailand) and lemon basil (*bai manglak* in Thailand). Ordinary basil and fresh mint are the best Western substitutes for the very aromatic South-East Asian basils.

BEAN CURD This is made of soaked, mashed and strained soya beans and takes the form of white, milky, custard-like squares. Bean curd is sold by all Chinese grocers and health food shops. It can be soft (silken tofu) or firm. For the recipes in this book, use firm bean curd. Bean curd squares are sold packed in water. If you do not intend to use them immediately after buying them, put them in a bowl, cover them with fresh water and refrigerate. Change the water every day.

BEANS, LONG Also known as asparagus beans and yard-long beans, these can indeed be very long. In the Far East they come in two colours, pale and dark green, the dark being the crisper of the two. In the West we have to use what we can get, though good Chinese grocers here usually stock long beans. The beans are generally cut into smaller lengths and then used just like string beans. The best substitute is, indeed, string beans.

BEAN SAUCE, BLACK Commercially prepared sauces made of fermented soya beans are used throughout Malaysia and other parts of South-East Asia. They can be very thick, filled with crumbled beans, or smooth and somewhat thinner. Use any bottled or tinned black bean sauce that is available, such as that sold under the brand name of Amoy. Once you have opened a bottle you should store it, tightly closed, in the refrigerator.

BEAN SAUCE, YELLOW Like black bean sauce, this is commercially prepared from fermented soya beans, only it has a very pale brown, almost yellowish colour. It can be smooth but I like to use the kind that has whole or halved beans in it, usually labelled as 'crushed yellow bean sauce'.

BEAN SPROUTS These are crisp sprouts grown from the same mung beans sold in Indian stores as whole moong. They can now be bought fresh in supermarkets and health food stores as well as all Indian and Chinese grocers' shops. They are good when they are crisp and white. When you buy fresh sprouts, rinse them in cold running water and then put them into a bowl of fresh water. The bowl should be covered and refrigerated. If the beans are not used by the next day, you should change the water again.

It is considered proper to 'top and tail' bean sprouts before using them. This means pinching off the remains of the whole bean at the top as well as the threadlike tail at the bottom, and requires a lot of patience. The sprouts do indeed look better after this treatment, but I have to admit that I very rarely bother with it. Bean sprouts are also sold in tins. I never use them as they do not have the necessary crunch.

BLACK BEANS, SALTED These are salted, spiced and fermented soya beans. In their dry form they are sold in plastic bags. They need to be rinsed slightly to remove any excess salt and then chopped before use. They are also available in tins as 'black beans in salted sauce'. These are whole black beans usually floating in liquid. Lift them out of their liquid, chop them and use them as the recipe suggests.

BONITO STOCK *See Dashi*

BONITO, DRIED Known as *katsuo-bushi* in Japan, this fish of the mackerel family is filleted and dried until it becomes as hard as wood. It is then shaved with a plane rather like wood. These shavings are an essential ingredient in Japanese soup stock. The shaved flakes are sold in specialist shops as *hana-katsuo*.

CANDLENUTS Called *kemiri* in Indonesia and *buah keras* in Malaysia, these nuts are used in curry paste to give it thickness and texture. As they are not easily available in the West, a reasonable substitute would be raw cashew nuts or macadamia nuts, both of which are sold in health food shops and many supermarkets.

CARDAMOM, WHOLE PODS These small green-coloured pods have the most aromatic black seeds inside them. The pods are used to flavour curries, rice dishes and Indian-style desserts. In the West bleached whitish pods can be found in most supermarkets. They are less aromatic but may be used as a substitute for the green variety.

CASHEW NUTS These nuts travelled from the Americas via Africa and India all the way to China. For the recipes in this book they are used in their raw form as a substitute for candlenuts. (In fact all so-called 'raw' cashews have been processed to remove the prussic acid which they contain in their natural state.)

CASSIA BARK This is Chinese cinnamon, sometimes known as 'false cinnamon'. It is thicker, coarser and generally cheaper than true cinnamon but with a stronger flavour.

CHILLI BEAN SAUCE This reddish-brown, very hot and spicy sauce is made of soya beans, red chillies and other seasonings. It is used in the cooking of Western China and is sold in jars by Chinese grocers. The Yu Kwen Yick brand is the best.

CHILLI OIL This is an orange-coloured oil that gets its heat and its colour from red chillies. Small amounts of it can be put into dishes as they are being cooked to add a bit of pep to them. Many Chinese restaurants have small bottles of chilli oil on the table for those who wish to season their own foods further. Chilli oil can be bought from any Oriental grocer. If you wish to make your own, see the recipe on page 227.

CHILLI PASTE, THAI The Thai chilli paste (*nam prik pow*) is made by frying shallots and chillies together and then combining them with sugar and tamarind until the seasonings have the consistency of a thick jam. *Nam prik pow* is sold by Thai grocers. Unfortunately, the bottles are not always labelled as such. It is best to ask for help and tell the shop attendant whether you want it hot, medium or mild, as it comes in all three strengths. If you cannot obtain it, you can add a certain amount of similar seasoning to your food by combining one part each of chilli powder and sugar with two parts vegetable oil.

CHILLI POWDER This powder is made by grinding dried hot red chillies. You can add as much or as little to a dish as you like, depending on how hot you like your food.

CHILLIES, DRIED RED These can be small and thin or long and fat. The small variety is the most easily available. When used for making a spice paste they are usually soaked in water before being ground with other spices.

CHILLIES, FRESH GREEN AND RED Chillies originated in the Americas and then travelled via Africa and India all the way to China and Korea. The East has adopted them with a passion almost unmatched in the countries of their origin. Red chillies are just ripe green chillies. However, their flavour is slightly different, though their intensity can be exactly the same. Red chillies are used in hundreds of South-East Asian curry pastes not only for their heat but also for the beautiful colour they provide to the sauce. I find that a combination of our more common sweet red pepper with paprika and chilli powder makes the best substitute when I cannot obtain fresh red chillies.

Chillies are a very rich source of iron and vitamins A and C. As they vary tremendously in size, shape and heat, it might take a little experimenting to find the chillies you like best. To store fresh red or green chillies, wrap them first in newspaper, then in plastic, and place in the refrigerator. They should last for several weeks. Any that begin to soften and rot should be removed as they tend to infect the whole batch. Chillies may also be washed, dried and then frozen whole in plastic containers. Hot chillies must be handled carefully. When you are cutting them, be careful not to touch your eyes or your lips with your fingers or they will burn. Wash your hands thoroughly afterwards.

Chillies are used for their taste and heat in South-East Asia, but also to provide a decorative element to a dish. Sometimes they are sliced into rings, at other times into slivers, and often they are cut to resemble flowers.

To make chilli flowers Just cut off a tiny piece of the very tip, leaving the stem attached. Make four cuts lengthways in the chilli, starting from a little below the stem and going all the way down to the tip. You should now have four sections still attached at the stem. Remove all the seeds and soak the chillies in cold water until they open into flowers.

CHINESE CABBAGE There is great confusion about what Chinese cabbage is. To me, Chinese cabbage is the very chunky, pale green, long, wide-ribbed cabbage that is generally about 5 in (13 cm) or more in diameter. Its leaves resemble those of the vegetable sold as Chinese leaves, tapering away from the base in much the same way. They are, however, much wider and have greater flavour. This is the vegetable that is used to make the Korean cabbage pickle called *kimchee*. If you cannot get it, use Chinese leaves, which are widely available, as a substitute.

CHINESE CELERY This resembles Italian flat-leafed parsley. It is larger and coarser and its thin stalks have a distinct celery flavour. Celery stalks, finely diced, and celery leaves can be used as substitutes: follow the directions in individual recipes.

CHINESE CHIVES The leaves of Chinese chives are flat and have a pronounced garlic-like flavour. During the season in which the plant is budding, buds, still attached to their stalks, are also sold. They add a wonderful touch to stir-fried dishes. Ordinary chives can be used as a substitute (use their young buds as well).

CHINESE LEAVES This is an exceedingly slim version of Chinese cabbage. *See above.*

COCONUT, FRESH When buying a coconut, look for one that shows no signs of mould and is free from cracks. Shake the coconut. If it has a lot of water in it, it has a better chance of being good. People generally weigh a coconut in each hand and pick the heavier.

To break open a coconut, use the unsharpened side of a cleaver or heavy knife and hit the coconut hard all around its equator. You can hold the coconut in one hand over a large bowl while you hit it with the other, or you can rest the coconut on a firm solid surface while you hit it and then rush it to a bowl as soon as the first crack appears to catch the coconut water. Some people like to drink it; I do. This coconut water is not used in cooking but it is a good indication of the sweetness and freshness of the coconut.

You should now have two halves. Before proceeding any further, cut off a small bit of the meat and taste it. It should have a sweet flavour. If it is lacking in sweetness, this can be endured, but if it is at all rancid or mouldy you must discard the coconut. Now remove the tough outer shell by slipping a knife between it and the meat and then prising the meat out. Sometimes it helps to crack the halves into smaller pieces to do this.

The coconut meat is covered on the outer side with a thin brown skin. If your recipe calls for grated fresh coconut, remove the skin with a vegetable peeler or knife, cut the meat into small cubes and put these into a food processor or blender. Instead of the paste you might expect, the result will resemble grated coconut. You can freeze what you do not use. Grated coconut freezes very well and it is a good idea to keep some at hand.

As a substitute for grated fresh coconut you can use unsweetened desiccated coconut which is sold in most health food stores. To get the equivalent of 2 oz (50 g) of grated fresh coconut, soak 1 oz (25 g) desiccated coconut in 4 tablespoons water for 1 hour.

COCONUT MILK This is best made with fresh coconut but is also available tinned or can be prepared using powdered coconut milk, unsweetened desiccated coconut or blocks of creamed coconut. No coconut milk of any sort keeps well – this includes tinned milk after it has been opened. Even if you refrigerate it, it generally does not last more than a few days.

Using fresh coconut First prise the flesh off the shell as described above. Whether you also peel off the brown skin depends on the dish you are making. If it needs to look pale and pristine, remove the skin; if not, leave it on. Grate the coconut meat in a food processor or blender as explained above.

To make about 12 fl oz (350 ml) coconut milk, fill a glass measuring jug to the 15 fl oz (450 ml) mark with grated coconut. Empty it into a blender or food processor. Add 10 fl oz (300 ml) very hot water. Blend for a few seconds. Line a sieve with a piece of muslin or cheesecloth and place it over a bowl. Empty the contents of the blender into the sieve. Gather the ends of the cloth together and squeeze out all the liquid. For most of the recipes in this book, this is the coconut milk that is needed. If you leave this milk to stand for a while, cream will rise to the top. That is why I recommend stirring the coconut milk before using it. If just the cream is required, spoon it off the top.

Tinned coconut milk is available from most Chinese and Indian grocers but the quality varies. A brand which I like very much and use frequently is Chaokoh from Thailand. It is white, creamy and quite delicious. As the cream tends to rise to the top in a tin as it does in fresh coconut milk, always stir it well before using it. Sometimes, because of the fat in it, tinned coconut milk tends to become very grainy. To rectify this you can either whirr the milk for a second in a blender or beat it well. I find that whereas you can cook, say, a fish in fresh coconut milk for a long time, tinned coconut milk, which behaves differently, is best added towards the end of the cooking time.

Powdered coconut milk You can now buy packets of powdered coconut milk from Oriental grocers and supermarkets. Their quality varies from good to poor, the poor ones containing hard-to-dissolve globules of fat. I like the Emma brand, which comes from Malaysia. Directions for using the powder are given on the packet. To use the powder in any of the recipes in this book calling for coconut milk, mix an equal volume of powder and hot water and then stir well until the powder dissolves. If unwanted granules or globules remain, strain the milk before using it. I find that it is best to add coconut milk made of powder towards the end of the cooking period as it tends to separate easily.

Using unsweetened desiccated coconut Put 12 oz (350 g) desiccated coconut into a pan. Add 1 pint (600 ml) water and bring to a simmer. Now pour the contents into a blender or food processor and blend for 1 minute. Strain the resulting mixture through a double thickness of muslin or cheesecloth, pushing out as much liquid as you can. You should get about 1 pint (600 ml) coconut milk.

Using creamed coconut This, available in block form, can also be turned into coconut milk. I do not advise you to use it if you need large quantities of milk, but if you require just a few tablespoons, mix equal quantities of creamed coconut and hot water. The thick coconut milk that will result should be put into dishes only at the last moment.

CORIANDER, FRESH This is the parsley of the eastern half of Asia. Generally just the delicate, fragrant, green leaves are used. In Thai curries, however, the white root is ground in as well, and in China the stems are dried and put into sauces. The best way to keep fresh coriander is to stand it in a glass of water, cover it with a plastic bag and refrigerate the whole thing. Break off the leaves as you need them.

CORIANDER SEEDS These are the round, beige seeds of the coriander plant. They are sold either whole or ground. You can grind them yourself in a coffee grinder and then put them through a fine sieve.

CUMIN SEEDS Cumin was brought into South-East Asia by Arab and Indian traders. Sometimes the seeds are used whole, though in this region they are generally ground with the spice paste for curries.

CURRY LEAVES These highly aromatic leaves are used in many areas of South-East Asia. In Indonesia, where they are known as *daun salaam*, they are always used in their fresh form. They are not easily available fresh in the West, however. You could use the dried leaf, but I think a better substitute is the Indian curry leaf (*kari patta*) which is sometimes available both fresh and dried. Fresh curry leaves may be frozen flat in a polythene bag or plastic box.

DASHI This is Japanese soup stock. The most common kind is made with a combination of shavings from dried bonito fillets and a dried kelp (*konbu*). See the recipe on page 66.

DASHI-NO-MOTO This is instant *dashi*, available in granules and generally salted. It is sold under many brand names. The kind I use requires 2 teaspoons of the granules to be mixed with 15 fl oz (450 ml) hot water to make a basic Japanese stock. To season this stock for soup, add 1 tablespoon sugar, 3 tablespoons Japanese soy sauce (shoyu) and 2 tablespoons *sake*. Simmer it gently for a few minutes until the sugar dissolves.

EVAPORATED MILK Available in tins, this is milk which has been condensed but not sweetened. It is popular in Malaysian and Filipino cooking.

FENNEL SEEDS These seeds look and taste like aniseed, but they are larger and plumper. To grind fennel seeds, put a few tablespoons into a clean coffee grinder or other spice grinder and grind as finely as possible. Store in an air-tight container.

FISH SAUCE Known as *nam pla* in Thailand, *nuớc mắm* in Vietnam and *patis* in the Philippines, fish sauce is used in these countries much as soy sauce is used in China. A thin, salty, brown liquid made from salted shrimp or fish, it has a very special flavour of its own. It is obtainable from Chinese and Far Eastern grocers. You can either use salt as a substitute or improvise a sauce by combining 1 tablespoon water with ½ teaspoon salt, ¼ teaspoon soy sauce and ¼ teaspoon sugar.

FIVE-SPICE POWDER A Chinese spice mixture, this contains star anise, fennel, cloves, cinnamon and Sichuan peppercorns. It is sold already ground by Chinese grocers and many supermarkets. To make it yourself, combine 2 whole star anise, 1 teaspoon whole fennel seeds, 1 teaspoon whole cloves, a 2 inch (5 cm) stick cinnamon or cassia bark and 1 tablespoon Sichuan peppercorns. Grind as finely as possible in a clean coffee grinder or other spice grinder and store in a tightly lidded jar.

FRUIT, FRESH See pages 244–8.

FUNGUS, BLACK Also known as *moer* mushrooms and cloud ears, this tree fungus is a speciality of Sichuan province. It is sold in Chinese grocers' shops in the form of little, dried, curled up, black chips. Once these have been soaked, they enlarge considerably. At this stage you should feel with your fingers for the little hard 'eyes' they have and snip them off. Rinse them well as they tend to be very gritty. They have no particular flavour of their own but add a very nice crunchy texture.

GAI LAN This is the Chinese name for a wonderful member of the cabbage family. Deep green in colour, it is close in taste to broccoli but has no head. It is basically all leaves with tasty stems and small flowers. It is usually available in Chinese grocers' shops, where it may be labelled in Cantonese as *kai lan*.

GALANGAL Known as *Laos* and *lengkuas* in Indonesia, *langkuas* in Malaysia and *kha* in Thailand, this ginger-like rhizome has a very distinct earthy aroma of its own. Unfortunately, it is rarely available in its fresh form in the West. In the recipes which require it, I have suggested that you use dried sliced galangal. This has to be soaked in water before being ground with other spices to make curry paste. The dried slices are available from some Chinese and Far Eastern grocers. Ground dried galangal (frequently labelled 'Laos powder') is also obtainable.

GARLIC This is used in large quantities in South-East Asia. Very often it is sliced, fried into crisp chips and either scattered over foods as a garnish or mixed in with them to give them an added delicious flavour.

GHEE This is butter that has been clarified so thoroughly that you can even deep-fry in it. As it has no milk solids left in it, it does not need refrigeration. It has a nutty, buttery taste. All Indian grocers sell it and I find it more convenient to buy it ready-prepared. If, however, you need (or want) to make your own, put 1 lb (450 g) unsalted butter in a pan over a low heat and let it simmer very gently until the milky solids turn brownish and cling to the sides of the pan or fall to the bottom. The time this takes will depend on the amount of water in the butter. Watch carefully towards the end of the heating period and do not let the *ghee* burn. Strain the *ghee* through a triple layer of muslin or cheesecloth. Home made *ghee* is best stored in a refrigerator.

GINGER, FRESH You almost cannot cook without fresh ginger in the Far East. This rhizome has a sharp, pungent, cleansing taste and is a digestive to boot. Its brown skin is generally peeled, though in Chinese cookery it is often left on.

When a recipe calls for finely grated ginger, it should first be peeled and then grated on the finest part of a grater so that it turns into pulp. If a recipe requires a 1 inch (2.5 cm) piece of ginger to be grated, you will find that it is easier to grate that length while it is still attached to the large knob, so saving you from grating your fingers.

Ginger should be stored in a cool dry place. Many people like to bury it in dryish sandy soil. This way they can break off and retrieve small portions as they need them, while the rest of the knob generously keeps growing.

HOISIN SAUCE This is a thick, slightly sweet, smooth Chinese bean sauce with a light garlic flavour. It may be used in cooking or as a dip. It is sold by Chinese grocers and many supermarkets. Store in a tightly lidded jar in the refrigerator.

HOLY BASIL (*bai kaprow*) *See* Basil.

JAGGERY A form of raw lump cane sugar. You should look for the kind that crumbles easily and is not rock-hard. It can be bought at Indian grocers' shops. This is the best substitute for the palm sugar that is used in South-East Asia.

JAPANESE SEVEN-SPICE SEASONING *See Shichimi.*

KAFFIR LIME, LEAVES AND RIND Kaffir lime is a dark-green knobbly lime whose peel and leaves are used in South-East Asian cookery. They are highly aromatic and there is no real substitute for their flavour. If you are lucky enough to obtain fresh leaves, you should tear them in half and pull off their coarse centre veins before using them. Left-over leaves can be stored in a plastic bag in the freezer. Whole limes may be frozen as well. Both leaves and rind are sometimes available dried. You should use them in whatever form you can find. The leaves, dried rind and the lime itself are sold by Far Eastern and some Chinese grocers. You may have to ask for help in locating the rind, which may be labelled in Thai as '*piwma grood*'.

KOCHU CHANG A spicy paste made with fermented soya beans and red chillies, this is a very common seasoning in Korea. You can improvise by using the recipe on page 229.

KOKUM Various souring agents are used in Indonesian cookery. *Asem candis*, the dried skin of a mangosteen-like fruit, is very popular in Western Sumatra. As it is hard to find in the West, I use the Indian *kokum*, which is very similar.

KONBU This green, calcium-rich, dried kelp used for making stock (*dashi*) in Japan is sometimes sold as *dashi-konbu*. It resembles large long leaves and is available either folded up or cut into small pieces. *Konbu* (sometimes called *kombu*) should never be washed as its flavour resides near the surface. It should be wiped with a damp cloth just before use. *Konbu* may be allowed to simmer gently but never boil vigorously. It is obtainable from Japanese and some Chinese grocers where its price is generally a good indication of its quality.

KRUPUK These Indonesian wafers, somewhat similar to Indian poppadums, can be served with most meals. They are available in different flavours. The base, however, is usually tapioca. When dried, they are hard and brittle. When fried, they expand and turn very crisp. They are obtainable from Far Eastern and some Chinese grocers. Once a packet has been started, any unused wafers should be transferred to a tightly lidded jar.

LEMON GRASS Known as *sereh* in Indonesia, *serai* in Malaysia and *takrai* in Thailand, lemon grass is a tall, hard, greyish-green grass often used in South-East Asian dishes for its aroma and flavour. It is available in many supermarkets and ethnic grocers' shops. Usually only the bottom 6 inches (15 cm) are used and the strawlike top is discarded. The lemon grass may be used whole, its bottom first bruised with a hammer or other heavy object, or it can be sliced.

Lemon grass is fairly hard. To slice it, first cut off the hard knot at the very end and then slice crossways into paper-thin slices. Even when lemon grass is to be ground to a pulp in a blender it needs to be sliced thinly first or it does not grind properly. Lemon grass is best stored with its bottom end in a little water. This prevents it from drying out. You can also freeze stalks of lemon grass.

In South-East Asia lemon grass is always used fresh. Unfortunately, many of us in the West have to make do with the dried variety. I buy the dried sliced lemon grass and then soak it before I use it. As its name suggests, lemon grass has a citrus flavour and aroma. The best equivalent is lemon rind, though it is nowhere near as good as the real thing.

LIME AND LIME JUICE Limes of various sorts are plentiful in East Asia and are used with some abandon. The Philippines have the very small *kalamansi* lime which is squeezed over many foods and makes excellent limeade. There is the kaffir lime of Indochina with its unmatched aroma, and then there is the lime that we know in the West, though here it is generally found in a smaller size. If you cannot get limes, use lemons as a substitute.

MINT Mints of various sorts fill the vegetable shops of South-East Asia. They are used in cooking and also nibbled at on the side during meals or, as in Vietnam, added to morsels of food just as they are about to be eaten. Nothing but fresh mint can be used for this.

MIRIN This is sweetened *sake* which is used for cooking. Even though *mirin* is an essential ingredient in Japanese cookery, I have not used it too often in this book as it is exceedingly hard to find in the West. You can, however, make a reasonable substitute by combining equal parts of *sake* and sugar and then cooking them gently until the sugar dissolves and the liquid is reduced by half. I have tended to use this combination in my recipes instead of *mirin*. If you have access to a Japanese grocer, do try to get the real thing.

MISO A Japanese paste made from fermented soya beans, *miso* also contains other fermented grains. Among the *miso* easily available in the West is *aka-miso*, a reddish-brown variety. *Miso* can usually be found in health food shops. Sometimes it is labelled according to its colour – 'red', 'brown', 'yellow' or 'white'. In Japan, where *miso* is used a great deal, it is available in almost every shade and texture. It can be used for soups and stews, it can be lathered on to vegetables such as aubergines before they are grilled, and it can also be used in the preparation of pickles and dressings. To make soup, *miso* needs to be dissolved in water and then strained. It should never be allowed to boil vigorously.

MOOLI *See* Radish, white.

MUNG BEANS, WHOLE These yellow beans with green skins are sold in supermarkets, health food stores and Indian grocers' shops.

MUSHROOMS Hundreds of varieties of mushroom are sold in East Asia, from tiny pinheads to large meaty ones. In the West we can get only some of them and then only in their dried or tinned forms. (*See also* Fungus, black.)

Dried Chinese mushrooms These are available in Chinese shops. Price is generally an indication of quality. The thicker the cap, the meatier the texture. The mushrooms need to be soaked in warm water before they are used. The texture of the stalks remains hard, even after soaking, so they need to be cut off. The water in which the mushrooms have soaked should be strained and saved; it can be added to stocks or used to cook vegetables.

Straw mushrooms Smooth and meaty, there is nothing quite as delicious as a fresh straw mushroom. I eagerly await the day when they will be as commonly available in the West as they are in the East. Meanwhile, we have to make do with the tinned variety. Drain them first, rinse them and then use according to the instructions in the recipe.

MUSTARD SEEDS, BLACK AND YELLOW Black mustard seeds are used in curry pastes in some parts of South-East Asia. The seeds are tiny, round and of a blackish or reddish-brown colour. They can be brought from Indian grocers. Yellow mustard seeds may be substituted for the black ones.

NOODLES Noodles probably originated in the Far East. They are sold both dried and fresh, made of wheat or rice, and there are literally hundreds to choose from.

Fresh Chinese egg noodles These are usually sold in plastic bags in the refrigerated section of Chinese grocers' shops. A 1 lb (450 g) quantity usually serves 4–6 people. If you intend using smaller portions, divide the noodles as soon as possible after purchase, wrap well and freeze what you are not going to use that day; the rest can be refrigerated until you are ready to cook them.

The best way to cook fresh egg noodles is to put them into a large pan of boiling water. As soon as the water comes to the boil again, add a teacup of fresh water. Repeat this about three times or until the noodles are just tender. The noodles can now be drained and used as the recipe suggests. Frozen egg noodles defrost quickly and easily when dropped into boiling water: just stir them about at first to ensure that they separate.

Dried Chinese egg noodles When fresh noodles are not available, use dried ones. Put them into a large pan of boiling water and cook them as you would fresh noodles.

Fresh rice noodles These are white, slithery and absolutely delicious. In South-East Asia they are available in all sizes and shapes. Their freshness generally lasts for just a day. Many do not need to be cooked at all; others should be heated through very briefly. Unfortunately, these noodles are very hard to find in the West.

Dried rice noodles We usually have to make do with dried rice noodles in the West. For most of the recipes in this book, buy *banh phở* or any other flat rice noodles, soak them for about 2 hours or until they are soft and then cook them very briefly in a large pan of boiling water. Drain them and rinse them in cold water before using them as the recipe suggests. *Banh phở* is the noodle to use for making the Vietnamese noodle soup called *phở*.

Rice vermicelli Several recipes in this book call for rice vermicelli. These are very fine noodles which resemble cellophane noodles but are longer. Rice vermicelli are, of course, made from rice, whereas cellophane noodles are made from beans.

Cellophane noodles These noodles, also called bean thread or transparent noodles, are made from ground mung beans. Chinese grocers sell them dried. They are very fine and white in colour, and should be soaked for 10–15 minutes before use.

Udon These are white, slightly rounded or flat Japanese wheat noodles. They can be bought in the West only in their dried form. Cook them as you would Chinese fresh egg noodles, but then rinse them under cold running water.

OILS For most of the recipes in this book, I would recommend using groundnut (peanut) or corn oil. If the oil is used for deep-frying, it can be re-used. Skim off all extraneous matter with a slotted spoon or a Chinese mesh skimmer and then drop a chunk of ginger or potato into it and let it fry: this will absorb most of the unwanted flavours. When it is cool enough to handle, strain the oil through a triple thickness of muslin or cheesecloth or a large clean handkerchief. Let it cool completely and then store it in a bottle. When re-using, mix half old oil with half fresh oil.

Olive oil This is used only in the Philippines because of its Spanish heritage.

Sesame oil See the separate entry Sesame oil.

OYSTER SAUCE A thick, brown, Cantonese-style sauce made with oysters, this is salty and slightly sweet at the same time. It is used to flavour all sorts of dishes from vegetables to noodles. Once opened, a bottle of oyster sauce should be stored in the refrigerator. It keeps indefinitely. It can be obtained at some supermarkets and delicatessens and at Chinese grocers' shops. The Yu Kwen Yick brand is the best.

PALM SUGAR This is a delicious, raw, honey-coloured sugar used in many parts of South-East Asia. It comes in lump or fairly flowing forms. The best substitutes for it are either Indian jaggery or brown sugar.

PAPRIKA Not generally used in South-East Asian food. I use it frequently in place of fresh red chillies in order to give dishes their traditional colour.

PEANUTS Raw peanuts can be obtained at supermarkets, health food stores and ethnic grocers' shops. For roasting and crushing peanuts, see page 236.

PEPPERS, RED AND GREEN Cooked foods in South-East Asia are often garnished with strips of fresh hot red and green chillies. Since this tends to make the dishes even hotter than they already are, I frequently substitute strips of sweet red and green peppers. The curry pastes of this region often require a pounded paste made from fresh red chillies, which are very hard to obtain in the West. The best substitute is a combination of sweet red pepper, water and paprika.

PRAWNS Only raw prawns should be used for most of the dishes in this book. For instructions on peeling and de-veining a prawn, see page 291.

After you have prepared them, it is a good idea to wash prawns with salt to remove any sliminess and refresh them. To do this, put the peeled prawns in a bowl. Sprinkle a tablespoon or so of coarse salt over them and rub them lightly. Then wash them in cold water. Repeat once more, making sure that all the salt is washed away.

RADISH, WHITE Also known as mooli, this radish is large, long, thick and mild. It can be as large as 3 inches (7.5 cm) in diameter. It should be peeled before use.

RICE This is the staple in most parts of the Far East. Each country, sometimes each province within each country, favours its own special rice. For the purposes of this book, two types of rice should suffice: long-grain for all the dishes from Indonesia, Malaysia, Vietnam, Thailand, the Philippines and Hong Kong; and Japanese short-grain for Japanese and Korean dishes. The rice is generally washed before use. Directions for cooking these two types of rice can be found respectively on pages 203 and 204.

In some regions of Indochina, such as northern Thailand, glutinous rice is the staple. The grains are short and opaque. Directions for cooking glutinous rice are on page 205.

RICE PAPER, VIETNAMESE This is the thin translucent wrapper used to make Vietnamese spring rolls. It generally comes with the markings of the mats on which it was dried still imprinted on it. It needs to be dampened slightly in order to become soft. Rice papers are available in various sizes from just a few select Oriental grocers.

RICE WINE, CHINESE Several rice wines are used in Chinese cookery, the most common being Shao-Hsing. This is whisky-coloured with a rich sweetish taste. A reasonable substitute is dry sherry. I find that La Ina comes the closest in flavour.

SAFFRON This is the whole stigma of the autumn crocus, which is available dried and has a threadlike appearance. Look for a reliable source for your saffron as it is very expensive and there can be a great deal of adulteration.

SAKE This is the Japanese rice wine used for both cooking and drinking. It is available from many good off-licences and Japanese grocers. For more information see page 257.

SESAME OIL Oriental sesame oil is made from roasted sesame seeds. It therefore has a golden colour and a deliciously nutty taste and aroma. It is not used for cooking as such. Small amounts are added to dressings and foods just to give them a sesame flavour and sometimes a sheen. Store sesame oil in a cool place away from the light, but not in the refrigerator as it turns cloudy there.

SESAME PASTE Chinese and Japanese sesame pastes are made from roasted sesame seeds and have a darker colour than Middle Eastern sesame paste (*tahini*). If you cannot get the former, use the latter. All sesame paste has oil floating on the top. You need to mix the contents of the jar or tin thoroughly before using it. It can be very hard initially but mixing softens it up. Store sesame seed paste in the refrigerator. Sesame paste is available from ethnic grocers. *Tahini* is sold at most health food shops.

SESAME SEEDS You may use white sesame seeds or the beige ones for all the recipes in this book calling for these seeds.
   To roast sesame seeds, set a small cast-iron frying-pan over a medium-low heat. When it is hot, put in 1–3 tablespoons of sesame seeds. Stir them around until they turn a shade darker and give out a wonderful roasted aroma. Sesame seeds do tend to fly about as they are roasted. You could turn down the heat slightly when they do this, or cover the pan loosely. Remove the seeds from the pan as soon as they are done. You may roast sesame seeds in advance of when you need to use them. Cool them and store them in a tightly lidded jar. They will last several weeks in this way, though they are best when freshly roasted.

SHALLOTS For Westerners who tend to use shallots in small quantities, it is always rather startling to see South-East Asians use them in massive amounts. The shallot is the onion of this region. It is ground into curry pastes, sliced into salads and fried into crisp flakes to be used both as a garnish and as a wonderful flavouring.

SHICHIMI This Japanese seven-spice seasoning is also sold as 'seven-spice red pepper' ('*shichimi togarashi*'). Available only from Japanese grocers, it contains a coarsely crushed mixture of red pepper, a special Japanese pepper called *sansho*, roasted sesame seeds, roasted white poppy or hemp seeds, white pepper and tiny bits of orange peel and seaweed. Use my easy mixture called Sesame Seed Seasoning as a substitute.
   To make Sesame Seed Seasoning, set a small cast-iron frying-pan over a medium-low heat. When it is hot, put in 1 tablespoon sesame seeds, 1 tablespoon Sichuan peppercorns and 1 small dried hot red chilli. Stir these around until the sesame seeds turn golden-brown. Allow the mixture to cool, then grind it together with ¼ teaspoon salt in a clean coffee grinder or mortar until you have a fairly smooth powder.

SHRIMP PASTE This paste made of fermented shrimp is used as a seasoning throughout South-East Asia. It comes in many forms ranging from a grey watery paste to crumbly brown blocks. Only South-East Asian grocers sell an array of shrimp pastes.

To make your own substitute for the thin grey shrimp paste, buy a tin of 12 anchovy fillets in oil, drain well and then blend them with about 1½ tablespoons water.

There is really no substitute for the blocks, which are known variously as *blachan* and *terasi*. I have used anchovy paste in desperation. When *blachan* or *terasi* are used in uncooked dishes, they need to be roasted first. To do this, break off the amount you need and either hold it over a low gas flame with a pair of tongs, turning it around until it is roasted, or spread it out on a piece of aluminium foil and grill it. You could, if you like, fry it in a tiny amount of oil instead.

SICHUAN PEPPERCORNS Reddish-brown, highly aromatic pods, these are very slightly larger than ordinary peppercorns. They are available from Chinese grocers. Store them in a tightly lidded jar.

To roast Sichuan peppercorns, set a small cast-iron frying-pan over a medium-low heat. When it is hot, put in the peppercorns. Stir and fry until they release their fragrance. They might smoke a little, but the smoke will be highly aromatic. To grind roasted Sichuan peppercorns, allow them to cool, then put them into a clean coffee grinder or mortar and grind until you have a powder.

SOY SAUCE Many different soy sauces are used in East Asia. Not only do countries have their own brands of soy sauces but regions, towns and even individual villages within these countries sometimes proudly boast of producing their very own. All soy sauces are made from fermented and salted soya beans. They range from salty to sweet, from light to dark, from thick to thin, and have many different textures. Dark soy sauces tend to be thicker than the light ones and generally add a dark colour to the dish to which they are added. Light soy sauce tends to be thinner and saltier. There are several thick, textured, slightly sweet sauces that are used in parts of South-East Asia, many of which are unavailable in most Western markets. Very often black bean sauce is the best substitute. Since soy sauces vary so much in their saltiness, it is always advisable to use slightly less than the amount required in the recipe – you can always add more later.

Kecap manis is a thick, very sweet – indeed, syrupy – soy sauce used in Indonesia. If you cannot find it, you can make an approximation of it yourself by combining 8 fl oz (250 ml) dark soy sauce with 6 tablespoons treacle and 3 tablespoons brown sugar and simmering them gently until the sugar has dissolved.

Japanese and Chinese soy sauces have very different flavours. Hence, it is best to use Japanese soy sauces (sold in health food shops as shoyu) when called for and Chinese soy sauces as required. The best brand of Chinese soy sauce is Pearl River which is sold by Chinese grocers. It is most confusingly labelled: 'soy superior sauce' is dark and 'superior soy' is light. The best-known Japanese soy sauce is Kikkoman.

STAR ANISE A flower-shaped pod of a brownish colour, this spice has a decided aniseed flavour. It is used in Chinese-style braised dishes. Store it in a tightly lidded jar.

TAMARIND This is a bean-like fruit of a tall tree. When ripe, the beans are peeled, de-seeded and packed in lumps or bricks. Tamarind is sold by South-East Asian and Indian grocers.

To make your own tamarind paste, break off 8 oz (225 g) from a brick of tamarind and tear it into small pieces. Put them into a small china, glass or stainless-steel bowl, cover with 15 fl oz (450 ml) very hot water and set aside for 3 hours or overnight. (You could achieve the same result by simmering the tamarind in a pan for 10 minutes.) Set a sieve over another china, glass or stainless-steel bowl and empty the tamarind and its soaking liquid into it. Push down on the tamarind with your fingers or the back of a wooden spoon to extract as much pulp as you can. Put whatever tamarind remains in the sieve back into the soaking bowl. Add 4 fl oz (120 ml) hot water to it and mash a little more. Return it to the sieve and extract as much more pulp as you can. Some of this pulp will be clinging to the underside of the sieve: do not fail to retrieve it.

This quantity will make about 12 fl oz (350 ml). Whatever paste is left over may either be put into the refrigerator, where it will keep for 2–3 weeks, or it can be frozen.

TURMERIC Many countries of South-East Asia use fresh turmeric. Fresh turmeric is a rhizome not unlike ginger but smaller in size and more delicate in appearance. Many Indian stores sell it. Even though the ground tumeric available in most supermarkets is adequate, use fresh turmeric whenever possible. A 1 inch (2.5 cm) piece of fresh turmeric is equal to about ½ teaspoon ground turmeric. Like ginger, it needs to be peeled and ground. This grinding is best done with the help of a little water in an electric blender.

VINEGAR There are probably as many vinegars in the East as there are soy sauces, with every district in every country producing its very own brand. China, for example, has red, black and white vinegars. The Philippines have a pale, slightly milky vinegar made from palm toddy, and Japan is proud of its very mild rice vinegars. To make matters easy for those of you who are going to use this book, I have specified distilled white vinegar almost all the way through. Occasionally, when Japanese rice vinegar is called for and you cannot obtain it, make your own version by combining 3 parts distilled white vinegar with 1 part water and ¼ part sugar.

WATER CHESTNUTS Dark-skinned and chestnut-sized, these grow in water. They are sold fresh only by some Chinese grocers. The inside flesh is deliciously crisp and white. Tinned water chestnuts do not compare but may be used in cooked dishes.

YELLOW BEAN SAUCE *See* Bean sauce, yellow.

ANCHOVY PASTE

AUBERGINE

BAMBOO SHOOTS

AGAR-AGAR

THAI BASILS

BEAN CURD

ENGLISH BASIL

CHINESE LONG BEANS

BLACK BEAN SAUCE

CRUSHED YELLOW BEAN SAUCE

BEAN SPROUTS

TINNED BLACK BEANS

DRIED SALTED BLACK BEANS

BONITO FLAKES

CANDLENUTS

CASHEW NUTS

CARDAMOM PODS

CASSIA BARK

CHILLI BEAN SAUCE

DRIED CHILLIES

CHILLI OIL

CHILLI PASTE

CHILLI POWDER

CHILLIES

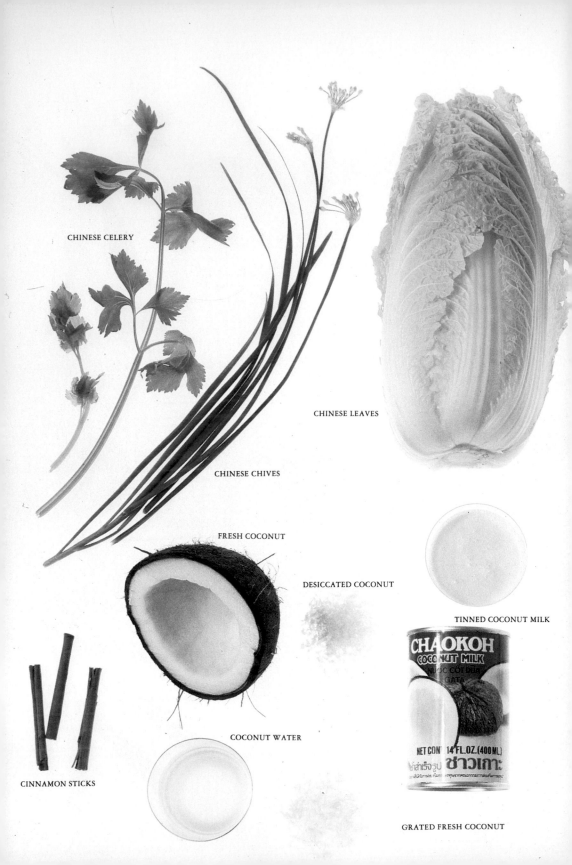

CHINESE CELERY

CHINESE LEAVES

CHINESE CHIVES

FRESH COCONUT

DESICCATED COCONUT

TINNED COCONUT MILK

CINNAMON STICKS

COCONUT WATER

GRATED FRESH COCONUT

CREAMED COCONUT

COCONUT POWDER

INSTANT coconut milk powder

FRESH CORIANDER

CORIANDER SEEDS

CUMIN SEEDS

GROUND CORIANDER

GROUND CUMIN

277

CURRY LEAVES

POWDERED SEASONING
"Dashi no Moto"
Ingredients: Bonito, Salt
Sugar, Monosodium glutamate
NET WT: 50g.
Distributed by
ARIMOTO TRADING CO., LTD.
No.10-12 Sotokanda 3-chome
Chiyoda-ku, Tokyo, Japan.
Made in Japan.

DASHI-NO-MOTO

DASHI STOCK

EVAPORATED MILK

DILL

FENNEL SEEDS

GROUND FENNEL

FISH SAUCE

FIVE-SPICE POWDER

BLACK FUNGUS

GAILAN

DRIED SLICED GALANGAL

FRESH GALANGAL

GALANGAL OR LAOS POWDER

GARLIC

GHEE

GINGER

HOI SIN SOSSE
海鮮醬
TƯƠNG ĐEN
250ml NETTO

HOI SIN BARBECUE SAUCE

HOISIN SAUCE

JAGGERY

KAFFIR LIME FRUIT

DRIED KAFFIR LIME RIND

FIRST WORLD
PIW MA GROOD
Peau de Cumbawa

DRIED AND FRESH KAFFIR LIME LEAVES

KOCHU CHANG

KOKUM

KOHLRABI

KRUPUK

KONBU

LEMON GRASS

DRIED SLICED LEMON GRASS

LIME JUICE

281

MIRIN

MISO

MINT

MUNG BEANS

DRIED CHINESE MUSHROOMS

STRAW MUSHROOMS

YELLOW MUSTARD SEEDS

BLACK MUSTARD SEED

CELLOPHANE NOODLES

DRIED RICE *PHO* NOODLES

FRESH RICE NOODLES

RICE VERMICELLI

DRIED EGG NOODLES

FRESH EGG NOODLES

UDON NOODLES

GROUNDNUT OIL

OLIVE OIL

OYSTER SAUCE

PALM SUGAR

PAPRIKA

PEANUTS: RAW, ROASTED, AND ROASTED AND GROUND

RAW PRAWNS

PEPPERS

JAPANESE RICE

LONG-GRAIN RICE

GLUTINOUS RICE

MOOLI

RICE PAPERS

SAFFRON

CHINESE RICE WINE

SAKE

SESAME OIL

SESAME PASTE AND TAHINI

SESAME SEEDS

SHALLOT

SCHICHIMI

SHRIMP PASTE

SICHUAN PEPPERCORNS

SICHUAN PEPPERCORNS, ROASTED AND GROUND

CHINESE DARK SOY SAUCE

CHINESE LIGHT SOY SAUCE

JAPANESE SOY SAUCE

INDONESIAN SOY SAUCE

STAR ANISE

TURMERIC

FRESH TAMARIND

BLOCK TAMARIND

DISTILLED WHITE VINEGAR

JAPANESE RICE VINEGAR

WATER CHESTNUTS

TECHNIQUES

The general techniques used in Far Eastern cookery are not all that different from those used in the West. A few pointers may, however, be of some help.

Cutting meats and vegetables

Meats and vegetables are frequently cut into strips or dice before they are cooked, so that the pieces cook evenly. This is particularly important for quick stir-frying and for the general look of the food. Aesthetics play a very special role in this region, reaching a pinnacle in Japan where restaurants are judged on the look of their food as much as on its taste.

To de-bone a chicken leg (see below)
The chicken recipes in this book often call for boneless dark leg meat as it stays much more moist than white meat and has a better flavour. De-boning a chicken leg is actually quite easy. (a) Using a sharp knife, make a deep slit along the length of the bone and drumstick. (b) Free the meat at both ends, cutting at right angles to the bones. (c) Now cut – almost scrape – the meat off the thigh bone and drumstick, freeing the meat from the middle joint as you do so. (d) The chicken meat may now be cut into pieces of the desired size.

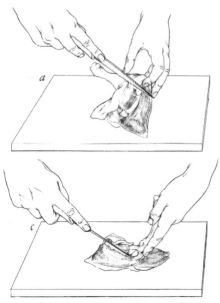

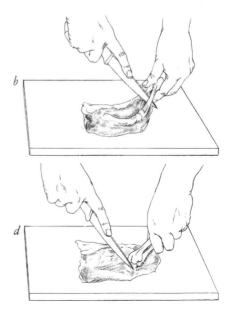

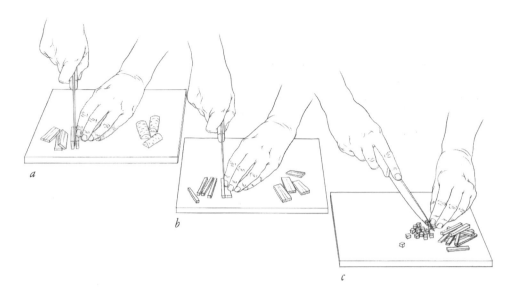

To cut vegetables into julienne strips and dice (see above)

Each vegetable demands its own cutting technique. Generally speaking, you should first cut the vegetable into slices of the required width. Then cut them lengthways into strips. These strips can be cut crossways if small dice are required.

To cut a carrot into julienne strips of 2 inches (5 cm) long, cut off the top and tip and then cut the carrot crossways into 2 inch (5 cm) chunks. (a) Cut each chunk lengthways into slices of the desired thickness. (b) Cut each slice lengthways again, to make the strips. (c) Cut each strip into dice, if required.

To slice meat into thin slices and strips

It frequently helps (though it is not essential) to partially freeze, say, a beef steak, before you cut it against the grain into thin slices. If strips are called for, stack a few slices together at a time to make the cutting quicker.

To peel and de-vein a prawn

These instructions and illustrations (*see below*) apply to the large uncooked prawns known as Pacific or king prawns. These are usually sold frozen and in the shell, but with the heads already removed.

(a) First pull off the tail. Then peel off the shell and, with it, the tiny legs. (b) Make a shallow cut down the back of the prawn. (c) Remove the fine digestive cord which runs the length of it.

To clean squid

Twist off the head (with the tentacles). The inner body sac will probably come away with it. Discard the sac and the hard eye area, which you may have to cut off with a knife. Retain the tentacles. If possible, pull off some of the brown skin on the tentacles. (You may safely leave this, if you wish.) Peel the brownish skin from the tubelike body. Discard this skin and pull out the smooth inner cartilage (or pen). The squid can now be washed and used as your recipe requires.

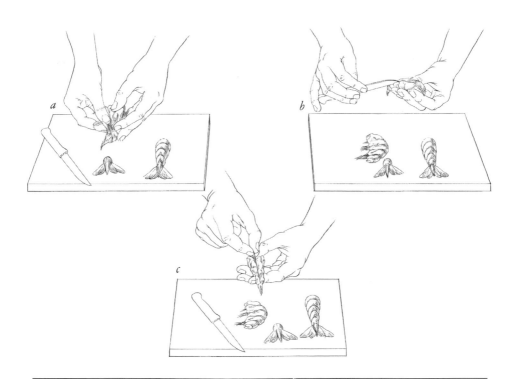

Marinating

Meats are often cut up and put into marinades before they are cooked. A marinade tenderises meat and injects it with all the flavours and aromas of its myriad ingredients. The meat can then be grilled or quickly stir-fried while retaining the tastes of all its seasonings.

Basting sauces

As meat, fish or poultry is grilling, it is often basted. Sometimes, as in Japan, the basting sauce has sugar in it so it not only provides flavour but a final glaze as well. In Malaysia basting sauces may contain coconut milk which provides the lubrication needed to keep the meat, poultry or fish from drying out. In Indonesia a most practical (and aromatic) brush is made from a stick of lemon grass which is lightly pounded at the end!

Spice pastes

Most curry-style dishes require that a spice paste be prepared first. To this end, fresh and dried spices are pounded in a mortar and then fried in oil to get rid of their raw taste. Freshly pounded spice pastes of good quality are sold in most Thai and Malaysian markets. We in the West have to prepare our own, but we have blenders and coffee grinders to make our lives easier.

Fresh hot red chillies, pounded to a paste, are a major ingredient in Thai, Indonesian and Malaysian dishes. While many people pound their own chillies at home in a mortar, others are content to buy them, already pounded, in small plastic bags. When I cannot get fresh hot red chillies, I blend together sweet red peppers and chilli powder; this mixture gives just the right colour to the dishes where it is needed.

Cooking coconut milk

When cooking coconut milk, care must be taken that it does not curdle. Stir it constantly as it cooks. I often add it only towards the end of the cooking period and then just bring it to a simmer and leave it at that. Coconut milk may be simmered for a long period, but only if it is stirred most of the time.

Garnishes which are flavourings

A garnish in the West often means a radish or a tomato cut into a flower. This sits on the edge of the plate, to be admired and perhaps even nibbled upon. It frequently has no real connection with the food it enhances. In the East what might look like a garnish is often an integral part of a dish. For example, crisply fried shallots and crushed roasted peanuts may be sprinkled over a dish at the last minute. They are there because without their flavour and texture the dish would be incomplete.

Grilling

Grilling is very popular throughout the Far East. Tiny pieces of meat skewered on bamboo sticks (*satays*) and freshly grilled on charcoal are sold in the bazaars of Indonesia, Malaysia and Thailand, as everyone loves to eat out. The Koreans cut their meat into strips, marinate it and grill it on their dining tables. Each home is equipped with special portable burners and grills just for this purpose. The Japanese pierce a fillet of fish with several skewers, then grill it with frequent bastings of sweetish sauces. The skewers are very helpful when it comes to turning the fillets over. As they are inserted against the grain, the fish does not fall apart. Bamboo skewers should be soaked in water for 30 minutes before use so that they do not burn.

Although most of the grilled dishes in this book can be cooked under a domestic grill, the taste will be more authentic if you are able to use a barbecue instead. When grilling on charcoal, it is important to get the coals white-hot before you start.

Steaming

Steaming is used for cooking anything from plain rice to complete dishes such as Fish Steamed with Lemon Grass and Savoury Egg Custard with Prawns and Mushrooms. Just as every home in the West has a roasting tin, so every home in the Far East tends to have a steamer. Steaming cooks gently and preserves flavour.

One of the most satisfactory utensils for steaming is a wok because its width easily accommodates a whole fish, a casserole or a large plate of food. Use a wok with a flat base or set a round-based wok on a wire stand. Put a metal or wooden rack into the wok. (You could use a small inverted empty tin can instead.)

Now pour in some water. Bring it to a gentle boil and lower in the food. The water should stay about ¾ inch (2 cm) below the level of the food that is being steamed. Extra boiling water should be kept at hand just in case it is needed to top up the level.

Cover the whole wok, including the food, with a wok lid or a large sheet of aluminium foil.

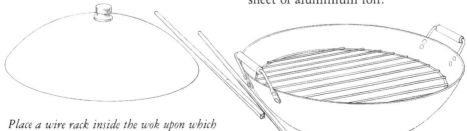

Place a wire rack inside the wok upon which the food is put for steaming.

Stir-frying

This is fast cooking over high heat in a small amount of oil. A wok is essential for this. The oil is heated and often flavourings such as garlic and ginger are tossed around in it before cut meats and vegetables are added. These, too, are tossed around quickly until they are cooked.

Deep-frying

You need several inches of oil in a wok or frying-pan and a good deal more in a deep-fat fryer in order to deep-fry. The oil must be heated to the required temperature before you drop in a single morsel of food. Properly deep-fried foods are not at all greasy; the outside is beautifully crisp while the inside is completely cooked.

Oil that has been used for deep-frying may be re-used. Let it cool completely and then strain it. Store it in a bottle. When you cook again, use half old oil and half fresh oil. Oil that has been used for frying fish should be re-used only for fish.

Dry-roasting

Spices are often dry-roasted before use. It is best to do this in a heavy cast-iron frying-pan which has first been heated. No oil is used: the spices are just stirred around until they brown lightly. Roasted spices develop a heightened, nutty aroma. They can be stored for at least several months in an air-tight jar.

Blanching and refreshing

In order to keep vegetables crisp and their colour bright, they may, after preparation, be plunged very briefly into a large pan of water at a rolling boil – that is, boiling furiously. The reason for using a lot of boiling water is that you do not want the temperature of the water to drop when the vegetables are put into it: this would slow their cooking time and therefore affect both their colour and crispness. The vegetables should be cooked in the water until barely tender (but still crisp), drained quickly and then either plunged into a large quantity of iced water or rinsed under cold running water. This helps to set their colour and stop the cooking process.

Poaching

Many recipes require that chicken breasts be poached in water to just cover. Breast meat is fairly dry and it toughens easily. To poach properly, it is important that the water be barely simmering. If it boils too rapidly, it will toughen the meat.

Braising

This also involves cooking foods slowly in liquid but over a long period. Whole birds and fish can be cooked in this way. The liquid is always flavoured. It may be stock or water flavoured with wine, herbs and spices; or, as in one recipe in this book, the braising liquid could be tea.

EQUIPMENT

This book does not require unusual equipment. However, it does help to have the following:

A wok

This is an all-purpose utensil that may be used for steaming, simmering, stir-frying or deep-frying.

A wok is traditionally a round-bottomed pan. Because of its shape, flames can encircle it and allow it to heat quickly and efficiently. It is most economical for deep-frying as it will hold a good depth of oil without needing the quantity a straight-sided pan would require. It is ideal for stir-frying as foods can be vigorously tossed around in it. As they hit nothing but well-heated surfaces, they cook fast and retain their moisture at the same time.

Choosing a wok What kind of wok should you buy? Advances are being made all the time and every year seems to bring new woks into the market place. Traditional woks of good quality are made either of thin tempered iron or carbon steel. The ideal wok is 14 inches (35 cm) in diameter and fairly deep. (Saucer-shaped shallow woks are quite useless.) A round-bottomed wok works well on a gas hob. A new,

somewhat flat-bottomed wok has been invented for people who have electric hobs. I cannot say I love it. Instead I have opted for a yet newer invention in my country house in the USA which has an all-electric kitchen. This is an electric wok – but a very special one. The brand name is Maxim. It is the only electric wok I know which heats very quickly, becomes *very* hot and allows foods to be both stir-fried and simmered.

Seasoning a wok The iron and carbon steel woks leave the factory coated with oil. This needs to be scrubbed off with a cream cleanser. Then a wok needs to be seasoned. Rinse it in water and set it over a low heat. Now brush it all over with about 2 tablespoons vegetable oil. Let it heat for 10–15 minutes. Wipe the oil off with a piece of kitchen paper. Brush the wok with more oil and repeat the process 3–4 times. The wok is now seasoned. Do not scrub it again; just wash it with hot water and then wipe it dry. It will *not* have a scrubbed look. It will, however, become more and more 'non-stick' as it is used.

Wok accessories For use on a gas hob, a wok needs a stand that not only stabilises it but allows air to circulate underneath. The perfect stand is made of wire. The collar variety with punched holes seems to kill free circulation of air and heat and should not be used on gas hobs.

When you buy a wok, it is also a good idea to invest in a curved spatula, a steaming tray and a lid.

Cast-iron frying-pans

I find a 5 inch (13 cm) cast-iron frying-pan ideal for roasting spices and a large one perfect for pan-grilling thin slices of meat. All cast-iron frying-pans can be heated without any liquid and they retain an even temperature. Once properly seasoned, they should never be scrubbed with abrasive cleansers.

Blender and coffee grinder

In the Far East mortars, pestles and grinding stones of varying shapes, sizes and materials are used to pulverise everything from sesame seeds to fresh hot red chillies. I find it much easier to use an electric blender for wet ingredients and a clean electric coffee grinder for dry ones.

Grater

The Japanese make a special grater for ginger and horseradish. It has tiny hair-like spikes that are perfect for their purpose. If you ever find one, do buy it. Otherwise use the finest part of an ordinary grater for grating fresh ginger.

Double-boiler

This is simply one pan balanced over another. The lower pan holds boiling water and allows the ingredients in the other pan to cook very gently. Double-boilers are available from good kitchenware shops but can be easily improvised.

Electric rice-cooker

Many households in the Far East seem to have one of these gadgets. Its main use it to free all burners on the hob for other purposes and make the cooking of rice an easy, almost mindless task. I do have one and use it only for plain rice.

Deep-fat fryer

For those who are afraid of deep-frying, this is a god-send. Because it has a lid that closes over all splattering foods, this piece of equipment also helps to make deep-frying a painless, safe and clean task.

Racks for grilling fish

In Indonesia hinged double racks are used for grilling fish over charcoal. The fish lies sandwiched between the two racks and can be easily turned and basted. Many types of fish racks are available in the West, some even shaped like a fish. I find them exceedingly useful.

MENUS

There is no reason why you should feel compelled to put together meals with dishes from just one country. However, in case you want to, here are typical menus from each of the eight countries I visited. In each case the first menu is for a simple family meal, the second for a more elaborate dinner party. At the end of this list I also suggest a couple of mixed menus.

THAILAND
HOT AND SOUR PRAWN SOUP

MINCED CHICKEN STIR-FRIED WITH BASIL

GREENS WITH GARLIC AND OYSTER SAUCE

PLAIN RICE

CHICKEN, PRAWN AND FRUIT SALAD

FISH STEAMED WITH LEMON GRASS

EASY BEEF CURRY

PLAIN RICE

FRESH FRUIT OR COCONUT MILK CUSTARD

JAPAN
FERMENTED BEAN PASTE SOUP WITH BEAN CURD

BREADED PORK CUTLETS

EAST-WEST SAUCE

PLAIN JAPANESE RICE

GREEN BEANS WITH SESAME DRESSING

GREEN BEANS WITH SESAME DRESSING

STUFFED MUSHROOMS

GRILLED MACKEREL WITH SWEET SOY SAUCE

ASPARAGUS AS BOTH FOOD AND GARNISH

PLAIN RICE

FRUIT

INDONESIA
WHOLE GRILLED FISH, SOUR AND SPICY

CAULIFLOWER AND CARROTS WITH A COCONUT DRESSING

PLAIN RICE

FRESH FRUIT

SPICY CHICKEN KEBABS WITH PEANUT SAUCE

BEEF CHUNKS COOKED IN COCONUT MILK

SPICED MUSHROOMS IN A PACKET

PLAIN RICE

PRAWN WAFERS

FRESH FRUIT

KOREA
STIR-FRIED PORK WITH RED PEPPER

SEASONED SPINACH

PLAIN JAPANESE (OR KOREAN) RICE

CABBAGE PICKLE

SAVOURY EGG CUSTARD WITH PRAWNS AND MUSHROOMS

MARINATED AND GRILLED BEEF STRIPS

STIR-FRIED COURGETTES WITH SESAME SEEDS

PLAIN JAPANESE (OR KOREAN) RICE

CABBAGE PICKLE

FRESH FRUIT

VIETNAM
PORK AND CRAB SOUP

EASY BEEF KEBABS

PLAIN RICE

A GREEN SALAD WITH LETTUCE, MINT
AND BASIL

SAVOURY PORK AND CRAB TOASTS

AROMATIC AND SPICY BEEF STEW

SMOKY AUBERGINES IN A LIME SAUCE

KOHLRABI OR BROCCOLI STEM SALAD

PLAIN RICE

FRESH FRUIT

MALAYSIA
RICE NOODLES IN A COCONUT CURRY
SOUP

BEAN SPROUTS WITH A SPICY COCONUT
DRESSING

SQUID IN CHILLI AND GARLIC SAUCE

SPICY PRAWN AND CUCUMBER CURRY

PERFUMED RICE WITH VEGETABLES
NONYA-STYLE

AUBERGINES IN A THICK, HOT, SWEET
AND SOUR CHILLI SAUCE

FLUFFY PANCAKES WITH SWEET SESAME-
PEANUT FILLING

PHILIPPINES
PORK COOKED IN A PICKLING STYLE

PLAIN RICE

MANGE-TOUT STIR-FRIED WITH PRAWNS

CARAMEL CUSTARD FILIPINO-STYLE

MACKEREL 'COOKED' IN LIME JUICE

GLORIOUS SEAFOOD SOUP

LAMB OR GOAT STEW WITH POTATOES,
PEPPERS AND OLIVES

PLAIN RICE

MANGE-TOUT STIR-FRIED WITH PRAWNS

APPLE OR GUAPPLE PIE

HONG KONG
COLD SESAME NOODLES WITH CHICKEN
AND VEGETABLES

LAMB WITH SPRING ONIONS

PLAIN RICE

BRAISED BROAD BEANS

FRESH MELON

COLD CHICKEN WITH SESAME AND
CHILLI SAUCE

GLAZED GINGERY SPARERIBS

FISH FILLETS WITH BLACK BEAN SAUCE

SALAD OF CARROTS, CELERY, CUCUMBER
AND HAM

PLAIN RICE

SWEET WALNUT SOUP

MIXED MENUS
HOT AND SOUR PRAWN SOUP

AROMATIC AND SPICY BEEF STEW

STIR-FRIED COURGETTES WITH SESAME
SEEDS

PLAIN RICE

FRUIT

CHICKEN BITS ON A SKEWER

FISH, SHELLFISH AND BEAN CURD STEW

GREEN BEANS AND CARROTS
WITH GINGER AND CHILLIES

PLAIN RICE

GINGER TEA

CARAMEL CUSTARD FILIPINO-STYLE

CANDIED WALNUT HALVES

MAIL ORDER LIST

There are now many ethnic grocers throughout the UK. Here is a list of those which offer a mail-order service.

LONDON

Welcome Supermarket,
31–37 Wardour Street, London W1
Tel: 01 437 7963
Matahari Supermarket,
102 Westbourne Grove, London W2
Tel: 01 221 7468
Tawana Supermarket,
18 Chepstow Road, London W2
Tel: 01 221 6316
Sri Thai,
56 Shepherds Bush Road,
London W6 7PH
Tel: 01 602 0621
Curry Shop,
37 The Market, Covent Garden,
London WC2
Tel: 01 240 5760
**Golden Gate Hong Ltd, Chinese
Supermarket,**
14 Lisle Street, London WC2H 7BE
Tel: 01 437 0014
Harrods Pantry Dept,
Harrods Ltd, Knightsbridge,
London SW1X 7XL
Tel: 01 730 1234
Ken Lo's Kitchen,
14 Eccleston Street, London SW1 0NZ
Tel: 01 730 4276/7734
Patel Brothers,
187–191 Upper Tooting Road,
London SW17
Tel: 01 672 2792 or 767 6338
Yoshino,
15–16 Monkville Parade,
Temple Fortune, Finchley Road,
London NW11
Tel: 01 209 0966/7
(Japanese foods)

SOUTH EAST

The Curry Club,
PO Box 7, Haslemere, Surrey
GU27 1EP
Tel: (0428) 2452
Lotte Supermarket,
126 Malden Road, New Malden,
Surrey
Tel: 01 942 9552

WEST

Tajmahal International Store,
146 Charminster Road, Bournemouth
BH8 8UU
Tel: (0202) 526963

NORTH

Soe Soe Oriental Foods,
Unit 69–70, Morley Market, Queen
Street, Morley, Leeds LS27 9BU
Tel: (0532) 380282
Tai Sun Supermarket,
49 College Road, Waterdale,
Doncaster, South Yorkshire DN1 3JH
Tel: (0302) 344360

SCOTLAND

Hong's Chinese Supermarket,
7a Bath Street, Glasgow G2 1HY
Tel: (041) 332 4492

MADHUR JAFFREY'S FAR EASTERN COOKERY STARTER KIT

A BBC Starter Kit of special Far
Eastern ingredients is available by mail
order. Details from:

**Madhur Jaffrey's Far Eastern
Cookery Starter Kit,**
PO Box 7, Haslemere, Surrey
GU27 1EP
Tel: (0428) 2452

INDEX

CONVERSION TABLES

All these are *approximate* conversions, which have been rounded either up or down. In a few recipes it has been necessary to modify them very slightly. Never mix metric and imperial measures in one recipe. Stick to one system or the other.

Weights		Volume		Measurements	
½ oz	15 g	1 fl oz	25 ml	¼ inch	0.5 cm
1	25	2	50	½	1
1½	40	3	85	1	2.5
2	50	5 (¼ pint)	150	2	5
3	75	10 (½)	300	3	7.5
4	100	15 (¾)	450	4	10
5	150	1 pint	600	6	15
6	175	1¼	750	7	18
7	200	1½	900	8	20
8	225	1¾	1 litre	9	23
9	250	2	1.1	11	28
10	275	2¼	1.25	12	30
12	350	2½	1.5		
13	375	2¾	1.6	**Oven temperatures**	
14	400	3	1.75	Mk 1	275°F 140°C
15	425	3¼	1.8	2	300 150
1 lb	450	3½	2	3	325 160
1¼	500	3¾	2.1	4	350 180
1½	750	4	2.25	5	375 190
2	1 kg	5	2.75	6	400 200
3	1.5	6	3.4	7	425 220
4	1.75	7	4.0	8	450 230
5	2.25	8 (1 gal)	4.5	9	475 240

Teaspoon and tablespoon measures are level, not heaped.